Bible
CROSSWORD
PUZZLES

Bible CROSSWORD PUZZLES

200 crossword puzzles
to enhance your Bible knowledge

 Tyndale House Publishers, Inc.
Wheaton, Illinois

The puzzles in this book were designed and created by Terry Hall, Media Ministries, Wheaton, Illinois, and by Randy Petersen.

Cover design by Beth Sparkman

Crossword puzzles in this book were previously published in *74 More Fun and Challenging Bible Crosswords, 78 Great Fun and Challenging Bible Crosswords, 365 Bible Crosswords and Word Searches 1992 Calendar, Tyndale Crossword Puzzles 1-2* by Terry Hall, and *Tyndale Crossword Puzzles 3-4* by Terry Hall and Randy Petersen.

ISBN 0-8423-0077-5
Printed in the United States of America

04	03	02	01	00	99	98	97	96
9	8	7	6	5	4	3	2	1

OLD TESTAMENT OCCUPATIONS

ACROSS

1 "_____ a child to choose the right path, and when he is older, he will remain upon it" (Prov. 22:6)
4 Money institution workers (Isa. 24:2)
8 Hometown of Hebrew Temple attendants (Neh. 3:26)
9 Cloth makers (2 Chron. 2:7)
10 Animal group tenders (Gen. 13:7)
11 Carpenter; half brother of Jesus; N.T. author
13 Secret information gatherers (Gen. 42:8)
15 Maker of bread, cakes, and pastries (Gen. 40:1)
19 O.T. author who saw Jerusalem tested with a plumbline

20 Counselors (Acts 25:12)
23 Improve in value (Esther 2:13)
24 One to whom something belongs (Exod. 21:28)
25 Ones who shape and harden clay (Matt. 27:7)
26 "My strength evaporated like water on a _____ day" (Ps. 32:4)

DOWN

1 Prize gained by a victory (1 Thess. 2:20)
2 Loathe; reject (Ps. 5:6)
3 Ship steerers (Ezek. 27:8)
4 Archers (Jer. 51:3)
5 First boat builder (Gen. 6:13, 14)
6 Carry out a function or task (Exod. 12:12)
7 Regular order; set of procedures (2 Chron. 34:9)

12 Custodians (Esther 1:5)
14 Spokesman for God; foreteller of future (Deut. 13:1)
16 Fabricated; fictitious: 2 wds. (Jer. 23:32)
17 Deadly snakes of Middle East (Isa. 11:8)
18 "A curse on those who lead _____ the godly. But men who encourage the upright to do good shall be given a worthwhile reward" (Prov. 28:10)
21 Owner of threshing-floor that became Temple site (2 Chron. 3:1)
22 "At the name of Jesus every _____ shall bow in heaven and on earth and under the earth" (Phil. 2:10)

(Solution on p. 203)

NEIGHBORS

ACROSS

1 Separate grain from chaff (Jer. 51:2)
5 N.T. author who said, "Faith is dead if it is not the kind that results in good deeds"
9 Fixed the eyes in a steady, intent look (Acts 7:55)
10 Fisherman with two sons who became disciples (Matt. 4:21)
11 Managers of large sheep farms (2 Kings 3:4)
13 Plow's circular steel part with sharp edge (1 Sam. 13:21)
15 Main activity of evil men (Prov. 2:11-14)
16 Take a long walk (Gen. 13:17)
20 Lie in wait to attack (Ps. 10:8)
21 Those who deal in objects of precious metal often set with gems (Exod. 35:35)
24 Discipline (Hab. 1:12)
25 Son of Aaron judged for using unholy fire (Lev. 10:1)
26 Indulged to excess (Jer. 50:10)
27 Assistant authority; one acting on behalf of another (1 Kings 22:47)

DOWN

2 Judge of Israel between Jephthah and Elon (Judg. 12:7-11)
3 Where Cain settled, east of Eden (Gen. 4:16)
4 Sorcerer; skillful person (Dan. 2:27)
5 Tasks to be done (Exod. 5:4)
6 Woman who aids at childbirth (Gen. 35:17)
7 Artist's rough drawing (2 Kings 16:10)
8 Belonging to author of Proverbs chapter 30 (Prov. 30:1)
12 Pursue game for food (Gen. 27:5)
14 Employ for pay (Lev. 25:50)
15 Occupation of Hagar and Gehazi, for example (Gen. 16:1, 2; 2 Kings 5:20)
17 What shepherds work with (Gen. 29:8)
18 Controlled a horse with bridle lines (2 Kings 9:23)
19 Officially distribute (2 Chron. 31:19)
22 Royal decree or proclamation (Esther 3:14)
23 Unspecific very small amount: 2 wds.
25 End of book supplementary material: abbr.

2

(Solution on p. 203)

BIBLE ANIMALS

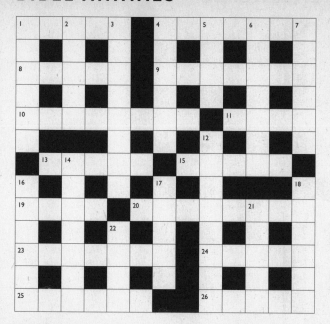

ACROSS

1 Excavated again, such as a well (Gen. 26:18)
4 Large bird in coastal areas (Lev. 11:16)
8 A hard gem (Exod. 28:17)
9 Tempted by arousing desire (Nah. 3:4)
10 Deerlike mammal related to the ox (Deut. 14:5)
11 Hebrew tribe appointed to offer animal sacrifices (1 Sam. 2:28)
13 Remains from burnt offerings (Lev. 4:12)
15 "The boy became so hungry that even the pods he was feeding the _____ looked good to him" (Luke 15:16)
19 Jacob's funeral site in Canaan; threshing place (Gen. 50:10)
20 Young steers used as sacrifices (Ps. 50:9)
23 O.T. prophet who spoke against offering God sick animals; O.T. book
24 Brother who was angry when the Prodigal Son returned home (Luke 15: 28)
25 Settle snugly into a sheltered location (Isa. 34:15)
26 Scattered (Lev. 19:9)

DOWN

1 Ceremonial form or traditional procedure (Hos. 8:13)
2 Storage and distribution site (Jer. 38:11)
3 Slender, swift-running mammals of Africa and Asia (1 Kings 4:23)
4 "Your teeth are white as _____ wool, newly shorn and washed" (Song. 4:2)
5 Industrious insects working in colonies (Prov. 6:6)
6 Not pure; unapproved for Hebrew consumption (Lev. 7:19)
7 Endearing term for young boy (Luke 7:14)
12 Small, migratory birds associated with sparrows (Ps. 84:3)
14 Horse barns (1 Kings 4:28)
16 Large game fish of northern waters (Matt. 1:4)
17 Short-winged, stout-bodied game birds given to Hebrews in wilderness (Exod. 16:13)
18 Large hawk (Deut. 14:13)
21 Evergreen tree with aromatic, reddish wood used in Hebrew ceremonies (Lev. 14:49)
22 Recipient of proverbial messages from Agur (Prov. 30:1)

(Solution on p. 203)

3

SHEEP AND SHEPHERDS

ACROSS

1 "There is a friend who sticks _____ than a brother" (Prov. 18:24)
5 "I took two shepherd's _____, naming one Grace and the other Union, and I fed the flock" (Zech. 11:7)
8 Me, reflexively (Gen. 16:5)
9 Elevated structures on which sheep are sacrificed (Exod. 20:24)
10 Curved upper support over an opening (Acts 4:11)
11 Contagious disease that spreads rapidly (1 Kings 8:37)
13 Quote from Psalm 100:3 about our relationship to God: 4 wds.
16 Annual Hebrew ceremony when roast lamb is eaten with bitter herbs (Exod. 12:8, 11)
18 Salt Lake City's state
20 Flow of water from underground (Gen. 26:19)
22 "He leadeth me beside the still _____" (Ps. 23:2, KJV)
23 To David: "I chose you to be the _____ of my people Israel when you were tending your sheep in the pastureland" (2 Sam. 7:8)
24 Songs sung by abrupt alternations between a natural voice and a falsetto

DOWN

2 "On top of these blankets is placed a _____ of rams' skins, dyed red" (Exod. 26:14)
3 Sheep tenders (Gen. 46:32)
4 Rouse; stimulate; make like new again (Isa. 32:2)
5 Hindu religious teacher; yogi
6 Small, unusually wise insect (Prov. 30:24, 25)
7 Capable of producing abundant plant life (Gen. 13:10)
12 Completely tired or worn out (Gen. 25:29)
14 "Follow God's _____ in everything you do just as a much loved child imitates his father" (Eph. 5:1)
15 Thin; gaunt (Ezek. 34:20)
17 Energy; force; determination (Ps. 38:19)
19 Month of the Hebrews' exodus from Egypt (Deut. 16:1)
21 Ohio's neighbor: abbr.

(Solution on p. 203)

BUILDING A HOUSE

ACROSS

1 Boxlike containers (2 Chron. 34:17)
5 Building location (1 Kings 6:7)
9 Quartz with various colors (Isa. 54:12)
10 External window covers or shades (Ezek. 27:7)
11 Frameworks of crossed wood or metal strips (1 Kings 7:21)
13 City given to tribe of Manasseh (1 Chron. 6:70)
15 Handheld implement (Exod. 20:25)
16 Table supports (Exod. 25:26)
20 Unusually fine; valuable (Luke 7:46)
21 Roof or ceiling window, such as in Noah's ark (Gen. 6:16)
24 Hardened wall coating (Dan. 5:5)
25 Where God gave Moses blueprints for building the Tabernacle (Heb. 12:18)
26 Short, weak sound, such as from a bird (Isa. 10:14)
27 Impress as important; give emphasis (Lev. 6:17)

DOWN

2 Central or essential part (Gen. 10:10)
3 Bring legal action; petition (Ezek. 7:25)
4 Long, thin slats of wood (Num. 21:18)
5 "Those who hear my instructions and ignore them are foolish, like a man who builds his house on _____" (Matt. 7:26)
6 Occupants of a rented dwelling (Lev. 25:23)
7 Pointed metal fasteners for wood (Exod. 38:20)
8 Lending money at excessive interest (Amos 5:11)
12 "Do not bring an _____ into your home and worship it" (Deut. 7:26)
14 Eternal home of the wicked (2 Thess. 1:9)
15 Balcony or patio (Ezek. 41:9)
17 Permanent underground home (2 Kings 21:26)
18 Garment that hangs below the waist (Exod. 20:26)
19 "It is better to live in the corner of an _____ than with a crabby woman in a lovely home" (Prov. 21:9)
22 Groups of people, often assembled for crime (Hos. 6:9)
23 Place for the foot to go up or down (1 Kings 10:20)
25 Respectful direct address to a man (Gen. 24:18)

(Solution on p. 203)

GRAB BAG

ACROSS

1 Requests (Gen. 46:33)
5 Shortened form
9 Long period of time
12 Blue: Ger.
13 Single stinging insect: 2 wds.
14 Make leather (Acts 9:43)
15 Condemn to eternal punishment
16 Most powerful one (Gen. 17:1)
18 Dwell
20 Related to ground: pref.
21 Imitated in mockery: slang
24 Ruth's mother-in-law (Ruth 1:15)
27 Deluded (Job 15:31)
31 Twist fibers into thread (Exod. 35:26)
32 What Peter sliced off (John 18:10)
33 Microscopic hairs
35 Participle ending
36 Employed (Gen. 47:24)
38 Communication system (Gen. 10:5)
40 Celestial bodies (Gen. 1:16)
42 Knitting material (Ezek. 27:19)
43 Obtain; select (Gen. 7:2)
45 Swine sounds
49 Initial (Exod. 22:15)
53 Witticism
54 Pidgeon talk
55 Pedestal part
56 Elbow-wrist connector
57 The _____ Commandments
58 Polluted fog
59 Wapitis

DOWN

1 Adoniram's father (1 Kings 4:6)
2 Broad, flat piece
3 _____kaze
4 Topped ice cream
5 Motorists' aid organization: abbr.
6 Round, wooden cask: abbr. (2 Sam. 16:1)
7 Victor's award site: Gk. (Rom. 14:8)
8 Dominion (Gen. 10:11)
9 North African country (2 Kings 19:9)
10 Long-tailed rodent (Lev. 11:29)
11 One, no matter which (Gen. 2:16)
17 Mardi _____
19 Long narrative poem
22 Began in the Garden (Gen. 3:5)
23 Tarry (Num. 22:37)
25 Chinese dynasty
26 Present action suffix: med.
27 _____ ex machina
28 Earth's orbit direction (Gen. 2:8)
29 The world and all its parts (Rom. 8:19)
30 Mighty: pref.
34 Belonging to the fields: pref.
37 Forcefully pull (Exod. 21:14)
39 One-of-a-kind (1 Chron. 17:21)
41 Slide
44 Judean city (Josh. 15:34)
46 Invalid
47 Tight twist
48 Mineral spring resorts
49 Tenth month: abbr. (1 Kings 8:2)
50 Fish eggs
51 Fuss
52 Felled tree (2 Chron. 2:16)

(Solution on p. 203)

IN THE COURTROOM

ACROSS

1 "Melchizedek had no father or mother and there is no ____ of any of his ancestors" (Heb. 7:3)

5 Interfere; fool with (2 Chron. 25:19)

8 First person to be deceived (2 Cor. 11:3)

9 "Their ____ in the truth that they have been taught must be strong" (Titus 1:9)

10 Widespread honor (2 Sam. 23:22)

11 Ornamental case for small articles used daily

12 "The Lord is the great Prosecuting ____ presenting his case against his people" (Isa. 3:13)

13 Outlawed; prohibited (1 Sam. 28:3)

15 Annoy with hostile intent (Ezra 6:7)

17 Unintentional or chance mishap (Num. 35:22)

20 Catch one's breath with amazement (Jer. 49:17)

22 Sum of one's possessions (Luke 12:13)

23 "He who ____ grace and truth is the king's friend" (Prov. 22:11)

24 Conservative Protestant organization of churches: abbr.

25 State firmly and positively (Esther 1:22)

26 Secretly watching to gather information (1 Sam. 28:9)

DOWN

2 Choose by vote (Num. 14:4)

3 "In my ____, nothing is worthwhile; everything is futile" (Eccles. 1:2)

4 Steal by trickery or deception (Lev. 19:11)

5 Rights and wrongs of a legal case (Dan. 9:18)

6 One who gives (Lev. 27:10)

7 "The king was furious but first consulted his ____, for he did nothing without their advice" (Esther 1:12, 13)

14 Charges with an offense (1 Cor. 6:6)

15 "A man's conscience is the Lord's searchlight exposing his hidden ____" (Prov. 20:27)

16 Lawfully; rightly (Gen. 31:16)

18 Visual representation of a likeness (John 3:14)

19 "It would be an annual ____ from generation to generation" (Esther 9:28)

21 "In their foolishness they worshiped heathen idols despite the Lord's ____ warnings" (2 Kings 17:15)

(Solution on p. 203)

HIDDEN MESSAGE

ACROSS

1 Ceremonial procession (1 Cor. 4:9)
5 Strong winds and heavy rain, hail, or snow (Isa. 30:30)
8 Not private; visible and accessible to the community at large (Isa. 4:5)
9 "Never _____ yourselves. Leave that to God, for he has said that he will repay those who deserve it" (Rom. 12:19)
10 Olympic awards site: Gk.
11 Praises publicly, often by hand clapping (Ps. 49:18)
13 Quote from Jesus about his return to earth: 4 wds. (Rev. 22:6)
16 "One shall come who rules righteously.... He shall be ... as _____

after rain" (2 Sam. 23:3, 4)
18 Food served and eaten at one sitting (Gen. 18:16)
20 Standards of excellence; worthy goals (Ps. 26:3)
22 Malta and Patmos, for example (Rev. 1:9)
23 Ruler; son of God, the King (Acts 5:31)
24 Flying, biting insect that annoys livestock (Jer. 46:20)

DOWN

2 Mistreatment (Matt. 27:39)
3 "Kingdoms will try to strengthen themselves by forming _____ with each other" (Dan. 2:43)
4 "Fill the followers of God with joy. Let those who love your salvation _____, 'What

a wonderful God he is'" (Ps. 70:4)
5 Pound upon with one's feet or other heavy objects (Gen. 49:19)
6 "I _____ no one anything. Everything under the heaven is mine" (Job 41:11)
7 "They gathered all the armies of the world near a place called, in Hebrew, Armageddon—the Mountain of _____" (Rev. 16:16)
12 Gathered together (Acts 10:27)
14 "What therefore God hath joined together, let not man put _____" (Mark 10:9, KJV)
15 Requiring (2 Cor. 1:4)
17 Point of controversy (Judg. 11:26)
19 Jesus "died to _____ that whole system of Jewish laws"; make legally void (Eph. 2:15)
21 Eastern border town of the Hebrews' Promised Land (Num. 34:10, 11)

8

(Solution on p. 203)

TOO MANY TITLES

ACROSS

1 Great Hebrew law-giver (John 1:17)
4 Paupers; solicitors of charity (Luke 14:21)
8 Public announcer (Isa. 40:9)
9 Senior commissioned military officer (Judg. 4:7)
10 Trained participants in competitive sports (2 Kings 2:16)
11 Spouse (Jer. 5:8)
13 Person doing business on behalf of another (Luke 10:22)
15 "These teachers in their _____ will tell you anything to get hold of your money" (2 Pet. 2:3)
19 Coarse, woven fabrics to sleep on (Mark 6:55)
20 Twelve disciples (Luke 9:1)
23 Protected by a defen-sive covering (Ezek. 38:4)
24 A pharaoh of Egypt in Jeremiah's prophecy (Jer. 46:2)
25 One in charge of daily operations for a business or household (Gen. 43:16)
26 Cook by dry heat (Exod. 12:8)

DOWN

1 Saul's daughter; David's wife (2 Sam. 3:13)
2 "I have created the _____ who blows the coals beneath the forge and makes the weapons of destruction" (Isa. 54:16)
3 Noncommissioned military officer (Matt. 27:54)
4 Military trumpeter (1 Cor. 14:8)
5 "Young men who are wise obey the law; a son who is a member of a lawless _____ is a shame to his father" (Prov. 28:7)
6 Land area measure-ment (Ezek. 36:34)
7 "In every contract of sale there must be a stipulation that the land can be redeemed at any time by the _____" (Lev. 25:24)
12 Person incarcerated or on trial (Acts 25:14)
14 Keepers of Hebrew Temple entrances (Ezek. 44:11)
16 What morticians do to a corpse (Gen. 50:2)
17 "Every house built by the wicked is as fragile as a _____ web" (Job 27:18)
18 One who accompanies another (Gen. 12:20)
21 Roman province on southern coast of Asia Minor (Acts 27:5)
22 "Don't _____ about your plans for tomor-row—wait and see what happens" (Prov. 27:1)

(Solution on p. 203)

STUCK IN SIN

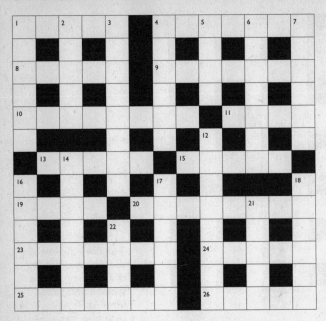

ACROSS

1 "Stay away from where the prostitute walks, lest she _____ you and seduce you" (Prov. 7:25)
4 Itinerant Levitical teacher (2 Chron. 17:8)
8 Dishonest or mischievous person; scoundrel
9 Distress arising from a sense of guilt (Ps. 51:17)
10 Charging another with wrongdoing (Luke 23:14)
11 Dull, persistent pain; yearning (2 Cor. 6:10)
13 Used profane language (Exod. 5:21)
15 "If you call your friend an _____ [foolish person], you are in danger of being brought before the court" (Matt. 5:22)
19 Skills; branches of learning, such as the occult (Exod. 7:22)
20 Sexual unfaithfulness of a married person (Exod. 20:14)
23 Feeling humiliated, disgraced, or guilty (2 Sam. 19:5)
24 Person outstanding in size, power, or achievement
25 Expected deliverer of the Jews (Ps. 110:1)
26 Periods of about 365 days (Gen. 5:3)

DOWN

1 Expression of intention to harm (2 Sam. 12:10)
2 "No Israeli may practice black _____, or call on the evil spirits for aid, or be a fortune teller" (Deut. 18:10)
3 "Wherever your _____ is, there your heart and thoughts will also be" (Luke 12:34)
4 Harsh ruler having absolute power (Rev. 11:7)
5 Idle, worthless vagabonds (Isa. 5:11)
6 Canaanite city where Achan angered God by stealing loot (Josh. 6:26–7:1)
7 "He heard the warning and wouldn't listen; the fault is his. If he had _____ the warning, he would have saved his life" (Ezek. 33:5)
12 Worshiping images of a god (Num. 31:1)
14 Women believed to have occult powers (Isa. 8:19)
16 Prophet hired by Moab to curse the Hebrews (Num. 22:7)
17 Southern Judean city near Edom (Josh. 15:21, 22)
18 Carnivorous African and Asian mammals with powerful jaws (Isa. 13:22)
21 Additional (Lev. 21:18)
22 Ahab's father; one of Israel's most wicked kings (1 Kings 16:25, 28)

(Solution on p. 203)

TRICKY ONES

ACROSS

1 Sweet, yellow-rinded melon
7 Where Jacob wrestled with the Angel (Gen. 32:30)
13 Sacred choral composition (Isa. 27:2)
14 Treat as equals
15 Difficult to control (Gen. 49:4)
16 "____ wrong way": 2 wds.; cause irritation
17 Cathedral
18 More just and equitable than another (Lev. 19:15)
19 "Father who is over us ____ in us": 2 wds. (Eph. 4:6)
21 Woman's name
22 Characterized by great effort and care (Ezra 6:12)
24 Current enlistment date: mil. abbr.
25 Placed; positioned (Gen. 1:17)
26 Cathode ray tube: computer abbr.
29 Tenth book of the N.T.
35 Father of Azareel (Neh. 11:13, KJV)
37 Trademark for polyester fiber
38 Repeated statements of falsehood (1 Kings 22:23)
39 Chins
40 Run a stake through a body: var.
41 Class of criminal gangs in India
42 Scorcher (Isa. 49:10)
43 Tree trunk extension (Ezek. 15:2)
44 Betty ____
45 Intervals of passing time

DOWN

1 Toward the posterior end
2 Annual rings of trees
3 Walk leisurely (2 Sam. 11:2)
4 One of the two Zorathite clans (1 Chron. 4:2)
5 Be the property of (Gen. 32:18)
6 Friend: law
7 Completed; matured (John 17:23)
8 Moses "performed miracles that have never been ____d" (Deut. 34:11)
9 Ancient kingdom along the southern Nile River
10 Relating to medical treatment: suff.
11 Colorless, flammable, gaseous hydrocarbon
12 Looked at another maliciously
20 Those who regard with contempt or disdain (Acts 13:41)
23 O.T. book between Ezra and Esther: abbr.
26 Philippine two-wheeled carriage
27 Poet
28 A great merchant in China
29 Large birds
30 Winged fruit of ash or elm tree
31 Extensive frozen perennial cover
32 Pertaining to Moab's northern border river (Num. 21:13)
33 Observe (Num. 15:39)
34 Scythe handles
36 Something entangling the unwary (Ezek. 17:20)
41 Twice as much: abbr. (Deut. 21:17)

(Solution on p. 203)

11

BIBLE FOREIGNERS

ACROSS

1 Country just north of Israel (Judg. 1:26)
4 Inhabitants of major Mediterranean island (Acts 2:11)
8 King of Egypt during battle of Carchemish (Jer. 46:2)
9 Giant race in ancient Transjordan (Deut. 3:11)
10 Descendants of Abraham through Ishmael (Neh. 4:7)
11 Circle of light around a body (Ezek. 1:27)
13 "Issue a royal edict, a law of the ____ and Persians that can never be changed" (Esther 1:19)
15 "The heart of Nimrod's empire included Babel, ____, Accad, and Calneh in the land of Shinar" (Gen. 10:10)
19 Scent as perceived by one's sense of smell (Num. 28:6)
20 Abraham's ancestral race (Deut. 26:5)
23 Ancient Roman region in Golan Heights; Texas city (Luke 3:1)
24 Put to death by mob action (Jer. 12:6)
25 "'Show me a coin. Whose portrait is this on it?' They replied, '____—the Roman emperor's'" (Luke 20:24)
26 Another name for Mount Hermon (Deut. 3:9)

DOWN

1 Day of Jesus' resurrection (John 20:1)
2 Ruled: Lat.; Last part of the intestine: pl.
3 Original Canaanite tribe in north Trans-jordan defeated by Moses (Deut. 1:4)
4 Home of Simon, who carried Jesus' cross (Matt. 27:32)
5 Broad public display of goods or services: abbr.
6 Language of ancient Babylon (Dan. 2:4)
7 Hebrew champion captured and blinded by the Philistines (Judg. 16:23)
12 Prickly shrubs; meaning of threshing place of Atad (Gen. 50:10)
14 Descendant of Esau living south of the Dead Sea (Gen. 36:9)
16 Type of law given by God at Mount Sinai (John 7:22)
17 "We are no longer Jews or ____, but we are all the same—we are Christians; we are one in Christ Jesus" (Gal. 3:28)
18 Jewish queen of Persia
21 Moab's northern border river (Num. 21:13)
22 One of Ishmael's 12 sons; ancestor of tribe bearing his name (Gen. 25:12-16)

(Solution on p. 203)

BIBLE WARS

ACROSS

1 "Suddenly, the angel was joined by a vast host of others—the ____ of heaven—praising God" (Luke 2:13)

5 Devices for holding things together (Exod. 26:6)

8 ____ and aah

9 "The Lord God said to the serpent, 'You shall ____ in the dust as long as you live.'" (Gen. 3:14)

10 Pierce with a pointed pole (Gen. 40:19)

11 Ran away (Gen. 14:10)

12 Foot soldiers (2 Sam. 8:4)

14 Intense fear and panic (Gen. 42:21)

17 Plant bearing pods

19 Humility; shame; dishonor (Ezek. 32:30)

21 Objects used to make a decision by chance (1 Chron. 6:61)

23 Chronological records of a king's wars and history (1 Kings 14:19)

25 Association for a common purpose (Jer. 41:2)

26 Highest possible: abbr. (Ezek. 27:10)

27 Flee (Gen. 19:17)

28 Hebrew name for God

DOWN

2 Nonurban; related to the country (Neh. 10:37)

3 One who enters for conquest (Jer. 50:44)

4 Person in military service (1 Sam. 18:17)

5 Highest in rank (Gen. 37:36)

6 Poisonous African snake

7 "I am but a ____ here on earth: how I need a map—and your commands are my chart and guide" (Ps. 119:19)

13 "A dull ____ requires great strength; be wise and sharpen the blade" (Eccles. 10:10)

15 "King Uzziah produced ____ of war manufactured in Jerusalem, invented by brilliant men to shoot arrows and huge stones" (2 Chron. 26:15)

16 Unit of electrical resistance

17 "Neither you nor anyone else can serve two masters. You will hate one and show ____ to the other" or vice versa (Luke 16:13)

18 Philistine giant David defeated (1 Sam. 17:48, 49)

20 "Without making a big ____ over it, God simply shatters the greatest of men and puts others in their places" (Job 34:24)

22 Agreement to not fight (Deut. 20:10)

24 Solomon's great-grandson, a mostly good king of Judah (Matt. 1:7)

(Solution on p. 204)

13

GOD'S WORK

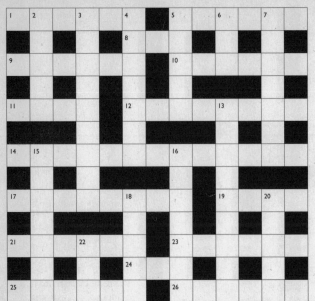

ACROSS

1 "The Lord accepted Job's prayer on their ____"; interest or benefit (Job 42:9)
5 Plain or wasteland of the Jordan River valley (Deut. 3:17)
8 "Don't ____ the poor and sick! For the Lord is their defender"; steal from (Prov. 22:22)
9 Outdoor sports arenas
10 O.T. book predicting Jesus' virgin birth
11 "You made all the delicate, inner parts of my body and ____ them together in my mother's womb"; interlaced (Ps. 139:13)
12 Schooled; trained (1 Chron. 27:32)
14 Fulfilling; bringing about (Gen. 11:6)
17 "What a foundation you stand on now: the ____ and the prophets; and the cornerstone of the building is Jesus Christ himself"; disciples (Eph. 2:20)
19 "What fools the nations are to ____ against the Lord! How strange that men should try to outwit God"; be violently angry (Ps. 2:1)
21 On fire
23 "I was not called to be a missionary by any group or ____. My call is from Jesus Christ himself"; administrative department (Gal. 1:1)
24 One's relatives (Gen. 16:12)
25 Starts (1 Cor. 14:36)
26 Indelibly mark human skin (Lev. 19:28)

DOWN

2 "What dainty morsels rumors are. They are ____ with great relish"; consumed (Prov. 18:8)
3 Supplements (2 Cor. 7:13)
4 Making another appear guilty (Mark 15:10)
5 Son of Aaron killed for using unholy fire (Num. 3:2, 4)
6 Expression of triumph (Ps. 35:25)
7 Rebekah's race (Gen. 25:20)
13 "A woman must not wear men's clothing, and a man must not wear women's clothing. This is ____ to the Lord your God"; detestable (Deut. 22:5)
15 "Find some ____, godly, honest men who hate bribes, and appoint them as judges"; competent (Exod. 18:21)
16 Moment (Luke 1:44)
18 Onionlike herbs (Num. 11:5)
20 Small, insect-eating lizard (Lev. 11:30)
22 Descendant of King Solomon's officials who came to Jerusalem with Zerubbabel (Ezra 2:55, 57)

(Solution on p. 204)

TRUTH OR CONSEQUENCE

ACROSS

1 Moses' father-in-law (Exod. 3:1)
5 "_____ fear and doubt! For remember, the Lord your God is with you wherever you go"; expel (Josh. 1:9)
8 "What's the _____ of saying that you have faith and are Christians if you aren't proving it by helping others?"; sense (James 2:14)
9 Struck with amazement or horror (Dan. 4:19)
10 "Solomon was the _____ of 3,000 proverbs and wrote 1,005 songs"; originator (1 Kings 4:32)
11 Flesh of a steer or cow (Isa. 25:6)
12 "Don't associate with _____"; persons advocating extreme change (Prov. 24:21)
14 Music played as support or embellishment (1 Chron. 25:1)
17 Refrains from (Acts 15:29)
19 Slippery liquids for fuel or lubrication (2 Kings 20:13)
21 "I give them eternal life and they shall never perish. No one shall _____ them away from me"; suddenly grab away (John 10:28)
23 "Caiaphas, who was High Priest that year, said, 'You stupid _____let this one man die for the people'"; foolish persons (John 11:49)
24 Judean village given to Caleb (Josh. 21:12, 16)
25 Conscious but not sensible, as in a drunken _____ (Gen. 9:24)
26 "Foolish and unlearned questions avoid, knowing that they do _____ strifes"; cause (2 Tim. 2:23, KJV)

DOWN

2 "They that wait upon the Lord shall renew their strength. They shall mount up with wings like _____": sing. (Isa. 40:31)
3 Frozen dew (Exod. 16:14, KJV)
4 Part of a rock stratum that appears above the ground (Song 2:14)
5 Facial hair on a man (Lev. 14:9)
6 Hard-shelled fruit with edible kernels (Gen. 43:11)
7 Enlarged from within (Deut. 8:4)
13 Disturbance; ruckus (Mark 5:39)
15 A body of advisers (Esther 1:5)
16 Building an egg shelter (Num. 24:21)
18 One of King David's sons (1 Chron. 3:6)
20 Despise (Ezek. 36:31, KJV)
22 Pointed end of something (Luke 16:24)

(Solution on p. 204)

PROVERBIAL POTPOURRI

ACROSS

1 Restaurant
5 Smallest particle
9 Engaged services of
(2 Sam. 10:6)
10 Major Philistine city (Gen. 26:1)
12 Treat with scorn (Lam. 2:16)
13 Careened (Ps. 18:7)
15 Fool: Gk.
16 Notice of intent: abbr.
18 Hitler's party
19 Sick (Luke 9:11)
20 Tabernacle choir leader
(1 Chron. 16:7)
22 Achieve victory (Gen. 32:25)
23 False; fake: pref.
25 Hole (Ezek. 8:7)
27 Same: Br.
29 Auto club: abbr.
30 Dilute solution of acetic acid
(Ps. 69:21)
34 Stretch (Exod. 4:6)
38 Single unit (Gen. 2:24)
39 Decree (Exod. 20:1)
41 Female deer
42 Yellow Dutch cheese balls
44 Basketball organization: abbr.
45 Radical religious group
(Acts 6:9)
46 Long, angry speech
48 Another name for Kiriath-
jearim (Josh. 15:9)
50 Bottomless pit (Luke 8:31, NIV)

51 Encourages; incites
52 Sweet potatoes
53 Glass part of camera

DOWN

1 Sphere (Ps. 25:13)
2 Operetic vocal solo
3 Provided food (Exod. 16:32)
4 "The land lies fair as ____ Garden in all its beauty" (Joel 2:3)
5 King hearing Paul's defense
(Acts 26:1)
6 Letter before u
7 Son of Jerahmeel (1 Chron.
2:25)
8 Lake in African Rift Valley
9 "I am the Lord who ____
you" (Exod. 15:26)
11 Syrian king (2 Kings 15:37)
12 Fall in drops (Joel 3:18)
14 Minor surface damage
17 One-and-only: abbr.
20 Short proverb
21 "Love the Lord your God
with all your ____" (Matt.
22:37)
24 Employ for a purpose (Gen.
9:2)
26 National Association of Evangelicals: abbr.
28 Lack of restraint or reason
(Eccles. 10:12)

30 ____ganger; immature African
locust
31 Eastern extent of Media-
Persia (Esther 1:1)
32 Not far away (Gen. 41:48)
33 A cut of meat (Num. 6:20)
35 Grown-ups (Luke 1:17)
36 Carbonated soft drinks
37 Son of Canaan (Gen. 10:15)
40 Group of secret conspirators
43 Language of Indians in southern Mexico
45 Recent or novel: pref.
47 District sales manager: abbr.
49 Honest ____ (Illinois politician)

(Solution on p. 204)

SING TO THE LORD

ACROSS

1 Song of praise or gladness (Isa. 27:2)
5 Hymn ending (Ps. 41:13)
9 Choir members' dress (1 Chron. 15:27)
10 "Always be full of joy in the Lord; I say it again, ____" (Phil. 4:4)
11 Pleasing arrangements of musical notes (Ps. 33:2)
13 Stimulate; heighten, such as a sense (Deut. 32:41)
15 "Sing his praises, accompanied by music from the harp and lute and ____"; ancient stringed instrument (Ps. 92:3)
16 Naomi's wealthy relative in Judah (Ruth 2:1)
20 Direct a choir (Neh. 12:46)
21 Small tambourines (Ps. 68:25)

24 High-pitched tune made through the lips and teeth (Zech. 10:8)
25 "The first musician— the inventor of the harp and flute" (Gen. 4:21)
26 Author of last part of book of Proverbs (Prov. 30:1)
27 Making an effort; attempting (Gen. 44:15)

DOWN

2 Abigail's first husband, a sheepherder (1 Sam. 25:3, 4)
3 Belonging to a man
4 Feel surprise and wonder (Ps. 48:5)
5 City of the tribe of Benjamin (Neh. 11:31)
6 Friend of Job's who came to comfort him (Job 2:11)
7 Skin-covered percus-

sion instruments (Ps. 81:2)
8 Rhythmic stresses in music
12 Plain where Nebuchadnezzar's band signaled worship of his 90-foot statue (Dan. 3:1, 5)
14 Toothed, hair arrangement tool (Job 33:10)
15 Jumping, often with joy (Mal. 4:2)
17 "In the twinkling of an eye, when the last trumpet is ____, all the Christians who have died will suddenly become alive" (1 Cor. 15:52)
18 "In everything you do, put God first, and he will ____ you and crown your efforts with success" (Prov. 3:6)
19 Sacred song giving its name to an O.T. book (Acts 13:33)
22 Son of Gad; grandson of Jacob (Gen. 46:16)
23 "I, Jesus, am the bright Morning ____" (Rev. 22:16)
25 "So be truly glad! There is wonderful ____ ahead, even though the going is rough for a while down here" (1 Pet. 1:6)

(Solution on p. 204)

BEACHED

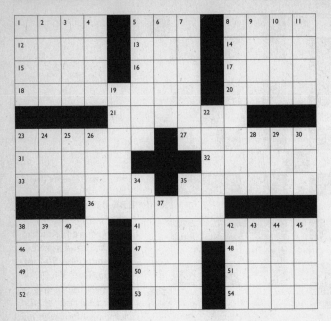

ACROSS

1 O.T. prophet and author: abbr.
5 Long, rigid, round item (Exod. 26:28)
8 Floating platform (1 Kings 5:9)
12 Religious teacher at Water Gate (Neh. 8:1)
13 Mist; haze: Scot.
14 Son of Shelah (Luke 3:35)
15 Family head in tribe of Gad (Num. 26:15, 18)
16 Reserve officer candidate: abbr.
17 Changed: pref.
18 Span of one's existence (Gen. 4:26)
20 Country Chedorlaomer ruled (Gen. 14:1)
21 Proceeded toward (Gen. 31:21)
23 Return to proper condition (Num. 4:32)
27 Refugee from a revolution
31 Growing older (1 Sam. 17:12)
32 Suitors
33 German author
35 Element used in antiseptics
36 Cyprus or Crete, e.g. (Jer. 2:11)
38 "So be it" (Deut. 27:15)
41 Meddlesome person (1 Pet. 4:15)
46 Person celebrated for accomplishments (2 Kings 5:1)
47 Rock mined for its contents
48 Australian Boating Industry Association: abbr.
49 Southern Judean city (Josh. 15:20, 26)
50 Women's Army Corps: abbr.
51 Deficiency (Exod. 16:18)
52 Extremely skinny (Gen. 41:19)
53 Satellite-to-satellite tracking: abbr.
54 Concept (Amos 5:18)

DOWN

1 Enthusiastic devotion (Ps. 69:9)
2 King David's estate manager (1 Chron. 27:26)
3 Highest-ranking teacher: abbr.
4 Unplowed strip in cultivated field
5 Mortician
6 Pleasant odor (Gen. 27:17)
7 Draw back (Ps. 18:15)
8 Cured (Deut. 28:27)
9 First martyr (Matt. 23:35)
10 White goat cheese
11 Streetcar: Br.
19 Legs between hips and knees (Job 40:17)
22 Include as part of a unified whole
23 Musical style
24 Self-image
25 Filled, baked pastry shell
26 Equally true but seemingly contradictory truths
28 Guaranteed annual income: abbr.
29 Operate regularly (Gen. 39:5)
30 Compass point about 4:00
34 Arm joints (Mark 7:3)
35 Small, multisegmented creature (Ps. 105:31)
37 Invisible emanations
38 Judean king in Elijah's time (1 Kings 17:1)
39 Short note (2 Sam. 11:6)
40 Ephraimite clan founder (Num. 26:34, 35)
42 Indonesian island near Java
43 O.T. prophet to Edom: abbr.
44 Numbered cubes (Josh. 14:2)
45 African Bantu people

(Solution on p. 204)

THE CORNERSTONE

ACROSS

1 Jesus ____
7 Local church leaders (1 Pet. 5:1)
13 Expression of pleasure or triumph
14 Related to body's main blood vessel
15 "Quick! Mix ____ pancakes!": 2 wds. (Gen. 18:6)
16 Crawly
17 Huge mammal with horned snout
18 Publisher William Randolph ____
19 Grease: Scot.
21 Deserter from Saul to David (1 Chron. 12:20)
22 "Is anything too ____ for God?" (Gen. 18:14)
23 Son of Hotham (1 Chron. 7:35)
26 Female sheep (Num. 6:14)
27 Male cat
28 South Africa Airways: abbr.
31 Languages including Lao, Shan, etc.
32 Fish; rockling
36 Featherlike column of smoke
38 Pushed out by force (Exod. 10:11)
40 Refuse to notice (2 Chron. 6:42)
42 "Carve ____ on it, and that's his god" (Isa. 40:20)
43 Light-sensitive eyeball lining
44 Son of Javan (Gen. 10:4)
45 Flower with narrow, sword-shaped leaves
46 Restless; troubled
47 Bloodsucking African fly
48 Spas: Br.

DOWN

1 "Upon this rock I will build my ____" (Matt. 16:18)
2 Egyptian Pharaoh aiding Judah (Jer. 37:5)
3 Brighter; more promising
4 Smoothed and pressed by a hot implement
5 Aegean island visited by Paul (Acts 20:15)
6 "He leads me beside ____ quiet streams" (Ps. 23:2)
7 "Let us practice loving ____ other" (1 John 4:7)
8 Pertaining to traditional knowledge
9 Anxious or fearful anticipation
10 Of endless duration: arch.
11 Large-toothed tool to cut with the grain
12 Long, round-bladed mowing tool
20 "What ____ God wrought"
24 Memorandum of agreement: abbr.
25 In the middle of
28 Third Person of the Trinity (1 Pet. 1:2)
29 Horatio ____: poss.
30 Father's or mother's sister: infor.
31 Steel sheets coated with lead and tin
32 Endowed with ability (Acts 15:32)
33 An exemplar; archetype
34 A determination: Lat.
35 Belonging to an estranged person (Exod. 23:4)
37 Damp (Ezek. 31:4)
39 Drippy day (Prov. 27:15)
41 Freedom from work and worry (Gen. 27:39)
44 Kushiro, Japan, airport symbol

(Solution on p. 204)

JACOB AND ESAU

ACROSS

1 His body was bound on an altar by his father (Gen. 22:9)
5 To make an effusive display of sentiment (Ps. 104:10)
8 "There will come a time when your limbs will tremble with age, your strong legs will become weak, and your ____ will be too few to do their work" (Eccles. 12:3)
9 "Where is the ____ King of the Jews? for we have seen his star in far-off eastern lands and have come to worship him" (Matt. 2:2)
11 Desire for food (Job 33:20)
13 Masticate; grind in the mouth (Lev. 11:26)
15 "When a good man ____, he leaves an inheritance to his grandchildren" (Prov. 13:22)
16 "Don't eavesdrop! You may ____ your servant cursing you" (Eccles. 7:21)
20 Lacking hair on the head (Lev. 13:40)
21 Unintentional mishap (Num. 16:29)
24 "The devil who had betrayed them will again be thrown into the Lake of Fire burning with ____"; nonmetallic chemical element (Rev. 20:10)
25 Group of church singers (Rev. 14:2)
26 Jaw part (Lev. 13:29)
27 People between childhood and maturity (Isa. 40:30)

DOWN

2 "If you love ____, you will end in poverty. Stay awake, work hard, and there will be plenty to eat" (Prov. 20:13)
3 Cremation remains (Exod. 27:3)
4 Soundness of mind (Dan. 4:34)
5 Woman's loose, flowing outer garment (Prov. 31:22)
6 Kill by depriving of air (1 Kings 3:19)
7 "A dry crust eaten in peace is better than ____ every day along with argument and strife"; thick slice of meat (Prov. 17:1)
10 Reports of recent events (Gen. 32:6)
12 One Philistine giant had six of these on each foot (2 Sam. 21:20)
14 Jesus' grandfather (Luke 3:23)
15 Samson's girlfriend and betrayer (Judg. 16:19)
17 Wanes, such as life; declines slowly (Lev. 26:16)
18 Vitamin-deficiency disease (Deut. 28:27)
19 Absolute, such as naked (Ps. 55:4)
22 First person who didn't die (Heb. 11:5)
23 Lean or slender (Job 33:21)
25 Hospital ward for heart patients: abbr.

(Solution on p. 204)

PERSONALITY CHARACTERISTICS

ACROSS

1 Is unwilling to acknowledge or accept (Ezek. 14:7)
5 Series of visions during sleep (Joel 2:28)
8 "Although the man and his wife were both _____, neither of them was embarrassed or ashamed" (Gen. 2:25)
9 Professional tree harvesters (2 Chron. 2:18)
10 "Tell them, '_____, the God of your ancestors Abraham, Isaac, and Jacob, has sent me to you.' This is my eternal name" (Exod. 3:15)
12 Judean king to whom God said, "Ask me for a sign. Ask anything you like, in heaven or on earth" (Isa. 7:11)
16 God's characteristic of being sympathetic, showing pity (Exod. 22:27)
18 "You will experience God's peace, which is far more wonderful than the human _____ can understand" (Phil. 4:7)
20 Declare ahead; foretell (Acts 11:28)
22 Even if you are stained as red as _____, I can make you white as wool"; deep red color (Isa. 1:18)
24 Surrender; cease resistance (Ps. 119:87)
25 Jericho woman who helped Hebrew spies (James 2:25)
26 "Lord, be _____ above the highest heavens"; glorified (Ps. 57:5)

DOWN

1 Money paid for use of another's property (Song 8:11)
2 City of Judah in hill country (Josh. 15:56)
3 Food chewed again by ruminating animals (Lev. 11:2)
4 Confidence in one's own abilities: 2 wds. (Isa. 3:18)
5 Canine (Exod. 11:7)
6 City in heart of Nimrod's empire (Gen. 10:10)
7 Conventional title for married woman: abbr. from Fr.
11 A son of Joktan (Gen. 10:26, 28)
13 Midianite general who gave his name to a winepress (Judg. 7:25)
14 Filthy film on a liquid (Ps. 119:119)
15 "The _____ of the Lord will last forever. And his message is the Good News that was preached to you" (1 Pet. 1:24, 25)
17 Belonging to times long past (Num. 13:22)
19 Horse's cry (Jer. 50:11)
21 Prophet of God in Samaria (2 Chron. 28:9)
22 People to whom seventh N.T. book was written: abbr.
23 Cry: wail (Gen. 27:34)
24 Affirmative salute given Jesus in jest by Roman soldiers (Mark 15:18)

(Solution on p. 204)

OLD TESTAMENT HODGEPODGE

ACROSS

1 American Association of Retired Persons: abbr.
5 Fixed charge (Exod. 22:15)
8 Boundary city for Asher (Josh. 19:25)
12 Burn evidence (Lev. 13:28)
13 Night-flying bird (Lev. 11:17)
14 ____hausen; German city
15 Black; dark
16 King: Sp.
17 Region in Ethiopia (Isa. 43:3)
18 Observing (1 Sam. 26:12)
20 Son of Naomi (Ruth 1:1)
22 Born as
23 Mimic: slang
24 Difficult situation (Gen. 30:22)
27 Walking sticks (Num. 21:18)
31 ____ Dodds (athlete)
32 Son of Bela (1 Chron. 7:7)
33 Cantaloupes, for one (Num. 11:5)
37 Colored, valuable quartz (Exod. 28:20)
40 Computer-aided instruction: abbr.
41 Father of Phinehas, a priest (1 Sam. 1:3)
42 Belonging to Othniel's uncle (Josh. 15:17)
45 Separate chaff from grain (Jer. 51:2)
49 Region (Gen. 13:13)
50 "____ for ____, tooth for tooth" (Lev. 24:20)
52 Recognition (1 Chron. 14:17)
53 Look over quickly
54 Belief system: abbr.
55 An institution of higher learning: abbr.
56 Belonging to Zophah's son (1 Chron. 7:36)
57 Donkey (Gen. 16:12)
58 After a certain time (Exod. 13:10)

DOWN

1 Tag on sale item: 2 wds.
2 Face disease
3 Smooth with tines
4 Snooping
5 Unable to recall (Deut. 6:13)
6 Female sheep (Num. 6:14)
7 Cyprian sorcerer (Acts 13:8)
8 King of Israel (2 Kings 15:30)
9 Israeli city (2 Sam. 20:14)
10 ____Hamath; Israeli border town (Num. 34:7)
11 Iraq's eastern neighbor
19 Rebuilder of Jerusalem's walls: abbr.
21 Suitable (Isa. 1:10)
24 Pacific Garden Mission: abbr.
25 Recline (Ruth 3:4)
26 Sick (1 Sam. 5:12)
28 Very important person: abbr.
29 Prior
30 Respectful address (Gen. 23:11)
34 Large bodies of salt water (Gen. 1:9)
35 Arrest: slang
36 Canaanite general (Judg. 4:2)
37 Polished, precious stones (Gen. 24:53)
38 Muhammad ____ (boxer)
39 Wicked (Deut. 10:16)
42 Currency (1 Kings 21:2)
43 Oil company name
44 Guide (Exod. 3:10)
46 Grandmother: infor.
47 Leave out (Lev. 5:16)
48 "____ a story to tell to the nations"
51 Affirmative statement (Gen. 3:12)

(Solution on p. 204)

THE I'S HAVE IT

ACROSS

1 Structures to offer sacrifices (Exod. 20:24)
5 Small magical symbols (Acts 19:19)
8 Father of Bezalel, the craftsman (Exod. 31:1)
9 "Everyone who asks, receives; all who seek, find; and the door is opened to everyone who ____"; raps (Luke 11:10)
10 Basely (2 Sam. 1:21, KJV)
11 Opposed to (Isa. 60:14)
12 Formal confederation between nations (Dan. 11:17)
14 "Have faith and love, and enjoy the ____ of those who love the Lord and have pure hearts"; close association (2 Tim. 2:22)
17 "The stone rejected by the builders has now become the ____ of the arch"; top piece (Ps. 118:22)
19 "Reverence for God ____ hours to each day"; increases (Prov. 10:27)
21 Acts of bearing young (Exod. 28:10)
23 "As the ____ pot for silver, and the furnace for gold; so is a man to his praise"; purifying (Prov. 27:21, KJV)
24 Time before night
25 Deceivers and swindlers (1 Cor. 5:10)
26 Moved quickly out of the way (1 Sam. 19:10)

DOWN

2 Cloth made from flax (Exod. 26:1)
3 "Say to ____, 'Be sure that you do all the Lord has told you to.'"; friend of Paul (Col. 4:17)
4 "A man's courage can ____ his broken body, but when courage dies, what hope is left?"; provide nourishment for (Prov. 18:14)
5 "Any kingdom filled with ____ war is doomed; so is a home filled with argument and strife"; domestic (Luke 11:17)
6 "God is Light and in him is no darkness at ____"; so much (1 John 1:5)
7 Last book of the O.T.
13 Refrained (Acts 15:29)
15 O.T. prophetic book to Edom
16 Served too much food (Deut. 32:15)
18 Fertile areas in a desert (Hos. 13:15)
20 Leap or skip about (1 Kings 18:26)
22 "They are asking a piece of wood to tell them what to do. 'Divine Truth' comes to them through ____ leaves! Longing after idols has made them foolish" (Hos. 4:12)

(Solution on p. 204)

WOMEN OF THE WORD

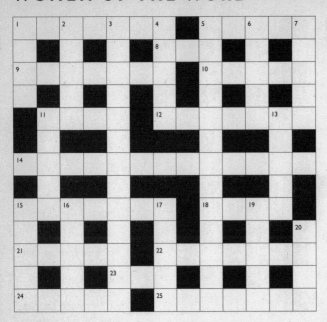

ACROSS

1 Sarah's response upon hearing she would have a son in her old age (Gen. 18:12)
5 "A short-tempered man must bear his own penalty; you can't do much to help him. If you try once you must try a ____ times"; number (Prov.19:19)
8 Commander of King David's Sixth Division (1 Chron. 27:9)
9 Ornamental borders of clothes (Mark 6:56)
10 Famous warrior joining David at Ziklag (1 Chron. 11:44)
11 "Martha was the jittery ____ and was worrying over the big dinner she was preparing" (Luke 10:40)
12 "Crafty men are caught in their own traps; God thwarts their ____"; stratagems (Job 5:12, 13)
14 Kind of altar outside the Tabernacle: 2 wds. (Exod. 30:28)
15 Condition of being secluded (Joel 2:16)
18 Famous warrior among David's men (1 Chron. 11:26, 29)
21 Break without completely separating (1 Kings 13:5)

22 Distributed as a share (Ezek. 48:21)
23 "____ father was Joshua" (Luke 3:29)
24 Moved away from fright (Num. 22:33)
25 Blocks or defeats (Job 5:13)

DOWN

1 "Anyone who listens to my message and believes in God who sent me has eternal ____, and will never be damned for his sins" (John 5:24)
2 Make into a coherent whole (Ezek. 37:22)
3 Placed at top, such as military officers: 2 wds. (1 Chron. 27:6)
4 Computer floppies
5 Relationship of Ruth to Naomi (Ruth 4:15)
6 Tribe of giants conquered by King Chedorlaomer (Gen. 14:5)
7 "When I return the world will be as indifferent to the things of God as the people were in ____ day" (Luke 17:26)
11 "There is no ____ statement than this: God is never wicked or unjust"; more genuine (Job 34:12)

13 Boredom
15 Compact groups (Hos. 6:9)
16 Inhabitant of country from which Abraham came (Acts 7:2)
17 Leavening agent forbidden during Passover (Exod. 12:19)
19 Elevated structure for religious ceremonies (Gen. 8:20)
20 "The people of the Lord marched down against great ____"; probabilities (Judg. 5:13)

(Solution on p. 204)

POLITICS

ACROSS

1 Break up an organization (1 Kings 12:24)
5 Direction on your left when facing east (Gen. 13:1)
8 "Bring to [the Lord] a free-will offering _____ in size to his blessing upon you"; commensurate (Deut. 16:10)
9 "Make use of the Light while there is still time; then you will become light _____"; carriers (John 12:36)
11 Head cook (1 Sam. 9:24)
15 Murder for political reasons (Esther 7:9)
17 "Lord, _____ me as you promised me you would. Tell me clearly what to do, which way to turn" (Ps. 5:8)
19 Fast gaits of horses (Ezek. 26:10)

22 Severe criticisms (Matt. 11:20)
24 Men (Lev. 7:6)
25 Sons of a brother or sister (2 Chron. 22:8)

DOWN

1 What Judas does with disciples' funds for his own use (John 12:6)
2 Digging tools (Num. 21:18)
3 Fuss or bother
4 Resolution (Acts 3:13)
5 Corner or private place (Luke 15:8)
6 "Stay always within the boundaries where God's love can _____ and bless you"; extend to (Jude 1:21)
7 Cultivate (Isa. 5:6)
10 "It is foolish and _____ to make a promise to the Lord before counting the cost"; prema-

turely hasty (Prov. 20:25)
12 "As for others, help them to _____ the Lord by being kind to them"; discover (Jude 1:23)
13 Missionary to the Gentiles (Eph. 3:1)
14 "Seek the Lord while you can find him. _____ upon him now while he is near" (Isa. 55:6)
16 "Pray for the happiness of those who curse you; _____ God's blessing on those who hurt you" (Luke 6:28)
18 Cancel (Eph. 2:15)
20 "Before every man there lies a wide and pleasant road that seems right but _____ in death"; terminates (Prov. 14:12)
21 "If God decides to argue with him, can a man answer even one question of a thousand he _____?" (Job 9:3)
22 Watercourse barrier (Eccles. 1:15)
23 "Finally, the innocent shall come out on _____, above the godless" (Job 17:8)

(Solution on p. 205)

CROSS MY HEART

26 Poured forth violently (Job 38:8)

DOWN

2 Aristocratic; of high and stately character, such as the name of Christ (James 2:7)
3 Continuous; without stopping (Eccles. 8:16)
4 Genuine; without hypocrisy, such as a prayer (Ps. 143:8)
5 Set free from restraint; not fixed (Jer. 50:6)
6 Foreign evangelistic support service organization: abbr.
7 Citizen of Hebrews' homeland (Num. 15:30)
13 "The Lord ____ the upright but ruins the plans of the wicked" (Prov. 22:12)
15 Late; past expected time (Hab. 2:3)
16 "If our consciences are clear, we can come to the Lord with perfect assurance and trust, and get whatever we ask for because we are ____ him" (1 John 3:21, 22)
18 "Keep ____ and pray. Otherwise temptation will overpower you" (Matt. 26:41)
20 Foot-leg joint (Acts 3:7)
22 Part of aerial guidance system: abbr.

ACROSS

1 "Everyone who asks, receives; and the door is opened to everyone who ____" (Luke 11:10)
5 Crystal clear; transparent, as a pool of water (Song 7:4)
8 Wedding vow response: 2 wds.
9 "To ____ these gifts, you need more than faith; you must also work hard to be good" (2 Pet. 1:5)
10 "Receive the love he ____ you—be reconciled to God" (2 Cor. 5:20)
11 Allot; deal out (Ezek. 23:45)
12 Freed from some liability or responsibility (1 Sam. 17:25)
14 Quote from Ps. 100:2; an invitation from God: 3 wds.
17 John the Baptist "will ____ many a Jew to turn to the Lord his God" (Luke 1:16)
19 "He traded his rights as the oldest son for a single meal" (Heb. 12:16)
21 Have high regard for (Luke 16:8)
23 "All who ____ a blessing or take an oath shall swear by the God of Truth" (Isa. 65:16)
24 "The rivers of God will not ____ dry" (Ps. 65:9)
25 "When you fast, put on festive clothing, so that no one will suspect you are hungry, except your Father who knows every ____" (Matt. 6:17, 18)

(Solution on p. 205)

ATTITUDE CHECK

ACROSS

1 "They will come to their ____ and escape from Satan's trap of slavery to sin" (2 Tim. 2:26)

5 "Some will come to me—those the Father has given me—and I will never, never ____ them" (John 6:37)

8 "____ that your hearts do not turn from God to worship other gods" (Deut. 11:16)

9 Placing; putting (Lev. 16:21)

10 "The love of money is the first ____ toward all kinds of sin" (1 Tim. 6:10)

11 Deliberate act of deception (Acts 13:10)

13 Quote from Psalm 100:2 about our response to God: 3 wds.

16 "We patiently endure suffering and ____ and trouble of every kind" (2 Cor. 6:4)

18 "A man will always reap just the kind of crop he ____" (Gal. 6:7)

20 Winner in a battle or contest (Zech. 9:9)

22 Free, open right of entry (Matt. 18:10)

23 Shocked, as by something terrible; appalled (Nah. 2:10)

24 Make sure or certain (Deut. 17:20)

DOWN

2 Choose by vote (2 Sam. 3:21)

3 "Wisdom is hid from the eyes of all mankind; even the ____ birds in the sky cannot discover it" (Job 28:21)

4 Distinctive odor (Song 4:11)

5 "Having started the ball ____ so enthusiastically, you should carry this project through to completion just as gladly" (2 Cor. 8:11)

6 "When the Holy Spirit controls our lives he will produce this kind of fruit in us: love, ____, peace" (Gal. 5:22)

7 "Anyone who says he is a Christian but doesn't ____ his sharp tongue is just fooling himself" (James 1:26)

12 Strapped, back bag to carry supplies: pl. (Mark 6:8)

14 "They are like trees along a river bank ____ luscious fruit" (Ps. 1:3)

15 Come into possession by legal succession (Luke 20:14)

17 "I am leaving you with a gift—____ of mind and heart" (John 14:27)

19 "Your words make me ____ than my enemies because they are my constant guide" (Ps. 119:96, 98)

21 Beverage made by steeping dried leaves in boiling water (Hos. 4:12)

(Solution on p. 205)

OBSCURE OLD TESTAMENT MEN

ACROSS

1 Pour forth; spill (Gen. 37:22)
5 Gentle blow
8 Obtains (Num. 31:28)
12 Hillside hollow (Gen. 19:30)
13 Hole maker (Exod. 21:6)
14 Yearn (2 Cor. 6:10)
15 "I don't give ____": slang; 2 wds
16 Perceive (Gen. 2:19)
17 National Collegiate Athletic Association: abbr.
18 Soften; mellow (Hos. 13:14)
20 Earnest; determined (Matt. 11:12)
22 Never: Ger.
23 Measure
24 Hebrews' departure from Egypt
27 Fit to be eaten (Matt. 13:48)
31 ____ Dodds (Christian athlete)
32 Sound receptacle (Ps. 80:1)
33 Hebrew returnee from Babylon (Ezra 2:55, 56)
37 Security (Gen. 38:17)
40 Gorilla or gibbon, e.g. (1 Kings 10:22)
41 Make a mistake
42 Levite; Temple gatekeeper (1 Chron. 9:17)
45 From one side to other (Gen. 2:11)
49 Costa ____

50 Town of Israel (2 Kings 9:27)
52 First shepherd (Gen. 4:2)
53 "Am I ____?" Goliath roared: 2 wds. (1 Sam. 17:43)
54 Hand clapping
55 Moses' death site (Deut. 34:1, 5)
56 ____-jaakan, wilderness site (Num. 33:31)
57 Daily time indicators: abbr.
58 Dull; plain

DOWN

1 Disease or injury mark (Lev. 13:23)
2 Large rabbit
3 Bad; wicked (Gen. 3:5)
4 "We ____ upon the Lord alone to save us" (Ps. 33:20)
5 Senses flavor (Prov. 23:2)
6 Reverence and wonder (Deut. 28:10)
7 Satisfy; give pleasure (Exod. 21:8)
8 Mahatma ____ (Indian leader)
9 "____ homo"
10 Comparison term (Gen. 25:23)
11 Sitting spot (Lev. 15:6)
19 Northern Illinois University: abbr.
21 Energy unit
24 Hen's product (Job 6:6)
25 Roman twelve
26 Specified age (Gen. 5:3)

28 Sleeping place (Gen. 47:31)
29 Fall behind (Deut. 25:18)
30 Prior
34 Harm; loss (Esther 7:4)
35 Environmental Protection Agency: abbr.
36 Measured distance (Exod. 26:12)
37 Oyster's gems (Matt. 13:46)
38 Learning Resource Center: abbr.
39 Short, specific mission (1 Sam. 15:18)
42 Semitic person; not a Jew (Neh. 2:19)
43 Keep undisclosed (Gen. 18:17)
44 Image symbol
46 ____ammergau, Passion Play site
47 Son of Cush (Gen. 10:7)
48 Crude or unkempt person: infor.
51 United Arab Republic: abbr.

(Solution on p. 205)

LEADERS

ACROSS

1 Son of Benjamin (Gen. 46:21)
4 Unenclosed (Lev. 14:53)
8 David's military head (2 Sam. 2:13)
12 Fish eggs
13 "Take ____ of yourself" (James 2:8)
14 Confined by: abbr. (Exod. 27:9)
15 Mine
16 Rounded handle
17 Covers with tears (Ps. 6:6)
18 Signer of Nehemiah's covenant (Neh. 10:16)
20 "The voice is Jacob's, but the hands are ____" (Gen. 27:22)
22 Drinking glasses with stem (1 Kings 7:26)
24 Duct
27 Loathe (Lev. 20:23)
29 Blot out (Ps. 51:9)
31 "Oh, that you were ____ proud!": 2 wds. (Jer. 13:15)
32 Roman governor trying Paul (Acts 23:24)
33 Healthy; thriving (Gen. 41:2)
34 Join together as one (Judg. 20:11)
35 Increase (Lev. 27:31)
36 Southern Judean town (Josh. 15:21, 30)
40 Forceful, noisy breathing (Job 39:25)
41 Research places: infor.
44 Intertwined (Lam. 1:14)
47 Good-bye
49 ____-o'-shanter
50 Arabian prince
51 Mastered
52 Old French coin
53 Lowest part of lampstand (Exod. 25:31)
54 First-century Roman emperor
55 ____ Hammarsköld (former U.N. secy-gen.)

DOWN

1 Kiriath- ____ (Judean city also called Hebron)
2 Vehicle passageway (Gen. 16:7)
3 Took great pleasure in (Luke 23:8)
4 Weight
5 Flat wall portion (1 Kings 7:31)
6 Irregular; uneven
7 Jeroboam's father (1 Kings 11:26)
8 Hebrews (Ezra 1:3)
9 A single (Gen. 2:21)
10 "Don't try to ____ big" (Rom. 12:16)
11 Large stone squares: abbr. (1 Kings 5:17)
19 Rope-loop trap (Job 41:1)
21 "The whole Bible was given to us by inspiration from God and is ____ to teach us" (2 Tim. 3:16)
23 Shattered (Lev. 6:28)
24 Legally substantiated
25 Jesus acted ____ he were going farther: 2 wds. (Luke 24:28)
26 Arousing passions
27 Advanced network systems architecture: computer abbr.
28 Daring (Josh. 1:9)
30 Related to kidneys
37 Horite chief (Gen. 36:22)
38 Visible evidence (Exod. 17:14)
39 Aquatic mammal
40 Withered (Ps. 129:6)
42 Valley in Palestine (Ps. 84:6, KJV)
43 Self-satisfied
44 Spider's trap (Job 8:14)
45 Airline code for major Nebraska city
46 Force; power
48 Fuss; trouble

(Solution on p. 205)

HARD TIMES

ACROSS

1 Angel; Persian city (Ezra 2:59)
5 Prophet Moabites hired to curse the Israelites (Num. 22:5-7)
8 "This truth was given me in secret, as though whispered in my ____" (Job 4:12)
9 Small compartment for clothes storage (1 Sam. 21:9)
10 "Cursed is he who is unjust to the foreigner, the ____, and the widow" (Deut. 27:19)
11 "We can ____ anything as long as we know that you remain strong in the Lord"; endure (1 Thess. 3:8)
12 "God tolerated man's past ignorance about these things, but now he ____ everyone to put away idols and worship only him"; orders (Acts 17:30)
14 "Anxious hearts are very heavy, but a word of ____ does wonders" (Prov. 12:25)
18 Soldiers' housing (Phil. 1:13)
20 "A lazy fellow has trouble all through life; the good man's path is ____"; free from difficulty (Prov. 15:19)
22 "You get no credit for being patient if you are ____ for doing wrong"; punished with blows (1 Pet. 2:20)
24 "Christ is the exact likeness of the ____ God"; invisible (Col. 1:15)
25 "Satan, the mighty prince of the power of the ____" (Eph. 2:2)
26 Walk leisurely (2 Sam. 11:2)
27 Belonging to the country holding Hebrews for 400 years (Exod. 14:7)

DOWN

2 Cut into two parts (Gen. 15:10)
3 Place to store liquid (Zech. 4:3)
4 City Philistines fled to when scared by God's thunder (1 Sam. 7:10, 11)
5 Flowering shrub (1 Kings 19:4)
6 Level part of a seated person (2 Kings 4:20)
7 "The Lord will not ____ his chosen people, for that would dishonor his great name"; desert (1 Sam. 12:22)
11 Honey maker (Ps. 118:12)
13 Without direction or a goal (Gen. 21:14)
15 Closest (Matt. 8:33)
16 Expressive body movement (Deut. 12:6)
17 "Work happily together. Don't ____ to act big"; attempt (Rom. 12:16)
19 Man-made waterway (Ezek. 1:1)
21 Distinctive odor (Song 4:11)
23 Also (Gen. 3:6)

(Solution on p. 205)

ALMOST THERE

ACROSS

1 Eye cosmetic (Jer. 4:30)
5 Engaged in, such as war (Rev. 17:14)
8 "Learn to be wise ... and develop good judgment and common sense! I cannot ____ this point"; stress too much (Prov. 4:5)
9 Position, such as an army (2 Chron. 33:14)
11 "May those curses return and cling to him like his clothing or his ____"; waistband (Ps. 109:19)
15 Lacking self-control
17 Weeps aloud with convulsive gasping (Gen. 27:34)
19 Breaks up plowed soil before planting (Hos. 10:11)
22 "When you hear of wars and ____ beginning, don't panic.... The end won't follow immediately"; revolutions (Luke 21:9)
24 "The man ____ his wife Eve (meaning 'The life-giving one')" (Gen. 3:20)
25 Longed for with an aching (Isa. 62:1)

DOWN

1 State of mind or emotion (John 7:32)
2 Filled with an odor (Song 5:13)
3 "You ____ the world's seasoning, to make it tolerable" (Matt. 5:13)
4 Nearly correct (Josh. 7:4)
5 "My power shows up best in ____ people"; lacking vigor (2 Cor. 12:9)
6 "We ____ along the tides of time as swiftly as a racing river, and vanish as quickly as a dream"; move smoothly (Ps. 90:5)
7 "In ____ season Christ will be revealed from heaven by the blessed and only Almighty God"; appropriate (1 Tim. 6:15)
10 "We beg you not to ____ aside this marvelous message of God's great kindness"; cast (2 Cor. 6:1)
12 Be enough to allow one to get by for a time (Heb. 9:10)
13 Partly-opened flowers that developed on Aaron's rod (Num. 17:5)
14 Aspersion (Gen. 30:23)
16 Neonatal infant (Exod. 1:22)
18 "We should behave like God's very own children, adopted into the ____ of his family, and calling to him, 'Father, Father'"; heart (Rom. 8:15)
20 Stepped upon (Rev. 19:15)
21 "Do not let any part of your bodies become tools of wickedness, to be ____ for sinning" (Rom. 6:13)
22 The Hebrew spies stayed at an ____ operated by Rahab (Josh. 2:1)
23 Beverage made by steeping shrub leaves (Hos. 4:12)

(Solution on p. 205)

DESERT DISCOVERY

ACROSS

1 Having a full, rounded form (Ezek. 34:22)
4 "Laziness lets the roof leak, and soon the ____ begin to rot"; roof supports (Eccles. 10:18)
8 "Give generously, for your gifts will return to you ____"; at a subsequent time (Eccles. 11:1)
9 Nomadic Arab (Jer. 3:2)
10 Unauthorized entry; illegal act (Ezek. 46:20)
11 "What a glorious Lord! He who daily bears our burdens ____ gives us our salvation"; in addition (Ps. 68:19)
13 "The Lord is close to those whose hearts are breaking; he rescues those who are humbly ____ for their sins"; regretful (Ps. 34:18)
15 Female servants (Mark 14:66)
19 Excessively dry
20 Close relationship (Ezra 9:14, KJV)
23 Extreme (Acts 22:11)
24 O.T. prophet who married a prostitute
25 "You have ____ him with eternal happiness. You have given him the unquenchable joy of your presence"; furnished (Ps. 21:6)
26 Abysses (Jer. 16:16)

DOWN

1 Roman official who authorized Jesus' execution (Matt. 27:24)
2 "Don't you ____ your cattle from their stalls on the Sabbath and lead them out for water?"; loose (Luke 13:15)
3 Sweat (Ezek. 44:18)
4 "The child Jesus became a strong, ____ lad, and was known for wisdom beyond his years; and God poured out his blessings on him"; vigorously healthy (Luke 2:40)
5 "Our natural lives will ____ as grass does when it becomes all brown and dry"; wither (1 Pet. 1:24)
6 "At God's command Moses performed amazing miracles that have never been ____"; duplicated or rivaled (Deut. 34:11)
7 Older or higher-ranking (Gen. 50:7)
12 Starved for food (Gen. 41:55, KJV)
14 Left out (2 Chron. 21:19)
16 Steep-sided valley (John 18:1)
17 Hurt or insult (John 6:61)
18 Side roads (Judg. 5:6, KJV)
21 "'Woe to unjust judges and to those who ____ unfair laws,' says the Lord"; pass down (Isa. 10:1)
22 "In this way each generation has been able to obey his laws and to set its hope ____ on God and not forget his glorious miracles"; over again (Ps. 78:7)

32

(Solution on p. 205)

THE MINISTRY OF JESUS

ACROSS

1 "He asked them, 'Who do you think I am?' Peter replied, 'The Messiah—the ____ of God!'" (Luke 9:20)

5 Deliver a sermon (Jon. 3:4)

8 "The days will come when all who ____ a blessing or take an oath shall swear by the God of Truth" (Isa. 65:16)

9 "No one needed to tell him how changeable human ____ is!" (John 2:24)

10 Admin's father (in Jesus' family tree; Luke 3:33)

11 Something taught or believed (1 Tim. 1:3)

12 Island where John wrote the book of Revelation (Rev. 1:9)

14 "Act in a way ____ of those who have been chosen for such wonderful blessings" (Eph. 4:1)

16 "God publicly endorsed Jesus of Nazareth by doing tremendous ____ through him" (Acts 2:22)

19 "Honor your marriage and its ____, and be pure" (Heb. 13:4)

21 Syrian false god (2 Kings 5:17, 18)

22 Commit money to another in hopes of a profit (Luke 19:13)

23 Large Mediterranean island near Syria (Acts 21:3)

24 City of homeless, demon-possessed man Jesus healed (Luke 8:27)

DOWN

2 "If you ____ your father and mother, yours will be a long life" (Eph. 6:3)

3 City near Antioch and Lystra where Paul preached (2 Tim. 3:11)

4 Insurrection leader killed by the Romans (Acts 5:36)

5 "When you hear of wars and insurrections beginning, don't ____. The end won't follow immediately" (Luke 21:9)

6 "This was his riddle: 'Food came out of the ____, and sweetness from the strong'" (Judg. 14:14)

7 Home city of Aquila and Priscilla (Acts 18:1, 2)

13 "God has given each of us the ____ to do certain things well" (Rom. 12:6)

14 "Master, you shouldn't be ____ our feet like this" (John 13:6)

15 "[Onesiphorus's] visits ____ me like a breath of fresh air" (2 Tim. 1:16)

17 "Use every piece of God's ____ to resist the enemy whenever he attacks" (Eph. 6:13)

18 "Eubulus sends you greetings, and so do Pudens, ____, Claudia, and all the others" (2 Tim. 4:21)

20 Solomon was ____ than any other man

(Solution on p. 205)

SUNDAY MORNING

ACROSS

1 Small place of worship (Amos 7:13)
5 "There's no use arguing with a fool. He only rages and _____, and tempers flare"; mocks (Prov. 29:9)
8 An official of King Solomon (Ezra 2:55, 57)
9 Short trip for specific task (Jer. 47:7)
10 Prophet who confronted David regarding Bathsheba (2 Sam. 12:13)
11 Main seaport of Syria (Acts 21:3)
12 After tenth (Num. 7:72)
14 Confidence in oneself (Isa. 3:18)
17 Swelled out in rolling waves (Exod. 19:18)
19 "It is hard to stop a quarrel _____ it starts, so don't let it begin"; after (Prov. 17:14)
21 "I will _____ all peoples of the earth, including my people in Israel, and he shall bring peace among the nations"; remove weapons from (Zech. 9:10)
23 One who understands written words (Mark 13:14)
24 "Since your real home is in heaven, I _____ you to keep

away from the evil pleasures of this world"; plead (1 Pet. 2:11)
25 Offensive; hateful; abhorrent (Prov. 30:23, KJV)
26 "Thank God that though you once chose to be slaves of sin, now you have _____ with all your heart the teaching to which God has committed you"; followed (Rom. 6:17)

DOWN

2 "Never be in a _____ about choosing a pastor"; rush (1 Tim. 5:22)
3 "Be glad for all God is planning for you. Be patient in trouble, and _____ always"; inclined to talk with God (Rom. 12:12)
4 Devices with rungs for climbing (Deut. 20:20)
5 "_____ God loved us as much as that, we surely ought to love each other too"; because (1 John 4:11)
6 "This cup is the new testament in my blood: this do ye, as _____ as ye drink it, in remembrance of me"; frequently (1 Cor. 11:25, KJV)
7 Wildly excited (Acts 5:24)

13 Complex and ornate (Exod. 39:5)
15 Built up spiritually (Acts 9:31, KJV)
16 "God will tenderly comfort you when you _____ these same sufferings"; endure; pass through (2 Cor. 1:7)
18 Places of earliest stages of development (Hos. 9:14)
20 Mediterranean island where Titus ministered (Titus 1:5)
22 Fuss (Mark 5:39, KJV)

(Solution on p. 205)

WHAT TO DO

ACROSS

1 Atmosphere (2 Sam. 16:13)
4 Respectful address to Indian: var.
8 To cover with icing
12 Southeastern U.S. state: abbr.
13 "Christ is the ____ of his body, the Church" (Eph. 4:15)
14 Italian city
15 Southern Judean city (Josh. 15:21, 32)
16 Energized; authorized (Luke 11:19)
18 An Ethiopian prince
19 Smoked salmon
20 Up to date with (Prov. 24:3)
25 Married
28 Narrate the facts (Heb. 11:32)
30 Fodder (1 Cor. 3:12)
31 Command from God: 3 wds. (quote excerpted from John 16:24)
35 ____ West
36 Broke from captivity (Gen. 14:13)
37 Assembled listeners: abbr. (Acts 25:24)
38 Prepared again for a task (2 Tim. 3:17)
40 Atomic Energy Commission: abbr.
41 Son of Caleb (1 Chron. 4:15)

44 David's wife; Solomon's mother (1 Kings 1:11)
50 Constantly complain (Judg. 16:16)
51 Body fluid compound
52 King of Israel (1 Kings 16:8)
53 Green indicator lamp: abbr.
54 Name of rock and winepress (Judg. 7:25)
55 Dyansen Corp. trademark
56 Cunning

DOWN

1 Long distance away (Isa 30:27)
2 Pelvis bones
3 Pillaged (1 Kings 14:26)
4 Her (Gen. 3:20)
5 Garment's folded edge (1 Sam. 24:11)
6 Talk freely and frankly
7 Worship images (Gen. 31:30)
8 Goat (Deut. 14:5)
9 Beth____ (1 Sam. 7:11)
10 Before
11 ____ Caesar
17 Know of
21 ____ constrictor
22 Operate steadily (Gen. 39:5)
23 Final extent (Gen. 9:13)
24 "Anyone who is hanged on ____ is cursed": 2 wds. (Gal. 3:13)
25 Repeated lashings (Gal. 6:17)

26 "Don't ____sdrop!" (Eccles. 7:21)
27 Changed color (Exod. 39:34)
28 ____h; baby massacre site (Matt. 2:18)
29 Birthright trader (Heb. 12:16)
32 Male courtesy title: abbr.
33 Coronary care unit: abbr.
34 Education Auditing Institute: abbr.
38 Follows do musically: pl.
39 Enlarged: obs.
40 King Omri's son (1 Kings 16:28)
42 Hurl insults (1 Sam. 25:14)
43 Not pretty
44 Nephew of Abraham (Gen. 22:20, 21)
45 "Humble men ____ very fortunate!" (Matt. 5:3)
46 Golf ball holder
47 Easterly: abbr.
48 Sheepish announcement
49 Army health nurse: abbr.

(Solution on p. 205)

OLD TESTAMENT STORIES

ACROSS

1 Joab's brother, who could run like a deer in battle (2 Sam. 2:18)
5 King who rid Israel of Jezebel and Baal worship (2 Kings 10:19, 20)
9 Curved seizing and holding devices used to capture King Manasseh (2 Chron. 33:10, 11)
10 Marches, as in a procession (Luke 20:46)
11 Liquid containers Gideon's army used to conceal their torches (Judg. 7:19, KJV)
13 Extended travel on an assignment (Num. 13:25)
15 Pack animal; offspring between donkey and horse (2 Sam. 18:9)
16 Two-wheeled hauling device, often pulled by animals (1 Sam. 6:7)
20 Shallow stream crossing site (Gen. 32:22)
21 "Some nations boast of armies and of _____, but our boast is in the Lord our God"; implements of war (Ps. 20:7)
24 Tribe of Israel; enemy of Judah (Isa. 9:21)
25 One of 12 spies; man in tribe of Benjamin (Num. 13:3, 9)

26 "God sometimes _____ sorrow in our lives to help us turn away from sin and seek eternal life"; employs (2 Cor. 7:10)
27 Intense desire for liquid (Exod. 15:24)

DOWN

2 "Select three men from each tribe, and I will send them to _____ the unconquered territory and bring back a report of its size and natural divisions so that I can divide it for you" (Josh. 18:4)
3 Possesses
4 "Ten _____ stood at a distance, crying out, 'Jesus, sir, have mercy on us'" (Luke 17:12, 13)
5 What Gideon's army broke so their torches blazed in the night (Judg. 7:19)
6 Place to remain out of sight (1 Sam. 20:19)
7 Large water navigation crafts (Gen. 49:13)
8 Seize and hold without right (Eccles. 4:15)
12 Sword handle (Judg. 3:22)
14 Temporary army quarters (1 Sam. 26:5)
15 "Though a mighty army _____

against me, my heart shall know no fear! I am confident that God will save me" (Ps. 27:3)
17 Present for acceptance (Ps. 4:5)
18 Protective covering for a soldier's head (1 Sam. 17:38)
19 King of Persia who conquered Babylon and freed the captive Jews (2 Chron. 36:22)
22 Back of the neck: pl.
23 Armed conflict between nations (2 Sam. 7:11)
25 A loyalist to King David (1 Kings 1:8)

(Solution on p. 205)

SEARCH FOR TRUTH

ACROSS

1 "Noah's _____ in God was in direct contrast to the rest of the world"; trust (Heb. 11:7)

5 Harmonious notes sounded together (Isa. 24:8)

8 Implement to propel a boat (Ezek. 27:6)

9 "In that day he who created the royal dynasty of David will be a _____ of salvation to all the world"; flag or standard (Isa. 11:10)

10 Not readily controlled or disciplined (Exod. 33:5)

11 "_____ friends, never avenge yourselves. Leave that to God"; highly valued (Rom. 12:19)

12 Years of rest for the Hebrews' land (Lev. 26:35)

14 Admitting something's true (1 Kings 1:47)

17 Seemed desirable (1 Sam. 15:9)

19 "God has given _____ of you some special abilities; be sure to use them to help _____ other" (1 Pet. 4:10)

21 "I have had to feed you with milk and not with solid food because you couldn't _____ anything stronger"; assimilate (1 Cor. 3:2)

23 "It is _____ for a camel to go through the eye of a needle than for a rich man to enter the Kingdom of God"; less difficult (Mark 10:25)

24 "My purpose is to give life in all _____ fullness (John 10:10)

25 Pattern or sketch (Num. 8:4)

26 Angelic creature that serves and worships God in heaven

DOWN

2 Manage to escape (Jer. 25:29)

3 "If anyone thinks he knows all the answers, he is just showing his _____"; lack of knowledge (1 Cor. 8:2)

4 Realized ahead of time; anticipated (Prov. 22:3)

5 Small fragment (Amos 5:11)

6 "If we confess _____ sins to God, he can be depended on to forgive us and to cleanse us from every wrong" (1 John 1:9)

7 Trainable sea mammal (Ezek. 16:9)

13 One who makes an unprovoked attack

15 Prisoner (Zech.1:14)

16 "I was the one chosen for this special joy of telling the Gentiles the Glad News of the _____ treasures available to them in Christ"; unlimited (Eph. 3:8)

18 Language of ancient Romans (John 19:20)

20 "Silver was too _____ to count for much in those days"; inexpensive (2 Chron. 9:20)

22 Father of Hophni and Phinehas (1 Sam. 1:3)

(Solution on p. 206)

SCHOOL DAZE

ACROSS

1 Carved pole used as tribal emblem or idol (Ezek. 43:9)
4 Hung to swing freely, such as Absalom by his hair (2 Sam. 18:14)
8 Equal Rights Amendment: abbr.
9 Engaged in regularly; exercised diligently (Luke 11:53)
10 Living without a permanent home (Jer. 25:24)
11 One who carves letters in stone or metal (2 Chron. 2:14)
12 The Jewish leaders "could think of nothing, for Jesus was a ____ to the people—they hung on every word he said" (Luke 19:48)
14 Private teacher (1 Chron. 27:32)
16 Group of civilians aiding law enforcement (2 Kings 21:24)
20 Speed contest (1 Cor. 9:24)
21 Shook; spoke with trembling (1 Sam. 22:12)
24 Player of a pipelike musical instrument (Isa. 30:29)
25 Jewish religious leader and teacher (Matt. 9:18)
26 Likely; suitable (Exod. 34:15)
27 "The Jewish leaders were surprised when they heard Jesus. 'How can he know so much when he's never been to our ____?' they asked" (John 7:15)
28 "O Belteshazzar, I know that the spirit of the holy gods is in you and no mystery is too great for you to ____" (Dan. 4:9)

DOWN

1 Having point covered or extended, such as a spear (1 Sam. 17:7)
2 Fastening together, such as with cord or ribbon (Exod. 39:21)
3 "Moses was the go-between—the ____ between the people of Israel and the Angel who gave them the Law of God" (Acts 7:38)
4 Moved rhythmically to music (Mark 6:22)
5 "God raised Jesus up to the heights of heaven and gave him a ____ which is above every other" (Phil. 2:9)
6 Runged climbing devices (Deut. 20:20)
7 Luke's occupation (Col. 4:14)
13 "Some who listened were persuaded and became ____"; new believers (Acts 17:4)
15 Rude and vulgar, like Nabal (1 Sam. 25:3)
17 Occupations requiring special skills (Exod. 35:35)
18 Production allotments; assigned minimums (Exod. 5:14)
19 Have high regard for (Luke 16:8)
22 "It is senseless to pay tuition to educate a ____ who has no heart for truth"; one who resists authority (Prov. 17:16)
23 Home of one of David's top thirty soldiers (2 Sam. 23:34)

(Solution on p. 206)

LIFE AND DEATH

ACROSS

1 Instrumental group
(2 Chron. 5:13)
5 Large tub (1 Kings 7:38)
8 Restrain or moderate
12 Spice used on Jesus' body
(John 19:39)
13 Piercing site (Exod. 21:6)
14 Hushai's father (1 Chron. 7:12)
15 Mourn (2 Sam. 1:24)
16 Woman: pron. (Gen. 2:23)
17 Circular jewelry (Gen. 41:41)
18 Holdups (Ezek. 12:25)
20 Belonging to Miriam's brother
(Exod. 15:20)
22 _____ vs. Wade
23 Particular
24 Door beam (Exod. 12:22)
27 Jerked (Judg. 16:14)
31 African or Asian people
32 Independent retirement
account: abbr.
33 Prepare for burial (Luke 23:56)
37 Stray (2 John 1:9)
40 Round, green vegetable (Gen.
25:34)
41 Industry standard architecture: computer abbr.
42 Defense device (Judg. 14:6)
45 Son of Cush (Gen. 10:7)
49 Eve's second child (Gen. 4:2)
50 Son of Leah and Jacob (Gen.
30:11)

52 Greasy; slick (Ps. 55:21)
53 Stab with a horn (Exod. 21:29)
54 Bible's second book: abbr.
55 Capture device (Josh. 8:22)
56 Grandson of Adam and Eve
(Luke 3:38)
57 Programming comment: computer abbr.
58 Present place (Gen. 13:9)

DOWN

1 Prostitute
2 Away from the wind
3 "The first _____, the angels did
say"
4 Leave (1 John 2:27)
5 Large boat (Ezek. 27:26)
6 Ooh and _____
7 Covenant; agreement (Gen.
26:28)
8 Childless (Gen. 11:30)
9 Abinadab's son (2 Sam. 6:3)
10 Eastern U.S. state: abbr.
11 Dyne's worth of energy units
19 Ye Olde Enoch: abbr.
21 Expression of surprise or triumph (Job 39:25)
24 Strong cleaning acid (Job 9:30)
25 "Just say, '_____' has sent me"
(Exod. 3:14)
26 Home town of Ahimelech, the
priest (1 Sam. 21:1)
28 Child: slang (1 Sam. 17:33)

29 Before
30 Daughters of the American
Revolution: abbr.
34 Hard, often red-skinned fruit
(Prov. 9:17)
35 Northern hemisphere constellation
36 Animals' feeding trough
(Luke 2:7)
37 Common sense; decision-making insight (Prov. 2:1)
38 Photographic film speed rating: abbr.
39 Vineyard owner Jezebel killed
(1 Kings 21:15)
42 Pay (Deut. 24:15)
43 Teak wood: arch. (Ezek. 27:15)
44 Related to aircraft: pref.
46 Grow weary (Prov. 30:2)
47 Controversial chemical
sprayed on fruit
48 Advertising claims
51 Woodchopping tool
(Deut. 19:5)

(Solution on p. 206)

FOR EXAMPLE

ACROSS

1 Double-cross; sell out (Josh. 2:14)
7 Thin, crisp crackers (Lev. 2:4)
13 "Beautiful bdellium and even lapis ____" (Gen. 2:12)
14 N.T. name for Edom (Mark 3:8)
15 Suitable for growing crops
16 Designating (Zech. 11:7)
17 Not genuine
18 Subject matters (Matt. 3:1)
19 Job's wife said, "Curse him and ____" (Job 2:9)
20 Miniature representations (1 Sam. 6:17)
25 Clatter in rapid succession (Job 39:23)
31 Humble; degrade
32 Bundle of grain stalks (Gen. 37:7)
33 One who owes something (Jer. 15:10)
35 Digits opposed to four (Lam. 5:12)
36 Self-esteem
37 "A ____ goes around spreading rumors" (Prov. 11:13)
42 King of Israel; enemy of Judah (1 Kings 15:16)
48 Layman living in a monastery
49 City of Manasseh (Josh. 17:11)
50 Dried grape (1 Sam. 25:18)
51 Burning
52 Levites replaced all the ____ sons of Israel (Num. 8:18)
53 Hurry (Job 20:2)

DOWN

1 Blue: Ger.
2 Deserve (Rom. 4:4)
3 Russian ruler before 1917
4 Awkward, unsophisticated person
5 ____ breve (musical notation)
6 Produces; bears (Ps. 85:12)
7 Season between autumn and spring (Prov. 6:8)
8 One of Esau's wives (Gen. 36:2)
9 Boil up; rage (1 Sam. 20:3)
10 Giant inhabitants of plain of Kiriathaim (Gen. 14:5)
11 ____ Pache, European theologian and author
12 Droops
20 Crazy (2 Cor. 11:23)
21 Ancient Laconian clan
22 Apply lightly
23 Calculate approximately: abbr. (2 Kings 25:16)
24 Fifth sign of zodiac
26 Combustion debris (Jer. 52:18)
27 Fifth day of week: abbr.
28 Not permanent: abbr. (1 Kings 8:64)
29 Experimental site
30 Sixth letter: pl.
34 "He is giving more time for sinners to ____" (2 Pet. 3:9)
35 Samaritan opposed to Nehemiah (Neh. 6:1)
37 Pierce with ox's horn (Exod. 21:29)
38 Son of Joktan (Gen. 10:26-28)
39 Moved smoothly down a surface
40 To be enclosed with a query: abbr.
41 "____ not good for the man to be alone": 2 wds.
43 Endearing term for father: Gk.
44 Fullest extents: pl.
45 "Blood that he sprinkled on the mercy ____" (Heb. 9:7)
46 Smog
47 So be it; prayer's end (Matt. 6:13)

(Solution on p. 206)

AREAS OF CAUTION

ACROSS

1 Ninth month in Hebrew calendar

5 What holds something closed (John 1:27, KJV)

8 God "heals the _____, binding up their wounds"; woeful (Ps. 147:3)

9 Guard plotting against King Ahasuerus (Esther 2:21)

11 The Lord "isn't getting _____! He can hear you when you call" (Isa. 59:1)

15 "Praise God for _____ such loving-kindness to me"; publicly exhibiting (Ezra 7:28)

17 Small rodent: pl. (Isa. 66:17)

19 Anyone who _____ a brother Israelite and treats him as a slave or sells him must die; carries away illegally by force (Deut. 24:7)

22 Irreverently against God or sacred things (Rev. 13:1)

24 "Who is this king of yours who _____ to plot against the Lord?" presumes (Nah. 1:11)

25 Hastened (Esther 8:14)

DOWN

1 "It is safer to meet a bear robbed of her _____ than a fool caught in his folly" (Prov. 17:12)

2 City where murderous mob stoned Paul (Acts 14:19)

3 "You must not _____"; prevaricate (Exod. 20:16)

4 Sickness (Ezek. 43:25)

5 Tree's green outgrowth (Rev. 7:1)

6 To give a tenth to God (Luke 11:42)

7 "[Wisdom] is _____ from the eyes of all mankind; even the sharp-eyed birds in the sky cannot discover it" (Job 28:17, 21)

10 "Nineveh is like a leaking water _____"; vat (Nah. 2:8)

12 "A tree is identified by the kind of fruit it produces. _____ never grow on thorns" (Luke 6:44)

13 Esau's nickname, meaning "Red Stuff" (Gen. 25:30)

14 Knitting strands (Ezek. 27:19)

16 Established as compulsory (Deut. 17:11)

18 Seat with a back (2 Kings 4:10)

20 Large, tailless primates imported by Solomon (2 Chron. 9:21)

21 "I remained clear-_____, so that I could evaluate all these things" (Eccles. 2:9)

22 "If there come any unto you, and bring not this doctrine, receive him not into your house, neither _____ him God speed"; express to (2 John 1:10, KJV)

23 Solemn lyric poem (Hab. 3:19)

(Solution on p. 206)

GIFTS OF GOD

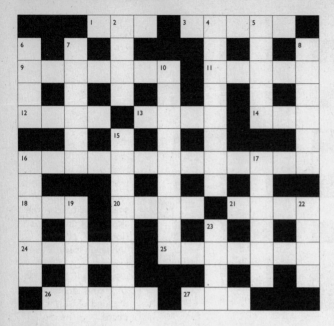

ACROSS

1 "The mountains melt like
____ before the Lord of all
the earth"; bees' secretion
(Ps. 97:5)

3 In the wrong way (Ps. 17:3)

9 Make provisions; settle details
(Mark 14:10)

11 An open sore (Lev. 13:10)

12 "God has reserved for his children the priceless gift of eternal life; it is ____ in heaven for
you, pure and undefiled"; preserved (1 Pet. 1:4)

13 Oxidation of exposed metal
(Hag. 2:17)

14 Drain away; gradually weaken
(Hos. 5:12)

16 Distinctive individuals
(Acts 18:15)

18 "A dull ____ requires great
strength; be wise and sharpen
the blade" (Eccles. 10:10)

20 Village where Jesus resurrected a widow's son
(Luke 7:11-14)

21 "Come, everyone, and ____
for joy! Shout triumphant
praises to the Lord"; applaud
(Ps. 47:1)

24 "When Christ comes back, all
his people will become ____
again"; animated (1 Cor. 15:23)

25 "Love forgets mistakes; ____
about them parts the best of
friends"; constantly scolding
(Prov. 17:9)

26 Person trained to care for
others (Gen. 24:59)

27 "Jehovah keeps his ____ upon
you as you come and go and
always guards you"; organ of
sight (Ps. 121:8)

DOWN

2 Sister of one's father or
mother (Lev. 18:13)

4 "The advice of a wise man
refreshes like water from a
____ spring"; elevated land
higher than a hill (Prov. 13:14)

5 Bags (Gen. 44:1)

6 Strong, sudden pull (Zech. 9:7)

7 "It is senseless for you to
work so hard from early
morning until late at night,
fearing you will starve to
death; for God wants his
loved ones to get their ____
rest"; suitable; right (Ps. 127:2)

8 Heavy curtains (Exod. 35:17)

10 "In this new life one's nationality or race or ____ or social
position is unimportant.
Whether a person has Christ

is what matters"; training by
formal instruction (Col. 3:11)

15 "I will bless the Lord who
____ me; he gives me wisdom
in the night"; advises (Ps. 16:7)

16 Public squares or markets
(Mark 6:56)

17 Set into a surface (2 Chron.
3:6)

19 Youngest of Job's four visitors
(Job 32:4)

22 What demons exorcised from
two men of Gadara went into
(Mark 5:13)

23 Offensive to look at

(Solution on p. 206)

UNHEALTHY RELATIONSHIPS

ACROSS

1 Robe's bottom (1 Sam. 24:11)
4 Window glass
8 Small valley (Ezek. 36:4)
12 Chopping tool (Deut. 19:5)
13 Son of Enoch (Gen. 4:18)
14 Judean city (Josh. 15:33, 34)
15 Samson's girlfriend (Judg. 16:3, 4)
17 18th letter of Hebrew alphabet
18 "Straw to ____ down the camels" (Gen. 24:32)
19 Anatomy between ribs and hip (John 13:4)
20 Unclothed (Gen. 2:25)
23 Asking as for charity (1 Sam. 2:36)
26 Major credit card company: abbr.
27 Speckled horse color
28 Canaanite city near Bethel (Gen. 13:3)
29 Droop
30 Long-legged wading bird (Jer. 8:7)
32 Doing business as: abbr.
33 Comparison term
34 "____ for those who persecute you!" (Matt. 5:44)
35 Edible seed pods (2 Sam. 17:28)
36 Disobedient to civil authority (Prov. 8:7)
38 Delivered; apportioned (Ruth 1:20)

39 Freedom from pain or worry (Gen. 27:39)
40 Coiling, crushing snake
41 Make a law (2 Chron. 24:6)
43 Most uncivilized (Ezek. 34:25)
47 Small, sheltered bay
48 Ordered; commanded
49 Son of Noah (Gen. 5:32)
50 Employed (Gen. 47:24)
51 ____-melech, Ethiopian palace official (Jer. 38:7)
52 Personal reference: Ger.

DOWN

1 Possessed (2 Kings 8:6)
2 Last three letters of runnable computer program's name
3 Honey
4 Heaped (Josh. 4:20)
5 Country near Edom (Num. 21:2-4)
6 Expression of negation: slang
7 Process of acquiring knowledge: abbr.
8 Plan (Num. 8:4)
9 Son of Elioenai (1 Chron. 3:24)
10 Boy (Gen. 21:19)
11 Uncle: Scot.
16 Mountain goat (Deut. 14:5)
17 ____d; clad in loose Roman garment
19 ____ Patillo (Christian musician)

20 Pertaining to the nose
21 Son of Abigail (2 Sam. 17:25)
22 Small beverage barrel
23 Donkeys' cries (Job 6:5)
24 Abigail's first husband (1 Sam. 25:3)
25 Goliath, for one (1 Sam. 17:4)
30 Top of a wave
31 Carve or engrave
32 Lay minister: abbr. (Phil. 1:1)
34 Put in position (Gen. 2:8)
35 Stringed jewelry item (Song 4:9)
37 Make cloth (Exod. 28:39)
38 Distributed to the poor (Lev. 26:26)
40 Await; stay
41 Old French coin with shield design
42 Negatives
43 Something woven: Scot.
44 Grandson of Jacob (Gen. 46:21)
45 Strategic Air Command: abbr.
46 Tons per man hour: abbr.
48 Exist

(Solution on p. 206)

PEOPLE APLENTY

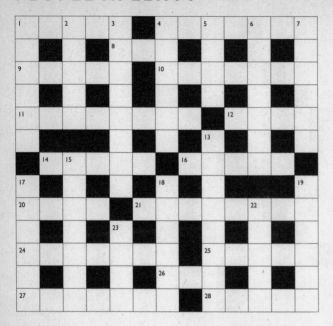

ACROSS

1 Make a swift diving attack (Neh. 4:11)
4 Child's name meaning "there is no glory" (1 Sam. 4:21)
8 Belonging to a male
9 Brother of Goliath the giant (1 Chron. 20:5)
10 Sapphira's husband, killed for lying to the Lord (Acts 5:1, 3, 5)
11 Queen Esther's adoptive father (Esther 2:5, 7)
12 A temporary Canaanite home of Israel was near the Tower of _____ (Gen. 35:21)
14 Father of the 12 patriarchs of the Jewish nation (Acts 7:8)
16 Author of many musical psalms during David's reign (2 Chron. 29:30)
20 "She was the brash, coarse _____, seen often in the streets and markets, soliciting at every corner for men to be her lovers" (Prov. 7:11)
21 Criminal Pilate released instead of Jesus (Matt. 27:26)
24 O.T. author seeing vision of valley of dry bones
25 Rebecca's husband; son of Abraham (Rom. 9:10)
26 Earlier than the present (Gen. 42:8)

27 "The king appointed Shadrach, _____, and Abednego as Daniel's assistants" (Dan. 2:49)
28 "God sent those fingers to write this message: 'Mene,' 'Mene,' '_____,' 'Parsin'" (Dan. 5:25)

DOWN

1 Wife of Zebedee; mother of James and John, Jesus' disciples (Matt. 27:56; Mark 15:40)
2 Source of gold for King Solomon (1 Kings 9:28)
3 Friend of Paul; Onesimus's master
4 O.T. prophet who said, "The year King Uzziah died I saw the Lord! He was sitting on a lofty throne, and the Temple was filled with his glory"
5 "Some people like to make cutting remarks, but the words of the wise soothe and _____"; make sound or whole (Prov. 12:18)
6 Act of amassing or increasing, such as military forces: 2 wds. (1 Sam. 17:2)
7 "Peter said to him, 'I will never _____ you no matter what the others do'"; abandon (Mark 14:29)

13 Judas _____, disciple of Jesus who betrayed him (John 12:4)
15 Father of Jesus' disciple Levi (Acts 2:14; NASB)
17 Steady flow of water (Deut. 9:21)
18 One of Zelophehad's five unmarried daughters (Num. 26:33)
19 Brother of Aner and Mamre, Amorite allies of Abram (Gen. 14:13)
22 Darkest color (Gen. 30:32)
23 Son of Mephibosheth; grandson of Jonathan befriended by King David (2 Sam. 9:11, 12)

(Solution on p. 206)

MURDERERS

ACROSS

1 Call to mind: abbr. (Gen. 9:15)
4 Bread form (Exod. 29:23)
8 Long distance away (Isa. 30:27)
12 Wood cutter (1 Sam. 13:21)
13 Single occurrence (Gen. 29:35)
14 Narcotic
15 Repentant (Ps. 51:17)
17 Midianite general (Judg. 7:25)
18 Combined (Gen. 30:39)
19 Short, light strokes
21 Communication standard: computer abbr.
24 Transactions (Ps. 101:3)
27 Tree wrap (Joel 1:7)
30 Figurative name for Israel (Hos. 2:1)
32 Parts collection to assemble
33 King of Judah (1 Kings 15:9)
34 City of Refuge (1 Chron. 6:58)
35 Rather than
36 Start of Eve (Gen. 2:22)
37 Ahira's father (Num. 1:15)
38 Judean lowland city (Josh. 15:34)
39 Abigail's husband (1 Sam. 25:3)
41 Frost
43 Same as before: Lat. abbr.
45 Son of Ishmael (Gen. 25:12, 14)
49 Water-to-wine site (John 4:46)
51 Formal recording of name (Num. 3:40)
54 Idi ____ (African dictator)
55 O.T. herdsman and prophet
56 Network: abbr.
57 Tribe killing five missionaries in 1956
58 Small insects
59 "____! Humbug!" (Scrooge)

DOWN

1 Fool: Gk.
2 Bible's second book: abbr.
3 Restore to wholeness (Gen. 6:3)
4 Dominators (Matt. 20:25)
5 "Ben____," Rachel's dying word (Gen. 35:18)
6 Behave (Gen. 31:28)
7 Animal's nourishment (Gen. 24:32)
8 Unfired brick
9 "My God, why have you ____ me" (Matt. 27:46)
10 Chimpanzee or orangutan, e.g. (2 Chron. 9:21)
11 Addressing synagogue leader: Yid.
16 Hard, Asian wood
20 Jewish subclan head (Ezra 2:15)
22 First murderer (Gen. 4:8)
23 Father of Micaiah, the prophet (1 Kings 22:8)
25 Italian currency
26 Main supporting part (Exod. 37:20)
27 Animal shelter (1 Sam. 6:7)
28 ____ Minor; Turkish province (Acts 16:6, KJV)
29 Pertaining to Jewish spiritual leader (Matt. 9:18)
31 Woman's period; pref. (Lev. 12:2)
34 Joseph's father (Luke 3:23)
38 Particular periods of history
40 River in Syria (2 Kings 5:12)
42 Out of order (Ps. 17:3)
44 Olive brown color
46 Pierce with a knife (2 Sam. 20:10)
47 Grandson of Ham (Gen. 10:6, 7)
48 "Stone rejected has become the capstone of the ____" (Acts 4:11)
49 Credit account agreement: abbr.
50 Atomic mass unit: abbr.
52 Ostrich's relative
53 King of Meshech and Tubal (Ezek. 38:2)

(Solution on p. 206)

KING DAVID

ACROSS

1 Swollen eyelid
5 Stringed instrument invented by Jubal (Gen. 4:21)
9 Part of Jacob's traded meal (Gen. 25:34)
12 Common; general: pref.
13 Son of Hotham (1 Chron. 7:35)
14 Computer-aided instruction: abbr.
15 Amalekite king Saul captured (1 Sam. 15:20)
16 Gifted with ability (1 Sam. 16:18)
18 Hill of _____ in southeast Jerusalem (Jer. 31:39)
20 Business agreement (2 Sam. 3:12)
21 Father: infor.
23 Prepare killed game (Prov. 12:27)
27 Samson's type of vow (Judg. 16:17)
32 Caused sound with air (Josh. 6:16)
33 Accelerated Christian Education: abbr.
34 Make a uniform mixture
36 _____ carte: 2 wds.
37 Face covering (Job 24:15)
39 Extravagantly (Isa. 46:6)
41 The way in (2 Sam. 11:13)
43 Affirmative expression

44 American Academy of Arts and Letters: abbr.
47 Second king of Israel (2 Sam. 5:3)
51 Divisions (Gen. 2:10)
55 Dreadful; urgent
56 Rowing implement (Ezek. 27:6)
57 Cod relative
58 Tamar's husband (Gen. 38:8)
59 Typist's speed rating: abbr.
60 Equals three teaspoons: abbr.
61 Passed (Gen. 8:14)

DOWN

1 Heroin: slang
2 Roman garment
3 365 days (Gen. 14:4)
4 Site of David's cave hideaway (1 Sam. 23:29)
5 Head covering (1 Cor. 11:4)
6 Boundary city of Asher (Josh. 19:25, 26)
7 Abnormal respiratory sound
8 Beg; implore (Exod. 8:8)
9 Fraction of whole: abbr.
10 Extended arithmetic element: abbr.
11 Help (Deut. 18:10)
17 National Labor Relations Board: abbr.
19 A sharp projection, as from the point of an arrow
22 Seasoning herb

24 King Hoshea's father (2 Kings 15:30)
25 Exchange for money (Gen. 23:4)
26 Move back and forth (Ps. 29:9)
27 Personal designation (Gen. 12:2)
28 A round metal container: 2 wds.
29 Gusto (Ezek. 23:44)
30 Leaves used for divining (Hos. 4:12)
31 Resentful awareness of another's advantage (Deut. 5:21)
35 Expired (Gen. 5:5)
38 Morton, TX radio station
40 A cast outline (2 Kings 20:9)
42 Expensive pleasure cruise vessel
45 False prophet in Babylon (Jer. 29:20, 21)
46 Units of Albanian currency
48 "I am the true _____" (John 15:1)
49 Country at war with Iraq for eight years
50 Surface depression from a blow
51 Arrow shooter (Gen. 27:3)
52 Modern poetry form?
53 Upper body limb (1 Kings 13:6)
54 Divide: abbr. (Gen. 1:6)

(Solution on p. 206)

BEING WISE

ACROSS

1 "A fool thinks he needs no _____, but a wise man listens to others" (Prov. 12:15)
5 Break in friendly relations (Gen. 13:8)
9 Having mental facilities impaired by alcohol (Gen. 9:20)
10 Understanding of the true nature of a situation (1 Cor. 2:15)
11 "A relaxed _____ lengthens a man's life; jealousy rots it away"; state of mind about something (Prov. 14:30)
13 "A friendly discussion is as stimulating as the sparks that fly when _____ strikes _____" (Prov. 27:17)
15 "A man may ruin his chances by his own foolishness and then _____ it on the Lord" (Prov. 19:3)
17 "Develop good judgment and common _____" (Prov. 4:5)
21 Spoken by mouth (Dan. 1:18)
22 "God loved the world so much that he gave his only Son so that anyone who _____ in him shall not perish but have eternal life" (John 3:16)
25 Verify; corroborate (Exod. 22:13)
26 Untrue; not in accordance with fact (Deut. 19:21)
27 Worthless; empty (Matt. 12:36)
28 "For he _____ down our foes" (Ps. 108:13)

DOWN

2 Be uncertain about; mistrust (Matt. 21:21)
3 Pigmented writing liquid (2 Cor. 3:3)
4 Great general from tribe of Benjamin (2 Chron. 17:17)
5 Trick; deception (Gen. 27:23)
6 Calculations (Num. 26:63)
7 "The intelligent man is always open to new _____"; imaginations in the mind (Prov. 18:15)
8 "The grass withers, the flowers fade, but the Word of our God shall _____ forever"; endure (Isa. 40:8)
12 Change from wild to controllable (James 3:8)
14 Another name for Matthew, tax collector turned disciple (Mark 2:14)
16 Gained understanding by study or experience (Isa. 29:13)
18 "Be sure you know a person well before you _____ for his credit"; give a personal guarantee (Prov. 11:15)
19 "You will need the _____ of salvation and the sword of the Spirit—which is the Word of God"; mind protector (Eph. 6:17)
20 Inquired about; put a question to (Gen. 3:13)
23 "It is a badge of honor to accept _____ criticism"; founded on truth or fact (Prov. 25:12)
24 Knowing and doing the right thing (Prov. 10:8)
26 "Are you friend or _____?"; enemy (Josh. 5:13)

(Solution on p. 206)

IN THE FAMILY

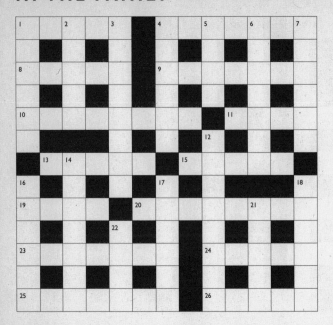

ACROSS

1 "You shall not leave in ____, running for your lives; for the Lord will go ahead of you"; rapid action (Isa. 52:12)

4 Provide care and feeding (Jer. 1:10)

8 Respond (Dan. 11:40)

9 Sudden, surprise attackers (1 Sam. 13:17)

10 "Since Christ is so much ____, the Holy Spirit warns us to listen to him"; higher or better (Heb. 3:7)

11 "Then I will ____ you of idolatry and faithlessness, and my love will know no bounds"; heal (Hos. 14:4)

13 "A true friend is always ____"; faithful (Prov. 17:17)

15 Joint between foot and leg (Acts 3:7)

19 "If the military demand that you carry their gear for a ____, carry it two"; 5,280 feet (Matt. 5:41)

20 Symbolic story (Gal. 4:24, KJV)

23 "The word of God has ____ them; they don't want it at all"; aroused strong feelings of displeasure (Jer. 6:10)

24 Taut (Dan. 3:21)

25 "A beautiful woman lacking discretion and ____ is like a fine gold ring in a pig's snout"; freedom from any trace of lewdness (Prov. 11:22)

26 Series of mountains in a row (Job 39:8)

DOWN

1 "The people of Israel began once again to worship other gods, and once again the Lord let their enemies ____ them"; continually annoy (Judg. 6:1)

2 Inundate (Luke 8:23)

3 Relating to the outside (2 Chron. 15:6)

4 "Heaven can be entered only through the ____ gate"; less wide than normal (Matt. 7:13)

5 "One who doesn't give the gift he promised is like a cloud blowing over a desert without dropping any ____" (Prov. 25:14)

6 Without rival or similarity (Ps. 150:2)

7 "It is ____ for a camel to go through the eye of a needle than for a rich man to enter the Kingdom of God"; less difficult (Luke 18:25)

12 Forefather (Heb. 7:9)

14 Compelled (Acts 18:14)

16 Preserve a corpse (Gen. 50:2)

17 "Anyone whose Father is God listens ____ to the words of God"; very willingly (John 8:47)

18 Shiny evergreen (Zech. 1:8)

21 Bodily part performing a special function (Lev. 16:27)

22 "The magicians tried to do the same thing with their secret ____, but this time they failed"; skills (Exod. 8:18)

(Solution on p. 206)

DETAILS, DETAILS

ACROSS

1 Cutting or tearing open (Amos 1:13)

5 "These trials are only to see whether or not your faith is strong and pure, as fire _____ gold and purifies it"; refines or evaluates (1 Pet. 1:7)

8 "God was afraid I might be puffed up; so I was given a physical condition which has been a _____ in my flesh" (2 Cor. 12:7)

9 An unbreakable stone (Zech. 7:12, KJV)

10 Next to one's sleeping space (Luke 4:39)

12 "I, Jesus, am both David's Root and his Descendant. I am the bright Morning _____"; visible celestial body (Rev. 22:16)

16 "Swallow your pride; don't let _____ stand in the way"; self-consciousness (Prov. 6:3)

18 "I strain to reach the end of the _____ and receive the prize for which God is calling us up to heaven because of what Christ Jesus did for us"; speed contest (Phil. 3:14)

20 Isa. similar to (Luke 5:36, KJV)

23 Not neat or combed

24 Cut with care, as a figure from wood (Isa. 40:20)

25 Freed from pressure or care (Ps. 73:12)

26 "Pray first that the Lord's message will spread _____ and triumph wherever it goes, winning converts everywhere"; quickly (2 Thess. 3:1)

DOWN

1 First Bible book named for a woman

2 "In the mouth of a fool a _____ becomes as useless as a paralyzed leg"; maxim (Prov. 26:17)

3 Hotel (Josh. 2:1)

4 Girl born to one's child (Lev. 18:17)

5 Platter (Matt. 14:8)

6 "My children are _____ enough at doing wrong, but for doing right they have no talent"; intelligent (Jer. 4:22)

7 "Since you became alive again when Christ arose from the dead, now _____ your sights on the rich treasures and joys of heaven"; fix (Col. 3:1)

11 Waves that break on shore (Jer. 50:42)

13 Religious liturgy or ceremony (Lev. 14:19)

14 Large, heavy mammal with shaggy hair (2 Sam. 17:8)

15 Small body of land surrounded by water

17 Went into (Exod. 20:21)

19 Sweet food made from baked batter (1 Sam. 25:18)

21 Among; during

22 "If anyone wants to be a follower of mine, let him _____ himself and take up his cross and follow me"; disavow (Matt. 16:24)

23 "The diligent man makes good _____ of everything he finds"; application (Prov. 12:27)

24 Head covering (Ezek. 27:10)

(Solution on p. 207)

TIME TO MOVE

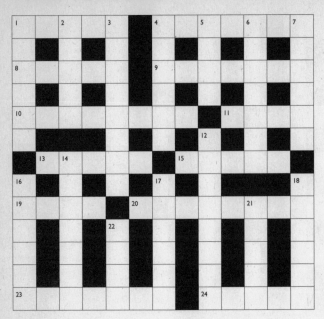

ACROSS

1 "Wisdom is far more valuable than gold and ____"; transparent vessel or mirror (Job 28:17)
4 Plant leaves (Ezek. 19:10)
8 "That is why we never give up. Though our bodies are dying, our ____ strength in the Lord is growing every day"; opposite of outer (2 Cor. 4:16)
9 "Of all the beasts, [the crocodile] is the proudest—____ of all that he sees"; sovereign (Job 41:1, 34)
10 "A good reputation is more ____ than the most expensive perfume"; of great importance (Eccles. 7:1)
11 "What is wrong cannot be righted; it is water ____ the dam; and there is no use thinking of what might have been"; past (Eccles. 1:15)
13 Small containers, usually enclosed (Mark 12:41)
15 "As all the people watched, Solomon ____ down, reached out his arms toward heaven, and prayed this prayer" (2 Chron. 6:13)
19 Beat with a whip (Acts 22:25)
20 Estrange (Ezek. 48:14, KJV)

23 "Your throne, O God, endures forever. Justice is your royal ____"; staff signifying authority (Ps. 45:6)
24 Gradually diminished (2 Cor. 3:11)

DOWN

1 Feel sorrow for (Ruth 1:13)
2 Render void (Eph. 2:15)
3 "I ____, 'I'm slipping, Lord!' and he was kind and saved me"; cried loudly" (Ps. 94:18)
4 "The fool who provokes his ____ to anger and resentment will finally have nothing worthwhile left"; parents and children (Prov. 11:29)
5 "There will always be some among you who are poor. You must ____ to them liberally"; give temporarily (Deut. 15:11)
6 "Everyone must straighten out his life to be ready for the Lord's ____"; coming (Mark 1:3)
7 "I ____ you to be of good cheer"; urge earnestly (Acts 27:22, KJV)
12 Jesus said, "The world's sin is ____ in me"; lack of trust (John 16:9)
14 Make dim or partly hidden (Hab. 3:11)

16 Solid pieces of a hard substance with flat sides (1 Kings 5:17)
17 Musician (1 Sam. 16:18)
18 Cut down (2 Kings 3:25)
21 "A sensible man watches for problems ____ and prepares to meet them"; in the future (Prov. 27:12)
22 "Those who still reject me are like the restless sea, which is never still, but always churns up mire and ____"; soil (Isa. 57:20)

(Solution on p. 207)

WISDOM AND FOLLY

ACROSS

1 People of country bordering Egypt (2 Chron. 16:8)
5 "The whole land is full of images, and the people are ____ in love with their idols"; wildly (Jer. 50:38)
8 "Jehoiada the priest bored a hole in the lid of a large chest ... and the doorkeepers put all of the people's ____ into it" (2 Kings 12:9)
9 "I want those already wise to become the wiser and become leaders by exploring the depths of meaning in these ____ of truth"; lumps of gold (Prov. 1:5)
11 God "____ swiftly to my aid with wings of wind" (Ps. 18:10)
15 Involuntarily (Num. 30:5)
17 "The priceless gift of eternal life ... is ____ in heaven for you, pure and undefiled, beyond the reach of change and decay"; preserved (1 Pet. 1:4)
19 Urban thoroughfares (Esther 6:11)
22 "Not using your liberty for a cloke of ____, but as the servants of God"; ill will (1 Pet. 2:16, KJV)

24 Disciple who walked on water (Matt. 14:29)
25 "We—every one of us—have ____ away like sheep"; wandered (Isa. 53:6)

DOWN

1 Stroke the tongue over (Ezek. 23:34)
2 "Let us be glad and rejoice and honor him; for the time has come for the wedding ____ of the Lamb"; ceremonial dinner (Rev. 19:7)
3 What Absalom dangled in by his hair (2 Sam. 18:9)
4 Replacements (Lev. 27:33)
5 Partner (Isa. 34:16)
6 "My health fails; my spirits ____, yet God remains! He is the strength of my heart"; sag (Ps. 73:26)
7 Expression of consent (Gen. 3:12)
10 "A lazy man won't even dress the ____ he gets while hunting" (Prov. 12:27)
12 "Our ____ here on earth are as transient as shadows"; 24-hour periods (Job 8:9)
13 "Let not the wise man ____ in his wisdom"; revel (Jer. 9:23)
14 "Our hearts ____, but at the

same time we have the joy of the Lord" (2 Cor. 6:10)
16 Drawing for prizes (Josh. 19:51)
18 "A tiny rudder makes a huge ship turn wherever the ____ wants it to go"; helmsman (James 3:4)
20 Lingering sign of damage (Gal. 6:17)
21 Employed (Exod. 3:15)
22 Travel guide (Ezek. 4:1)
23 Respectful address to a man (Gen. 24:18)

(Solution on p. 207)

TAKING A RISK

ACROSS

1 Violent outburst (Acts 19:23)
5 "My ____ to you is this: Go to God and confess your sins to him"; suggestion (Job 5:8)
8 "Rest in the Lord; wait patiently for him to ____"; produce an effect (Ps. 37:7)
9 "A wise man is mightier than a ____ man"; physically powerful (Prov. 24:5)
10 "God ____ displayed to the whole world Christ's triumph at the cross where your sins were all taken away"; publicly (Col. 2:15)
11 "It is wrong to sentence the poor and let the rich go ____"; at liberty (Prov. 24:23)
12 "The king appointed Shadrach, Meshach, and ____ as Daniel's assistants" (Dan. 2:49)
14 "To me, living means ____ for Christ"; favorable times (Phil. 1:21)
17 "I have ____ against thee, because thou hast left thy first love"; rather; to a certain degree (Rev. 2:4, KJV)
19 Affected, artificial manners (2 Cor. 11:20)
21 Performer (1 Sam. 16:18)
23 Divine revelation (Exod. 28:15)

24 Word meaning "son" in Hebrew (Amos 1:4)
25 Affairs or points of controversy (Judg. 9:35)
26 Regular wage for work done (1 Cor. 9:19)

DOWN

2 "Give generously, for your gifts will return to you ____"; at a subsequent time (Eccles. 11:1)
3 "Let us purify ourselves, living in the ____ fear of God, giving ourselves to him alone"; conducive to spiritual health (2 Cor. 7:1)
4 Elaborate procession (Rev. 15:1)
5 Make satisfaction or payment for (Lev. 4:28)
6 Contend (2 Chron. 35:18)
7 "Wear fine clothes—with a dash of ____"; perfumed liquid (Eccles. 9:8)
13 Disciple to whom Jesus said, "I could see you under the fig tree before Philip found you" (John 1:48)
15 "You shall be holy to me, for I the Lord am holy, and I have set you apart from all other ____ to be mine"; races (Lev. 20:26)

16 "The glory and honor of all the ____ shall be brought into the city of God"; political entities (Rev. 21:26)
18 Plants used for seasoning or medicine (Mark 15:23)
20 "Christ is the highest ____, with authority over every other power"; political figure (Col. 2:10)
22 "____ are the world's seasoning, to make it tolerable"; direct address (Matt. 5:13)

(Solution on p. 207)

TO GOD BE THE GLORY

ACROSS

1 Judge or faultfinder (Job 40:2)
5 Deprived of something (Jer. 18:21)
8 Son of Abdiel (1 Chron. 5:15)
9 Young woman (Gen. 24:16, KJV)
10 "When you give a gift to a _____, don't shout about it as the hypo- crites do"; panhandler (Matt. 6:2)
11 "Take off your _____, for you are standing on holy ground"; foot covering: sing. (Exod. 3:5)
12 One's name and personal recognition factors (Acts 7:13)
14 "I pray to the Father that out of his glorious, unlimited resources he will give you the mighty inner _____ of his Holy Spirit"; making healthier (Eph. 3:16)
18 "When darkness overtakes the man who delights in doing God's commands, light will come _____in"; suddenly breaking out (Ps. 112:4)
20 "Go _____ on others; then they will do the same for you"; not hard (Luke 6:37)
22 Cling to (Acts 15:1)
24 "If a soul commit a trespass, and sin through ignorance, he shall make _____ for the harm

that he hath done"; reparations (Lev. 5:15, 16, KJV)
25 Damage; jeopardize (Ruth 4:6, KJV)
26 "Release all the animals, birds, and reptiles, so that they will _____ abundantly and reproduce in great numbers"; propagate (Gen. 8:17)
27 "Do not bring an idol into your home and worship it, for then your doom is sealed. Utterly _____ it, for it is a cursed thing"; hate (Deut. 7:26)

DOWN

2 "Eternal peace was within your _____ and you turned it down"; grasp (Luke 19:42)
3 "Even honey seems _____ to a man who is full; but if he is hungry, he'll eat anything"; without flavor (Prov. 27:7)
4 Making watertight (Ezek. 27:9)
5 "A pastor must enjoy having guests in his home and must be a good _____ teacher"; Scripture (1 Tim. 3:2)
6 Soft floor covering (Lev. 11:32)
7 "No mountain, however high, can stand before Zerubbabel! For it will _____ out before him"; make smooth (Zech. 4:7)

11 Female sibling: inform. (Gen. 19:31)
13 Softest; most chewable (Amos 6:4)
15 "The mighty oceans _____ your praise"; sound following lightning (Ps. 93:3)
16 Worn or emaciated (2 Sam. 13:4)
17 Happy; lighthearted
19 Thing in a series or collection (Num. 3:31)
21 Front and back, as of a scroll (Ezek. 2:10)
23 Until (Hos. 8:5, KJV)

(Solution on p. 207)

THE POWER OF GOD

ACROSS

1 "Stand before the Lord in
_____, and do not sin against
him"; reverential wonder
(Ps. 4:4)

3 Walking (Mark 6:33, KJV)

9 Gathers; accumulates
(1 Chron. 29:25)

11 Become liable for

12 Dry and barren

13 Sign or warning for the future
(Luke 21:25)

14 Male sheep (Mal. 1:14)

16 "Adam's sin brought punishment to all, but Christ's _____
makes men right with God, so
that they can live"; moral
excellence (Rom. 5:18)

18 Edge of a curved object
(2 Chron. 4:2)

20 Turn an animal by a bridle
part (2 Kings 9:23)

21 "In our greatness we have
gathered up kingdoms as a
farmer gathers _____"; hard-
shelled reproductive bodies
(Isa. 10:14)

24 Mountain where Moses
received the Ten Command-
ments (Exod. 31:18)

25 "Some astrologers arrived in
Jerusalem, asking, 'Where is
the newborn King of the
Jews? for we have seen his
star in far-off _____ lands and
have come to worship him'";
direction (Matt. 2:1, 2)

26 Light-colored silicate mineral
(Rev. 21:20)

27 Body of water nearly surrounded by land (Josh. 15:2)

DOWN

2 "_____ me and I shall be
whiter than snow"; cleanse as
with a liquid (Ps. 51:7)

4 "God will judge them with
complete _____, for all heaven
declares that he is just"
(Ps. 50:6)

5 "This book unveils some of
the future activities soon to
_____ in the life of Jesus
Christ"; take place (Rev. 1:1)

6 "This miracle at _____ in Galilee was Jesus' first public dem-
onstration of his heaven-sent
power. And his disciples
believed that he really was the
Messiah" (John 2:11)

7 Cooking by dry heat (1 Kings
19:6)

8 "Even the puppies beneath the
table are permitted to eat the
_____ that fall"; small fragments
(Matt. 15:27)

10 Serve as the counterpart or
image of (Ezek. 21:14)

15 "God has planted _____ in the
hearts of men"; unending duration (Eccles. 3:11)

16 Most extraordinary; least seen
(Song 6:1)

17 Large birds of prey (Hab. 1:8)

19 Walk in a prim, affected manner (Isa. 3:16)

22 "A rebel's frustrations are
heavier than _____ and rocks";
loose, granular rock particles
(Prov. 27:3)

23 "Epaenetus was the very first
person to become a Christian
in _____"; Roman region north-
west of Syria (Rom. 16:5)

(Solution on p. 207)

NAME GAME

ACROSS

1 Cherished animal companions (2 Sam. 12:3)
5 Biographer of Solomon; O.T. prophet (2 Chron. 9:29)
9 Directly across from: abbr. (Num. 34:14)
12 Beginning; end; extremity: pref.
13 Mustard or God's message, e.g. (Luke 8:11; 13:19)
14 Father of Abner, King Saul's general (1 Sam. 14:51)
15 Brilliantly executed strategem
16 Survived fiery furnace (Dan. 3:23-25)
18 Aaron's son (Exod. 6:23)
20 Ship's distress signal
21 Unspoken; implied
23 Faint streak
26 Type of computer printer
29 Sarai's relation to Abram: infor.
31 ____ culpa
32 Conspirator (Num. 16:1, 2)
34 Prophet to Saul and David (1 Sam. 10:1; 19:18)
36 Last O.T. book: abbr.
37 Female domestic fowl (Luke 13:34)
39 Assigned work (1 Chron. 6:49)
40 Public notice: abbr.
42 King Jeroboam's father (1 Kings 11:26)
44 Eighth month: abbr. (Ezra 7:9)
46 ____ Pilate (Acts 4:27)
50 Woman who quarreled with Euodias (Phil. 4:2)
53 "Quota ____ est?": Lat.
54 Promissory note
55 Look intently into (Luke 24:12)
56 Female sheep: pl. (Gen. 30:40)
57 Long passenger carrier
58 Sharp-toothed tools (2 Sam. 12:31)
59 Habits; characteristics (Gen. 6:3)

DOWN

1 Walking step (Gen. 33:14)
2 Related to environment: abbr.
3 Consistent with reality (Gen. 45:28)
4 Paul's traveling companion (Acts 20:4)
5 Son nearly sacrificed by Abraham (Gen. 22:2)
6 Scattered remains (Acts 27:44)
7 Fourth letter
8 Probabilities (Judg. 5:13)
9 Converted runaway slave (Philem. 1:10)
10 Cylindrical fastener (Judg. 4:21)
11 Expert (Acts 4:13)
17 At present time (Gen. 2:25)
19 Son of Judah and Tamar (Gen. 38:30, KJV)
22 "____ the season to be jolly"
24 Search for (1 Chron. 16:11)
25 Chums: infor.
26 "Eli, Eli, ____ sabachthani" (Matt. 27:46)
27 "Won't risk having ____ conscience: 2 wds. (1 Cor. 10:27)
28 Paul's co-worker (2 Cor. 1:19)
30 Job's accuser (Job 1:6)
33 Adult males (Gen. 10:32)
35 Tax collector turned disciple
38 Lot's relation to Abraham (Gen. 12:4, 5)
41 Egyptian king
43 South Africans of Dutch descent
45 Swindle; defraud
47 Central U.S. state
48 Am. chemist, Harold Clayton ____
49 Impertinence; back talk
50 Blood relation
51 "What profit is there if ____ gain the whole world?" (Matt. 16:26)
52 Council of Economic Advisers: abbr.

(Solution on p. 207)

BAD HABITS

ACROSS

1 Polished, precious stone (Rev. 21:11)
4 Every (Gen. 6:20)
8 King of Amalekites (1 Sam. 15:8)
12 Physicians' organization: abbr.
13 Liver liquid
14 Summoned
15 Moses' wife (Exod. 2:21)
17 Father of Zechariah (Ezra 5:1)
18 Intentionally-set fire
19 Sea east of Judah (2 Kings 14:25)
21 Affirmative oral vote
23 Customary behavior (Rom. 12:13)
27 Sharp part of a plow (1 Sam. 13:21)
30 City of David; Jerusalem (2 Sam. 5:7)
33 Beer-like beverage
34 One of Lamech's wives (Gen. 4:19)
35 Complete; stop (Exod. 9:28)
36 Group of relatives (Gen. 36:17)
37 Normal; customary: abbr. (Exod. 5:18)
38 Passed-on practice: abbr. (John 7:22)
39 Flower garlands
40 King David's choir leader (Neh. 12:46)
42 Small Business Administration: abbr.
44 Piece of tree foliage (Gen. 8:11)
47 Prevaricators (Ps. 12:3)
51 Son of King Rehoboam (2 Chron. 11:18-20)
54 Jewish governor; returned exile
56 Single facial spasm: 2 wds.
57 Related to Confucians' beliefs
58 Acute care admission: abbr.
59 Open wide, as jaws (Job 16:10)
60 Make a long, narrow cut (1 Sam. 24:4)
61 Once owned

DOWN

1 Strip of land in western Israel (Gen. 10:19)
2 Arabian governor
3 Journey guides (Ps. 119:19)
4 Dark, valuable wood (Ezek. 27:15)
5 Atmosphere (Ps. 140:5)
6 Clothed
7 Foolish giggle
8 Son of Midian (Gen. 25:4)
9 Hebrew tribe (Num. 34:14)
10 Augment (Deut. 4:2)
11 Related to the earth: pref. (Gen. 10:31)
16 Take game by trespassing
20 Army health nurse: abbr.
22 Jewish cattle rustler (1 Chron. 7:21)
24 Bundled hay
25 Famous warrior (1 Chron. 11:26, 29)
26 Groups of 10 (Exod. 18:25)
27 Son of Zerah (1 Chron. 2:6)
28 Middle of month in ancient Roman calendar
29 Long, heroic narrative
31 "Like peas ____ pod": 2 wds.
32 Probabilities; chances (Judg. 5:13)
36 Legal right to a settlement (Gen. 20:16)
38 Particularization pronoun (Gen. 1:1)
41 Specific location (Gen. 2:21)
43 Generations "forever shall call me ____ of God" (Luke 1:48)
45 Diligent insects (Prov. 6:6)
46 Faithful; loyal: arch.
48 Rizpah's father (2 Sam. 21:8)
49 ____l; city (1 Sam. 30:27, 29)
50 Fish spawning upstream
51 Counterpart to zig
52 Lighter, slanted type: abbr.
53 Fast, energetic movement
55 ____ poloi

(Solution on p. 207)

GOD IS IN CONTROL

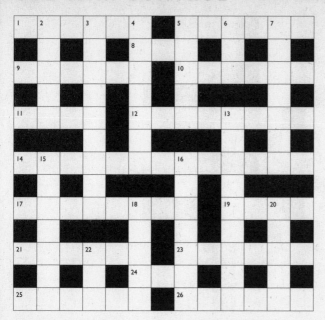

ACROSS

1 "No one can ____ them from me"; carry away by force (John 10:29)

5 "To enjoy your work and to ____ your lot in life—that is indeed a gift from God" (Eccles. 5:20)

8 "We toss the coin, but it is the Lord who controls ____ decision" (Prov. 16:33)

9 Nullify (Isa. 28:18)

10 Set on fire (Job 41:21)

11 Gave a new color to (Exod. 36:19)

12 "Because of this ____ upon Moses' face, Aaron and the people of Israel were afraid" (Exod. 34:30)

14 "This is the day ____ the atonement, cleansing you in the Lord's eyes"; celebrating (Lev. 16:30)

17 "I will reestablish the land of Israel and ____ it to its own people again"; allot again (Isa. 49:8)

19 "If the boss is angry with you, don't ____! A quiet spirit will quiet his bad temper"; resign (Eccles. 10:4)

21 One of Hazzelponi's brothers (1 Chron. 4:3)

23 "We are always confident, knowing that, ____ we are at home in the body, we are absent from the Lord"; at the time of (2 Cor. 5:6, KJV)

24 Abijam's son; king of Judah (1 Kings 15:7, 8)

25 Temporary indirect route (Isa. 33:8)

26 Nonmembers of the religious clergy (2 Chron. 11:16)

DOWN

2 Original country of Aquila and Priscilla (Acts 18:2)

3 Jewish leader to whom Jesus said, "Unless you are born again, you can never get into the Kingdom of God" (John 3:3, 4)

4 "I am but a ____ here on earth: how I need a map—and your commands are my chart and guide"; traveler (Ps. 119:19)

5 "This is what I have ____ of God for you: that you will be encouraged"; requested (Col. 2:2)

6 "I ____ do everything God asks me to with the help of Christ" (Phil. 4:13)

7 Large-billed sea bird (Deut. 14:17)

13 Ancient age (Isa. 23:7, KJV)

15 Late (Hab. 2:3)

16 A beginning again; restoration (2 Chron. 16:3)

18 A son of King David (1 Chron. 3:6)

20 "Without making a big ____ over it, God simply shatters the greatest of men and puts others in their places"; point of controversy (Job 34:24)

22 Prior (Deut. 1:6)

(Solution on p. 207)

STRONG BELIEFS

ACROSS

1 "I saw a great white throne and the one who _____ upon it" (Rev. 20:11)
4 Group of families (Gen. 19:32)
8 Boast (Amos 4:5)
12 Finnish seaport
13 Turkish or Syrian pound
14 Possess (Phil. 4:18)
15 Largest computer company: abbr.
16 Grandson of Noah (Gen. 10:21)
17 Twelfth month of Hebrew year (Esther 3:7, KJV)
18 Hard work (Jer. 22:13)
20 Assert positively
22 Years attained (Gen. 5:5)
24 "They shall mount up with wings like _____" (Isa. 40:31)
28 Ones killed for their faith (Rev. 14:13)
32 To blind or close eyes to: arch.
33 Intensive care unit: abbr.
34 Help or support (Rom. 15:27)
36 Pen point
37 "He is like a blazing fire refining precious _____" (Mal. 3:2)
40 _____ Ghandi
43 Valley (Num. 13:23)
45 Open: arch.
46 Black, solid fuel (Isa. 6:6)
48 Kingdom (2 Chron. 32:22)

52 Jesus "will _____ his people" (Matt. 1:21)
55 Appearance guarantee money (Acts 17:8)
57 Denial; no
58 As soon as possible: abbr.
59 4,840 sq. yds. of land (Isa. 5:10)
60 Yearly recurrence: abbr. (Deut. 16:6)
61 Small, arrowlike missile (Job 41:26)
62 Something required (Exod. 25:39)
63 New Zealand parrot

DOWN

1 Travel on wind (1 Kings 9:28)
2 Father: Gk.
3 Where Jesus' body placed (John 19:42)
4 Ordained ministerial order (1 Sam. 22:17)
5 Book collection: abbr. (Ezra 5:17)
6 Open space (Num. 3:38)
7 Courage (1 Sam. 13:6)
8 Command (Gen. 41:42)
9 Energy unit
10 Eggs
11 Who: Ger.
19 Edible cereal grass seed
21 Eastern Airlines System: abbr.
23 Period of history

25 Ash Wednesday to Easter
26 Wilderness oasis Hebrews visited (Num. 33:9)
27 Region of Ethiopia (Isa. 43:3)
28 Portray silently
29 Gets the better of: slang
30 King David's great-grandmother (Matt. 1:5, 6)
31 Sudan Interior Mission: abbr.
35 Father: infor.
38 "Be a living sacrifice, holy—the kind he can _____" (Rom. 12:1)
39 Old card game
41 Throw forcefully (1 Sam. 17:49)
42 Large primate (1 Kings 10:22)
44 Jacob's father-in-law (Gen. 29:23)
47 Delicate, open fabric
49 Father of three giants (Josh. 15:14)
50 Narrow road (Luke 14:23)
51 Asian starling
52 Unhappy; unfortunate (1 Kings 14:6)
53 Judean king
54 Change; alter: abbr.
56 Anger

(Solution on p. 207)

TIME TO GO

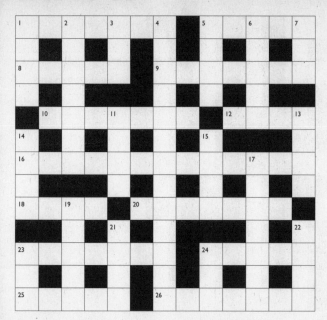

ACROSS

1 Driven or thrown out (Jer. 52:3)
5 Device for holding things together (Exod. 36:13)
8 "Your ____ is caused by your ignorance of the Scriptures and of God's power"; mistake (Matt. 22:29)
9 "Come, all of you who are skilled craftsmen having special ____, and construct what God has commanded us"; abilities (Exod. 35:10)
10 Rooms below ground level (1 Chron. 27:28, KJV)
12 Adult castrated bulls (Ps. 144:14)
16 "David prayed, 'O Lord God, why have you showered your blessings on such an ____ person as I am?'"; unimportant (2 Sam. 7:18)
18 "Don't ____ evil men but continue to reverence the Lord all the time, for surely you have a wonderful future ahead of you"; resentful awareness of another's advantage (Prov. 23:17)
20 Something purchased for less than its value (Prov. 20:14)
23 Member of Hebrew race (Exod. 5:14)

24 "____ his courts with praise. Give thanks to him and bless his name"; go in (Ps. 100:4)
25 Bloodsucking worm (Prov. 30:15)
26 "God took this list of sins and destroyed it by ____ it to Christ's cross"; fastening with metal spikes (Col. 2:14)

DOWN

1 Adam and Eve's home (Gen. 2:8)
2 Those receiving wages or profit for their efforts (Gen. 30:26)
3 Sealing liquid distilled from coal (Gen. 6:14)
4 Firm purpose (Acts 3:13)
5 Shape of golden idol the Hebrews made at Mount Sinai (Exod. 32:8)
6 Added-on building (1 Kings 6:5)
7 Yellowish fluid forming in an infected sore (Job 7:5)
11 Trees cut for lumber (Ezra 3:7)
13 "If you endorse a ____ for someone you hardly know, guaranteeing his debt, you are in serious trouble"; written promise to pay (Prov. 6:1)
14 "The man who finds a ____ finds a good thing; she is a blessing to him from the

Lord"; marriage partner (Prov. 18:22)
15 Male monarch (Gen. 12:15)
17 Father of the prophet Jonah (2 Kings 14:25)
19 "How constantly I find myself upon the ____ of sin; this source of sorrow always stares me in the face"; threshold (Ps. 38:17)
21 Rachel's older sister; Jacob's first wife (Gen. 29:16, 23)
22 "Don't ____ about your plans for tomorrow—wait and see what happens"; talk boastfully (Prov. 27:1)
23 Sick (John 5:6)
24 Samuel's priestly mentor and guardian (1 Sam. 2:11)

(Solution on p. 207)

QUALITIES

ACROSS

1 "Even the _____ of them, though they have hearts of lions, will be paralyzed with fear"; most courageous (2 Sam. 17:10)

5 The region of seven churches to which John wrote (1 Cor. 16:19)

8 "He _____ the little pet lamb in his arms like a baby daughter"; held close (2 Sam. 12:3)

9 "When there is _____ rot within a nation, its government topples easily"; according to basic principles of right (Prov. 28:2)

10 "Evil men have tried to _____ me into sin, but I am firmly anchored to your laws"; pull (Ps. 119:61)

11 Providers of money for temporary use (Isa. 24:2)

13 Mutual associations (Rom. 1:27)

15 "A man should only make a vow he _____ to keep" (Deut. 5:11)

17 "Jerusalem's streets _____ with the sounds of violence"; reflect sound (Jer. 6:7)

20 "Rich and poor are _____ in this: each depends on God for light"; similar (Prov. 29:13)

21 "How _____ are thy tabernacles, O LORD of hosts"; easy to get along with (Ps. 84:1, KJV)

22 "Where is the man who fears the Lord? God will teach him how to choose the _____"; most excellent (Ps. 25:12)

23 Pull taut (1 Chron. 18:3)

DOWN

1 "A rebuke to a man of common sense is more effective than a hundred lashes on the _____ of a rebel"; part nearest the spine (Prov. 17:10)

2 "In the end strong wine bites like a poisonous serpent; it stings like an _____" (Prov. 23:32)

3 "Daniel, I have heard that you have the spirit of the gods within you and that you are filled with _____ and wisdom"; spiritual insight (Dan. 5:14)

4 King of Goiim (Gen. 14:1)

5 "'We should spend our time preaching, not _____ a feeding program,' the Twelve said"; managing (Acts 6:2)

6 Member of the Hebrew nation (Exod. 9:6)

7 Most intimate (John 13:23)

12 "Proclaim that everyone must straighten out his life to be ready for the Lord's _____"; coming (Mark 1:3)

14 Framework of crossed strips (1 Kings 7:21)

16 Barely sufficient (Hag. 1:10)

18 "Get into the _____ of inviting guests home for dinner or, if they need lodging, for the night"; usual practice (Rom. 12:13)

19 Mentally alert; acute (Jer. 13:27)

(Solution on p. 207)

SIGNS AND WONDERS

ACROSS

1 Type of large boat Noah built (Gen. 8:18)

3 "Wisdom is better than weapons of war, but one rotten _____ can spoil a barrelful"; round, firm fruit with white flesh (Eccles. 9:18)

9 Work out by mutual agreement (Mark 14:10)

11 Make amends or satisfaction for (Lev. 4:28)

12 Bottom (Exod. 19:2)

13 "So that Christ could give her to himself as a glorious Church without a single _____ or wrinkle or any other blemish" (Eph. 5:27)

14 Second book of the Bible: abbr.

16 "Who else is like the Lord among the gods? Who is glorious in holiness like him? Who is so awesome in splendor, A _____ God?"; miracle-doing (Exod. 15:11)

18 Wane; decrease in strength (Deut. 32:36)

20 "Meanwhile little Samuel was helping the Lord by assisting Eli. Messages from the Lord were very _____ in those days"; infrequent (1 Sam. 3:1)

21 Affected, artificial manner (2 Cor. 11:20)

24 Transported goods (Jon. 1:5)

25 Reduced to a lower rank (1 Sam. 18:13)

26 Deadly pale (Jer. 30:6)

27 "You are a letter from Christ, written by us. It is not a letter written with pen and _____, but by the Spirit of the living God; not one carved on stone, but in human hearts" (2 Cor. 3:3)

DOWN

2 "Again and again their voices _____, 'Praise the Lord!'"; resounded (Rev. 19:3)

4 Ancient musical instrument similar to a zither (1 Sam. 10:5)

5 "Let _____ your lightning bolts, your arrows, Lord, upon your enemies, and scatter them"; unrestrained (Ps. 144:6)

6 Clothing (2 Kings 25:29)

7 Returned from the dead (Col. 1:18)

8 "If you _____ to the Lord, reverence him; for everyone who does this has everything he needs"; are related to (Ps. 34:9)

10 "If I am _____ by Satan, what about your own followers? For they cast out demons"; authorized by (Luke 11:19)

15 Terror-causing (Ps. 22:12)

16 Miserable, unhappy, vile person (Matt. 18:32)

17 Feeble-minded or foolish persons (John 11:49)

19 "Honor the Lord by giving him the first part of all your income, and he will fill your _____ with wheat and barley"; farm buildings (Prov. 3:9)

22 "Any story sounds true until someone tells the other _____ and sets the record straight" (Prov. 18:17)

23 "Don't bring us into temptation, but deliver us from the Evil One. _____" (Matt. 6:13)

(Solution on p. 208)

FAMILY RELATIONS

ACROSS

1 Mold for pouring metal (Exod. 38:30)

5 "As newborn ____, desire the sincere milk of the word, that ye may grow thereby" (1 Pet. 2:2, KJV)

8 Put identification slip on (Jer. 6:30)

9 "The Lord your God is merci- ful—he will not ____ you nor destroy you nor forget the promises he has made to your ancestors"; desert (Deut. 4:31)

10 Oval, edible nuts with soft, light-brown shell (Num. 17:8)

12 "The bird returned to him with an olive leaf in her ____. So Noah knew that the water was almost gone" (Gen. 8:11)

16 "Because of God's deep love and concern for you, you should practice ____ mercy and kindness to others"; com- passionate (Col. 3:12)

18 Postal service deliveries (Esther 8:14)

20 Frightened (Dan. 1:10)

23 Pillow or support (1 Sam. 26:16, KJV)

24 The devil (Rev. 12:9)

25 "It is ____ to make loans to strangers"; liability to loss (Prov. 20:16)

26 Closest (Gen. 28:19)

DOWN

1 Young cow (Gen. 18:7)

2 Extended family or tribal divi- sion (Num. 26:29)

3 "____gotten gain brings no lasting happiness; right living does"; wrongly (Prov. 10:2)

4 "An old man's ____ are his crowning glory"; offspring of one's son or daughter (Prov. 17:6)

5 The god of Moab (Num. 25:3)

6 "It is a ____ of honor to accept valid criticism"; symbol of status (Prov. 25:12)

7 "The wages of ____ is death, but the free gift of God is eter- nal life through Jesus Christ our Lord"; offense against God (Rom. 6:23)

11 "Evil men borrow and 'cannot pay it back'! But the good man returns what he ____ with some extra besides" (Ps. 37:21)

13 Young goats (Isa. 5:17)

14 "All the other commandments and all the demands of the prophets ____ from these two laws"; flow (Matt. 22:40)

15 Threadlike growths from skin (Gen. 25:25)

17 Auditorium (Acts 19:29, KJV)

19 "Hard work means prosperity; only a fool ____ away his time"; does nothing (Prov. 12:11)

21 "____ true to what is right and God will bless you and use you to help others"; remain (1 Tim. 4:16)

22 "Blind guides! You strain out a ____ and swallow a camel"; small, biting fly (Matt. 23:24)

23 Long, narrow strip of wood (Exod. 36:23)

24 Large body of salt water (Gen. 49:13)

(Solution on p. 208)

LEAD US NOT INTO TEMPTATION . . .

ACROSS

1 Oval fowl foods (Job 39:14)
5 Walk through impeding substance
9 Male sibling: abbr. (Gen. 4:2)
12 Public uproar (Acts 17:5)
13 Boat steering devices (Ezek. 27:6)
14 Army air base: abbr.
15 Prophetess Anna's tribe (Luke 2:36, KJV)
16 Lifting up: pl. (Ezek. 26:8)
18 Inflicted a blow (Gen. 32:25)
20 "In the day that thou _____ thereof thou shalt surely die" (Gen. 2:17, KJV)
21 Type of hat
22 Color changer (Ezek. 27:7)
23 Festival of Tabernacles month: abbr.
26 Resting place (1 Sam. 3:2)
28 Comparatively little (Gen. 19:20)
32 Leading citizen of Shechem (Judg. 9:26)
34 Basketball league: abbr.
36 Wound's crust (Lev. 14:56)
37 Spirited mount (Zech. 10:3)
39 Son of Benjamin (Gen. 46:21)
41 Major network: abbr.
42 Fair equivalent: abbr. (Exod. 22:4)
44 Defendant: var.

46 Tranquil (Isa. 18:4)
49 Changes (Ezra 6:12)
53 Subject of seventh commandment (Exod. 20:14)
55 "_____ every law of your government" (1 Pet. 2:13)
56 Nott and _____ (gods)
57 O.T. book after Proverbs: abbr.
58 Town where Jesus brought a boy back to life (Luke 7:11-14)
59 Physicians' professional organization: abbr.
60 Food fish
61 Other; in addition (Exod. 20:17)

DOWN

1 Distinguishable periods of time
2 Central idea
3 One who proceeds
4 Walk pompously (Ps. 73:9)
5 Skilled manual laborers (Exod. 28:5)
6 Chicago Motor Club, e.g.: abbr.
7 What God did to Red Sea and Jordan River (Josh. 4:23)
8 Short compositions on a theme
9 Cause of death or ruin
10 Worn-out scraps of cloth (Lam. 1:17)
11 Headstrong: abbr. (Isa. 48:4)
17 Specific parts of a collection (Exod. 29:33)

19 Taxi
23 "We turned toward King _____ land of Bashan" (Deut. 3:1)
24 Catches rats and mice
25 Take: Scot.
27 Sole proprietorship alias designation: abbr.
29 American Academy of Arts: abbr.
30 Scientific experimentation site: infor.
31 Units of weight = 16 oz.: abbr.
33 Flat; horizontal (Luke 6:17)
35 Arranged in order (Job 6:4)
38 Belonging to author of The Inferno
40 Computer command to erase a file
43 Blood sucker (Prov. 30:15)
45 Make amends for; cover (Lev. 4:28)
46 Seismic array data analyzer: abbr.
47 Experiment, drill, and maintainence: mil. abbr.
48 Visceral wrinkle
50 Son of Shobal (Gen. 36:23)
51 Belonging to a loyalist of King David (1 Kings 1:8)
52 Since then: Scot.
54 Electronics company

(Solution on p. 208)

63

ADD IT UP

ACROSS

1 "Let God _____ you, for he is doing what any loving father does for his children"; cause to grow as desired (Heb. 12:7)
4 Vertical sections of a printed page (Jer. 36:23)
8 "Some men enjoy cheating, but the cake they buy with such _____-gotten gain will turn to gravel in their mouths" (Prov. 20:17)
9 Paul had one of these in his flesh to keep him humble (2 Cor. 12:7)
10 An ephah equals about _____ bushel of dry measure: 2 wds. (Ezek. 45:11)
11 Number of men who died when the Tower of Siloam fell on them (Luke 13:4)
12 Sixth month (Ezra 3:8)
14 King Solomon "had seven hundred _____ ... and they turned his heart away from the Lord" (1 Kings 11:3)
16 "When a good man speaks, he is worth listening to, but the words of fools are a dime a _____" (Prov. 10:20)
20 "A lazy fellow has trouble all through life; the good man's path is _____"; not hard (Prov. 15:19)
21 "The _____ year shall be holy, a time to proclaim liberty throughout the land" (Lev. 25:10)
24 Large, level area raised above its surroundings (Num. 21:20)
25 Enthusiastic; anxious (2 Chron. 26:5)
26 Make delicate handmade lace
27 At farthest point; end of a range (Ezek. 46:19)
28 Angrily

DOWN

1 "Bring all the _____ into the storehouse"; tenths (Mal. 3:10)
2 In the number of (Gen. 7:1)
3 Number of cities given Hebrew tribe of Naphtali (Josh. 19:32, 39)
4 Divided into two; split (Lev. 11:7)
5 "_____ will get any man into trouble, but honesty is its own defense" (Prov. 12:13)
6 "Your care for others is the _____ of your greatness"; reference standard (Luke 9:48)
7 Examined closely; passed through a sieve (Amos 9:9)
13 Year after leaving Egypt that Aaron died (Num. 33:38)
15 Moment (Luke 8:44)
17 Hebrews' one allowable permanent worship center in Jerusalem (Exod. 25:8)
18 "It's wonderful to be young! Enjoy every _____ of it! Do all you want to... but realize that you must account to God for everything you do" (Eccles. 11:9)
19 Number of silver coins Judas paid for betraying Jesus (Matt. 26:15)
22 "_____ days later, at the baby's circumcision ceremony, he was named Jesus" (Luke 2:21)
23 Nothing more than what's specified (Prov. 29:19)

(Solution on p. 208)

MAJOR PROBLEMS

ACROSS

1 Dine (Rev. 3:20, KJV)
4 Midianite king (Num. 31:8)
8 ____-Hamath, Promised Land boundary marker (Num. 34:7)
12 Sin (2 Chron. 33:9, KJV)
13 Midianite general (Judg. 7:25)
14 Elderly (Deut. 32:7)
15 Untruth (Gen. 3:4)
16 Alienated (Job 19:13, KJV)
18 Donkey (Gen. 16:12)
19 Plus (Gen. 1:1)
20 Resource management (Isa. 29:23)
25 Cultivate (Isa. 5:6)
28 Disregarded (1 Kings 12:13)
30 Request (Gen. 24:14)
31 Cisterns (1 Kings 7:38)
32 Shout of disapproval (Job 27:23)
34 Without charge (Gen. 23:11)
35 Sum total (Gen. 1:8)
36 Without help (Isa. 63:5)
38 Attention getter (Mark 15:32)
39 Folks (Gen. 38:11)
41 What Jesus quieted (Mark 4:39)
42 Possessed
45 Mediate (Lev. 10:10)
51 Roman three
52 Ascertain (Gen. 45:16)
53 Spoken (Dan. 1:18)
54 Wide-mouthed cooking container (Lev. 2:7)
55 Contributes (Prov. 10:22)
56 Shealtiel's father (Luke 3:27)
57 Female reference (Gen. 2:23)

DOWN

1 City in Edom (2 Kings 14:7)
2 "____ son was Bezalel" (1 Chron. 2:20)
3 Now (Matt. 26:53, KJV)
4 Deer (2 Sam. 2:18, KJV)
5 ____ brother, Onan (Gen. 38:8)
6 Wager (2 Kings 18:23)
7 Sarai's husband (Gen. 11:31)
8 Country (Gen. 2:11)
9 Food from hen (Luke 11:12)
10 Relative of a hornet (Ps. 118:12)
11 Unusual (Eccles. 8:10)
17 One or another (Gen. 3:1)
21 Mediterranean island (Acts 21:1)
22 Alternative (Gen. 3:3)
23 Babylonian king: abbr. (2 Kings 24:1)
24 Scent (John 12:3, KJV)
25 Misfortunes (Neh. 9:32)
26 O.T. writer (Rom. 9:25, KJV)
27 ____ out a living
28 District of Babylon (2 Kings 18:34, KJV)
29 Windstorm (John 6:18)
33 Singular (Gen. 2:24)
34 Suitable (Gen. 49:20)
37 One (Gen. 8:11)
39 Cherished creature (Job 41:5)
40 First Hebrew priest (Exod. 28:1)
41 Honored ones (Gen. 18:3)
43 Father of Rizpah (2 Sam. 21:8)
44 Eat a main meal (2 Sam. 11:11)
45 Triumph cry (Ps. 35:21)
46 Crimson (Exod. 26:14)
47 Not good (Gen. 2:17)
48 "We ____ saved by trusting" (Rom. 8:24)
49 Waterproofing substance (Exod. 2:3)
50 Samuel's appointed guardian (1 Sam. 1:25)

(Solution on p. 208)

THE END IS NEAR

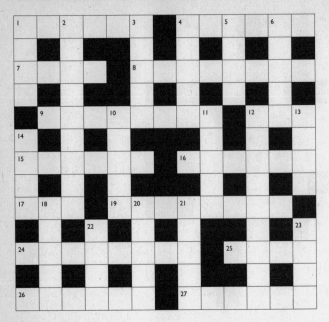

ACROSS

1 Jesus' apostle Simon was also called "The ____" (Acts 1:14)
4 Profane; lacking reverence for sacred matters (Lev. 10:1)
7 "It is destined that men die only ____, and after that comes judgment" (Heb. 9:27)
8 Ruler who exercises absolute power (Eph. 1:21)
9 Killed for one's beliefs (Rev. 16:6)
12 Plead; appeal (Gen. 50:17)
15 River branch in Garden of Eden (Gen. 2:14)
16 Realm of many countries (Ezra 1:2)
17 "The idols of Babylon, ____ and Nebo, are being hauled away on ox carts" (Isa. 46:1)
19 "God called the light 'daytime,' and the ____ 'nighttime'" (Gen. 1:5)
24 "Here on earth you will have many trials and sorrows; but cheer up, for I have ____ the world" (John 16:33)
25 City where Paul was under house arrest for two years (Acts 28:16, 30)
26 Harsh ruler with absolute power (Rev. 11:7)
27 Mourn; bewail (Isa. 16:9)

DOWN

1 City of David; Jerusalem (2 Sam. 5:7)
2 "The Lord himself will come down from heaven with a mighty shout and with the soul-stirring cry of the ____" (1 Thess. 4:16)
3 "Right now God is ready to welcome you. ____ he is ready to save you" (2 Cor. 6:2)
4 Laban's relationship to Jacob and Esau (Gen. 28:5)
5 "'This ____,' Laban continued, 'stands between us as a witness of our vows'" (Gen. 31:51)
6 Release from restraint (Ezek. 7:3)
10 "The star was called 'Bitterness' because it poisoned a ____ of all the water on the earth" (Rev. 8:11)
11 "Jesus spoke to the ____ within the man and said, 'Come out, you evil spirit'" (Mark 5:7)
12 "Fire and ____ rained down from heaven and destroyed them all" (Luke 17:29)
13 Mood of joy and high spirits (Judg. 15:14)
14 Wound with a pointed weapon (2 Sam. 20:10)
18 Diplomatic messenger (Isa. 37:8)
20 "His unchanging plan has always been to ____ us into his own family" (Eph. 1:5)
21 "Come, ____ before the Lord our Maker, for he is our God" (Ps. 95:6, 7)
22 Judean city given to Caleb (Josh. 15:13)
23 "Since everything around us is going to ____ away, what holy, godly lives we should be living!" (2 Pet. 3:11)

(Solution on p. 208)

BAD NEWS

ACROSS

1 "The holy Jerusalem was built on twelve layers of foundation stones ___ with gems"; decorated with a pattern set into a surface (Rev. 21:19)

5 Jeremiah's scribe and secretary (Jer. 36:18)

8 "Don't fail to correct your children; discipline won't hurt them! They won't die if you ___ a stick on them"; employ (Prov. 23:13)

9 "Shine out like ___ lights among people who are crooked and stubborn"; guiding or warning (Phil. 2:15)

10 Seat for riding on horseback (Gen. 31:34)

11 Restaurant's list of food (Esther 2:9)

12 "I have known from ___ days that your will never changes"; first-occurring (Ps. 119:152)

14 Eminent; perceived as better (1 Chron. 4:9)

18 Affecting many persons at one time (2 Chron. 7:13)

20 "Let me tell you how happy God has made me! For he has clothed me with garments of salvation and draped about me the ___ of righteousness"; long, outer garment (Isa. 61:10)

22 Drowsy (Gen. 2:21)

24 Release from restraint (Num. 5:18)

25 Wager (Isa. 36:8)

26 Cling (Acts 15:1)

27 Enclosed with a protective border of shrubs (Matt. 21:33)

DOWN

2 Daughter of one's brother or sister (Gen. 11:29)

3 "I will appoint responsible shepherds to care for them, and they shall not need to be afraid again; all of them shall be ___ for continually"; regarded or watched (Jer. 23:4)

4 Underground prison (Gen. 41:14)

5 Brook in Palestine (1 Sam. 30:9)

6 "You commanded the ___ Sea to divide, forming a dry road across its bottom. Yes, as dry as any desert" (Ps. 106:9)

7 "From: Paul, chosen by God to be Jesus Christ's messenger. To: The faithful Christian brothers— God's people—in the city of ___ "

11 Soft, wet earth (John 9:6)

13 "As for the one who conquers, he will have my new Name ___ upon him"; engraved (Rev. 3:12)

15 Pierced with something sharp and pointed (Gen. 41:13)

16 Rude or vulgar (1 Sam. 25:3)

17 "You shall give ___ honor and respect to the elderly, in the fear of God"; expected or proper (Lev. 19:32)

19 "The crowd was amazed. '___ Jesus is the Messiah!'"; perhaps (Matt. 12:23)

21 "Jehoram had married one of the daughters of Ahab, and his whole life was one constant ___ of doing evil"; spree (2 Chron. 21:6)

23 Before (John 4:49, KJV)

(Solution on p. 208)

AFFIRMATIONS

ACROSS

1 "Again Peter _____ it. And immediately a rooster crowed" (John 18:27)

5 "I even found great pleasure in hard work. This pleasure was, indeed, my only reward for all my _____" (Eccles. 2:10)

8 Not private (1 Cor. 14:19)

9 "God declares us 'not _____' of offending him if we trust in Jesus Christ" (Rom. 3:24)

10 Beat with a rod or whip (Mark 10:34)

11 "If it is an _____—a case in which something is thrown unintentionally, without anger" (Num. 35:22, 23)

12 This number (Mark 3:14)

14 "No one gets anything until it is _____ that the person who wrote the will is dead" (Heb. 9:16)

16 Carefully worked out plan of action (Gen. 32:20)

19 "God's truth stands _____ like a great rock, and nothing can shake it" (2 Tim. 2:19)

21 "He powerfully refuted all the Jewish arguments in public _____, showing by the Scriptures that Jesus is indeed the Messiah" (Acts 18:28)

22 "A man's poverty is no _____ for twisting justice against him" (Exod. 23:6)

23 "In the book of _____, we are told that the Lord knows full well how the human mind reasons" (1 Cor. 3:20)

24 To put forcibly into a position (Ps. 88:6)

DOWN

2 "'With whom will you compare me? Who is my _____?' asks the Holy One" (Isa. 40:25)

3 "It is _____ to take a millstone as a pledge, for it is a tool by which its owner gains his livelihood" (Deut. 24:6)

4 Speak to a person to record (Jer. 36:17)

5 "I will give you the right words and such _____ that none of your opponents will be able to reply!" (Luke 21:15)

6 "Many people can _____ houses, but only God made everything" (Heb. 3:4)

7 "A very great _____ of aides and servants accompanied the queen of Sheba" (2 Chron. 9:1)

13 "Do not cooperate with an evil man by affirming on the _____ stand something you know is false" (Exod. 23:1)

14 Return for goods or services (Gen. 42:25)

15 Person charged with law enforcement (Acts 22:26)

17 "All your feverish plans will not _____, for you never ask for help from God" (Isa. 22:11)

18 "The land lies fair as _____ Garden in all its beauty" (Joel 2:3)

20 Ceases action; stays (2 Kings 2:15)

(Solution on p. 208)

CALL THE DOCTOR

ACROSS

1 Excellent (Isa. 5:12)
5 "God's Messenger is like a blazing fire refining precious metal, and he can _____ the dirtiest garments"; whiten (Mal. 3:2)
8 "Even the birds of the _____ and the fish in the sea will perish" (Zeph. 1:3)
9 "God doesn't _____ to the prayers of those who flout the law"; pay attention to (Prov. 28:9)
10 "If your brother is bothered by what you eat, you are not _____ in love if you go ahead and eat it"; behaving (Rom. 14:15)
11 Class or kind (Mark 2:15)
12 "Forgive us our sins; for we also forgive every one that is _____ to us"; obligated (Luke 11:4, KJV)
14 "Give me an _____ mind so that I can govern your people well and know the difference between what is right and what is wrong" (1 Kings 3:9)
17 Discontentments aroused by others' possessions or abilities (2 Cor. 12:20)
19 Thought (1 Tim. 1:7)

21 "The Lord replies: 'I will be your lawyer; I will plead your case; I will _____ you'"; exact retribution (Jer. 51:36)
23 Man who tested God's will with a fleece (Judg. 6:39)
24 "At last the king gave the order for Daniel's arrest, and he was taken to the _____ of lions" (Dan. 6:16)
25 Loose head coverings (Ruth 3:15)
26 "Then they will come to their _____ and escape from Satan's trap of slavery to sin"; sound mental capacities (2 Tim. 2:26)

DOWN

2 "The Lord God says: 'I am bringing the people of Israel home from around the world to their own land to _____ them into one nation'"; make a coherent whole (Ezek. 37:21, 22)
3 Remotely; outermost (Ezek. 46:19)
4 Outlaws; robbers (Luke 10:30)
5 "When someone becomes a Christian, he becomes a _____ new person inside"; distinctively (2 Cor. 5:17)
6 "Stay awake, work hard, and

there will be plenty to _____!" (Prov. 20:13)
7 Water container (Gen. 21:19)
13 Unable to get up due to illness (Acts 9:33)
15 City where Jonah preached (Jon. 3:1)
16 Appoints as a task (Gen. 40:4)
18 "If you give to the poor, your _____ will be supplied"; lacks (Prov. 28:27)
20 "Don't store up treasures here on earth where they can _____ away or may be stolen"; gradually wear (Matt. 6:19)
22 "We will have wonderful _____ bodies in heaven, made for us by God himself"; not old (2 Cor. 5:1)

(Solution on p. 208)

TAKING SHAPE

ACROSS

1 "The mountains may ____ and the hills disappear, but my kindness shall not leave you"; go away (Isa. 54:10)
5 First O.T. prophetic book
8 Went quickly on foot (Luke 19:4)
9 "The power of the life-giving Spirit has freed me from the vicious ____ of sin and death"; round (Rom. 8:2)
10 "You have listened to my troubles and have seen the ____ in my soul"; strait (Ps. 31:7)
11 Jacob's son whose descendants became Tabernacle workers (Gen. 35:23; Num. 3:6)
12 "Any story sounds true until someone tells the other side and sets the record ____"; correct (Prov. 18:17)
14 "Enjoy the ____ of those who love the Lord" (2 Tim. 2:22)
18 Shape of the moon in its first quarter (Judg. 8:26)
20 "I have placed my rainbow in the clouds as a ____ of my promise" (Gen. 9:13)
22 "All the world will stand ____ at what I will do for you" (Mic. 7:16)
24 Models or standards of excellence (Ps. 26:3)
25 "Wisdom is its ____ reward, and if you scorn her, you hurt only yourself"; self (Prov. 9:12)
26 "God is not ____. How can he forget your hard work for him?" (Heb. 6:10)
27 "All the rest of the world around us is under ____ power and control"; the devil's (1 John 5:19)

DOWN

2 Banish from one's country (Deut. 28:36)
3 Co-recipient of Paul's letter to Philemon; "a soldier of the cross" (Philem. 1:1, 2)
4 Attempt to overthrow the government (2 Kings 11:14)
5 Become liable for
6 King Hezekiah's mother (2 Kings 18:1, 2)
7 Brother of Joab and Asahel; companion of David (1 Sam. 26:6)
11 Site: abbr. (Num. 3:24)
13 Firmly demanding (Acts 21:20)
15 Boat rowers
16 Gains or attains by planned action or effort
17 "Oh, that I could write my plea with an iron ____ in the rock forever"; writing instrument (Job 19:23)
19 Village where King Saul consulted a medium (1 Sam. 28:7)
21 Heights northeast of the Sea of Galilee (Josh. 20:8)
23 Head of one of the seven clans of the tribe of Gad (1 Chron. 5:11, 13)

(Solution on p. 208)

THE WORD

ACROSS

1 "God says, 'Your _____ came to me at a favorable time, when the doors of welcome were wide open'"; call for help (2 Cor. 6:2)
3 Orderly assemblage, such as of troops (1 Chron. 12:38)
9 "Run from sex sin. No other sin _____ the body as this one does"; has an influence (1 Cor. 6:18)
11 Jacob's uncle; father of Rachel (Gen. 27:43; 29:16)
12 Inflamed swelling; one of ten plagues on Egypt (Exod. 9:9)
13 For men only, such as a party (Mark 6:21)
14 "God made the _____ into a woman, and brought her to the man"; curved bone attached to the spine (Gen. 2:22)
16 God's characteristic of showing pity and sharing human sufferings (Exod. 22:27)
18 Woman belonging to a religious order
20 Fall in drops (Amos 9:13)
21 Move in leaps and steps (Ps. 29:5)
24 Body part performing a specific function (Lev. 1:9)
25 Put a riding seat on an animal (Gen. 22:3)
26 "If ye _____ in me, and my words _____ in you, ye shall ask what ye will, and it shall be done unto you"; remain or dwell in (John 15:7, KJV)
27 "The living beings darted to and _____, swift as lightning"; away (Ezek. 1:14)

DOWN

2 "May my spoken words and unspoken thoughts be pleasing even to you, O Lord my _____ and my Redeemer"; solid support (Ps. 19:14)
4 "When we teachers of _____, who should know better, do wrong, our punishment will be greater than it would be for others"; organized system of faith and worship (James 3:1)
5 Brownish-yellow color (Ezek. 8:2)
6 "John saw Jesus coming toward him and said, 'Look! There is the _____ of God who takes away the world's sin'"; young sheep (John 1:29)
7 Assert positively (Exod. 23:1)
8 Give power to (1 Tim. 1:12, KJV)
10 "The Lord _____ the thirsty soul and fills the hungry soul with good"; provides all that's needed (Ps. 107:9)
15 "Your body will die because of sin; but your spirit will live, for Christ has _____ it"; freed from penalty (Rom. 8:10)
16 Artillery to propel large balls (Isa. 65:23)
17 Basic, soluble mineral salt (Deut. 29:23)
19 Arid region in southern Palestine (Gen. 20:1)
22 "The boy became so hungry that even the _____ he was feeding the swine looked good to him"; fruit husks that split open (Luke 15:16)
23 Smell (Num. 28:6)

(Solution on p. 208)

THE BIG PARTY

ACROSS

1 "You furnish lovely music at your grand parties; the orchestras are ____! But for the Lord you have no thought or care"; outstanding (Isa. 5:12)
5 Long-haired (Dan. 8:21)
8 "____ fall short of God's glorious ideal"; everyone (Rom. 3:23)
9 Shield or hide (Exod. 40:21)
10 As much as one can carry with one arm (Acts 28:3)
11 "No one anywhere can ever ____ in the presence of God. For it is from God alone that you have your life through Christ Jesus"; boast (1 Cor. 1:29, 30)
12 Maximum or extreme (Ezek. 27:10)
14 "I am eighty years old today, and life has lost its excitement. Food and wine are no longer tasty, and ____ is not much fun"; diversion (2 Sam. 19:35)
18 Largest fabric to catch wind and propel a boat (Acts 27:40, KJV)
20 Behind or back (Matt. 26:58)
22 "A time to tear; A time to ____"; fix (Eccles. 3:7)

24 Eighteen-inch lengths (Exod. 25:10, KJV)
25 "With Rachel's last breath (for she died) she named him 'Ben____' ('Son of my sorrow')" (Gen. 35:18)
26 "To ____ this honor and renown you must be a holy people to the Lord your God, as he requires"; achieve (Deut. 26:19)
27 Ditch (1 Kings 18:32)

DOWN

2 Open sore (Lev. 13:10)
3 "I am like an ____ tree, yielding my fruit to you throughout the year. My mercies never fail"; having foliage that doesn't change color (Hos. 14:8)
4 Ceremonial dinner (Matt. 22:3)
5 "Do not ____ your testimony in favor of a man just because he is poor"; present with a special viewpoint (Exod. 23:3)
6 "If your ____ is to enjoy the evil pleasure of the unsaved world, you cannot also be a friend of God"; goal (James 4:4)
7 One who eats to excess (Matt. 11:19)
11 "They swarm around me like

____"; stinging insect: sing. (Ps. 118:12)
13 Worth remembering; noteworthy
15 Closest (2 Sam. 17:13)
16 Not lawful
17 "Moses' mother made a little boat from papyrus reeds, waterproofed it with ____, put the baby in it, and laid it among the reeds along the river's edge" (Exod. 2:3)
19 Miriam's brother (Exod. 15:20)
21 "It is better to live in a corner of an ____ than in a beautiful home with a cranky, quarrelsome woman"; space just below roof (Prov. 25:24)
23 A son of Ithran (1 Chron. 7:38)

(Solution on p. 208)

BIBLE FILL-INS

ACROSS

1 Contemptible, base people (Ps. 35:15, KJV)
5 Of the 12 Hebrew spies, only Joshua and _____ were allowed to enter the Promised Land (Num. 14:38)
8 "Don't envy the wicked. Don't _____ his riches"; desire enviably (Prov. 24:19)
9 "The Prince of the bottomless pit whose name in Hebrew is _____, and in Greek, Apollyon [and in English, the Destroyer]" (Rev. 9:11)
10 Warned; informed beforehand (Judg. 16:2)
12 "Obey your father and your mother, for their advice is a _____ of light directed into the dark corners of your mind to warn you of danger and to give you a good life"; ray (Prov. 6:20, 23)
16 "God gave Paul the power to do unusual miracles, so that even when his _____ or parts of his clothing were placed upon sick people, they were healed"; small pieces of cloth (Acts 19:11, 12)
18 "A happy _____ means a glad

heart"; countenance (Prov. 15:13)
20 "During the night some of Paul's converts let him down in a basket through an _____ in the city wall"; gap (Acts 9:25)
23 Welcome hug (Prov. 5:19)
24 Recurring round of events
25 Move rhythmically to music (Song 6:13)
26 "You constantly _____ the hunger and thirst of every living thing"; fulfill the desires or needs of (Ps. 145:16)

DOWN

1 "The stone rejected by the builders has now become the capstone of the _____"; top part of a doorway (Ps. 118:22)
2 Light spear (Job 39:23)
3 Sever with a sharp edge (Exod. 35:33)
4 "The land is mine, so you may not sell it permanently. You are merely my tenants and _____"; farmers who work another's land for produce (Lev. 25:23)
5 "As the _____ is in the potter's hand, so are you in my hand"; moist soil for shaping (Jer. 18:6)
6 Shelflike projection (Exod. 27:5)

7 Word meaning "son" in Hebrew (Gen. 35:18)
11 Long-handled garden tool with a row of projecting teeth at one end
13 "I've blotted out your sins; they are gone like morning _____ at noon"; visible water vapor (Isa. 44:22)
14 Head cook (1 Sam. 9:23)
15 Part of face below mouth (Lev. 13:29)
17 Castrated men (2 Kings 9:32)
19 Living compartment on a ship (Ezek. 27:6)
21 Infant (Exod. 2:6, KJV)
22 Large group (Esther 2:19)
23 "Proud men _____ in shame, but the meek become wise"; finish (Prov. 11:2)
24 Small, portable bed

(Solution on p. 209)

SOLVING PROBLEMS

ACROSS

1 "May God our Father and the
   Lord Jesus Christ mightily
   _____ each one of you and give
   you peace" (2 Cor. 1:2)
4 Instructive talk (Acts 19:9)
8 Sound of a pigeon
9 Bathsheba's first husband
   (2 Sam. 11:3)
10 Covering; disguising (Ps. 18:11)
11 Those who inform on others
   (1 Tim. 5:13, KJV)
12 "The Lord is my strength, my
   _____, and my salvation"
   (Exod. 15:2)
14 "In every battle you will need
   faith as your shield to stop the
   _____ arrows aimed at you by
   Satan"; burning (Eph. 6:16)
16 "What a _____ yes, how stupid!—to decide before knowing the facts" (Prov. 18:13)
20 "God has planted them like
   strong and graceful _____ for
   his own glory" (Isa. 61:3)
21 "Not until the heavens can be
   measured and the foundations
   of the earth _____, will I consider casting them away forever for their sins" (Jer. 31:37)
24 Brief look (Acts 1:10)
25 Hezekiah made a _____ of
   dried figs and spred it on his
   boil (2 Kings 20:7)
26 Drink in small quantities
   (Ezek. 12:19)
27 Uzziah produced _____ of war;
   invented by brilliant men
   (2 Chron. 26:15)
28 Haman asked the king to _____
   a decree that the Jews be
   destroyed (Esther 3:9)

DOWN

1 "Only a fool _____ out every
   thing he knows; that only
   leads to sorrow and trouble";
   utters suddenly (Prov. 10:14)
2 "What can you point to that
   is new? How do you know it
   didn't _____ long ages ago?; be
   (Eccles. 1:10)
3 "God gives wise men their
   wisdom and _____ their intelli-
   gence"; learned people
   (Dan. 2:21)
4 Sexual partners (Prov. 7:11)
5 "We toss the _____, but it is
   the Lord who controls its
   decision"; piece of metal used
   as currency (Prov. 16:33)
6 "The Lord himself will seat
   them and put on a waiter's
   _____ and serve them as they
   sit and eat!" (Luke 12:37)
7 Bring into battle contact
   (1 Chron. 19:10)
13 City to which Paul wrote,
   "Always be full of joy in the
   Lord; I say it again, rejoice!"
15 Hint or idea
17 "If you want a happy, good life,
   keep control of your _____,
   and guard your lips from telling lies" (1 Pet. 3:10)
18 Amount left over (Gen. 41:35)
19 Remain loyal; stick fast
   (Acts 15:1)
22 "The spirit of Elijah
   upon Elisha"; lies fixed upon
   (2 Kings 2:15)
23 "_____ my eyes to see wonderful things in your Word";
   remove obstructions from
   (Ps. 119:18)

(Solution on p. 209)

CHURCH RELATED

ACROSS

1 Hume Lake, e.g.
 (Gen. 32:21)
5 English foundation
9 Opera part
10 Fly high (Obad. 1:4)
11 ___ serif typeface
12 Not wavering
 (1 Pet. 1:5)
13 Chose to forego
 (Acts 15:29)
15 Acclaim another
 (Deut. 5:3)
16 Running commentary
20 ___ code (Josh. 9:1)
21 Missionaries'
 "umbrella" org.
22 Liquid sweet treat
23 Arranger ___ Mauldin
24 "Nobly to live, or ___
 nobly to die"
25 Narrow cut
 (1 Sam. 24:4)

DOWN

1 ___ Grande, Ariz.
2 Non-Jewish descen-
 dant of Abraham
 (Neh. 6:1)
3 Traveling variety
 troupe
4 Spiritual leadership
 position (Titus 1:5)
5 Supporting ministers
 (Titus 3:14)
6 Generous (James 1:5)
7 Solicitude (1 Pet. 5:2)
8 ___ Scott decision
14 Highest S&P rating
16 "In the ___ of Jesus.
 Amen" (1 John 2:12)
17 World's sixth-largest
 lake
18 Ind.-based missions
 agency: abbr.
19 Political cartoonist
 Thomas ___

(Solution on p. 209)

HIS

ACROSS

1 Familiar father
5 Gorges (Luke 16:26)
11 Styptic or astringent
12 Solid cylinder
13 Cut back
14 Faithless (John 10:35)
15 End of 22-across
   (Matt. 6:13)
16 Naturalness
17 Communion service
   (1 Cor. 11:33)
21 Leafy drink
22 Model invocation
   (Matt. 6:9-13)
30 Declare positively
31 Author Walter de la
   ___
32 Conductive elements
35 God's ___ (churchyard)
36 Original
37 Cast off (Isa. 58:8)
38 Constant
39 Ideals, for short

DOWN

1 Re Roman church head
2 "Remember the ___ "
3 Cleaner (Phil. 1:15)
4 Rectify
5 Computer's "brain"
6 Hebrew half gallon
7 Walk start: 2 wds.
   (1 Sam. 17:39)
8 Length of leather
9 Computer pointing
   device
10 Contempt expression
18 Avenues: abbr.
19 Ninth mo.
20 Egypt-Syria alliance
22 Light providers
   (Exod. 25:6)
23 Not concealed
24 Knot again
25 Play script
26 Collect
   (1 Chron. 29:25)
27 Pleasure boat
28 Strayed
29 Cane strips (Exod. 2:3)
33 Boy
34 Cunning

76

(Solution on p. 209)

A COMFORTING TRUTH

ACROSS

1 Descendent from Jacob (Ezra 7:13)
4 Arrest
7 Transfer rate: comp.
10 Tailless primate
11 Company runner
12 Career ended, for short (1 Sam. 8:1)
13 Beginning of comforting truth
16 Morgue-ready
17 Enthusiasm
18 Television interference (Job 6:16)
20 Sea north of Poland
22 "___ times are in your hands" (chorus)
23 Short food value
24 N.T. bk. to Jews
25 Ready to fit
27 Supervisor
28 Circular mix
29 Org. using "wordless book"
30 Conclusion of comforting truth
34 Before
35 Corrode
36 Northwestern U.S. state
37 End on-line session: comp.
38 Town without taverns
39 Pair

DOWN

1 Chat (Judg. 15:17)
2 Church in Asia, for short
3 "Gracious Saviour, ___ ___ ___" (hymn)
4 Univ. sports org.
5 Africa Evangelical Fellowship
6 In northern regions
7 "___ ___ ___, fill me with life anew" (hymn)
8 Thought payment
9 First word of 18-down: abbr.
14 Precedes *boat* or *rope* (Acts 27:16)
15 Harmful
18 Usual company policy (John 13:30, KJV)
19 Church cry room
20 "Casey at the ___"
21 Major network
23 Bent without angles
26 U.S. snoopers
27 London's Big ___
29 Larger than town
30 Fly catcher
31 Play it by ___
32 Tulsa Christian school
33 "Gloria in excelsis ___" (hymn)

(Solution on p. 209)

WEAR IT

ACROSS

1 Weak
5 Hebrew wise man
   (1 Kings 4:31)
10 Soft sanding stone
12 Scandinavian
13 Floral petals
14 Ala. civil rts. site
15 Garland
17 Radiate
18 Power raiser?
19 Site bet. Egypt and
   Canaan (Josh. 13:3, KJV)
21 Before
22 Middle: abbr.
23 Ooze
25 Denver's state: abbr.
27 Complain with oaths
28 Nine days' devotion
   (RCC)
30 Spoke holder
31 Bk. before Jer.
32 ___ Gantry
34 Feed
37 Evang. Teacher Training
   Assoc.
39 Lobe jewelery
41 Finding right spot
43 Document changer
44 Gush
45 Training overseer
46 Discern
47 Hide away

DOWN

1 Difficult position
2 Jumbled
3 Grain grinder
4 Chocolate confection
5 First letter of large
   boat
6 *Ish* ___ (Scand. expr.)
7 Hard hats
8 Regards highly
9 Tidier
10 Rhymer
11 To ___ his own
13 News network
16 End of file: comp.
20 Cycling
22 Ohio's main seaport:
   abbr.
24 *Red October*, for one
25 Halloween dress
26 Applause
28 Brother's daughters
29 Ginger is one
30 Roman Christian
   (Rom. 16:14, KJV)
33 Woman's address
34 Set up support
35 Follows *teen*
36 Computer pop-up
   pgm.
38 Earth movers
40 Amid
42 First letter in Cre-
   ator's name

(Solution on p. 209)

WOMEN AT WORK

ACROSS

1 Mrs. Marcos
7 Pago Pago's region
12 Virgin Mary
14 Hebrew dry measure:
   pl. (Exod. 16:36)
15 Settled in advance
16 Span
17 Lemonlike
18 Tony Acardo's org.
20 ___ of Worms
21 Affirmative cheer
22 Israeli politician ___
   Eban (Gal. 4:6, KJV)
24 Betti or Foscola
25 Store clerkess
   (Acts 16:14)
28 O.T. minor prophet,
   for short
29 ___ Cruces, New Mex.
30 Female foreteller
   (Exod. 15:20)
35 Turn on
36 Spinning material
37 Crash sound
40 Follows stomach or
   tooth

42 Absorbed energy unit
43 Celebrate
44 Pottery piece
46 Camel train
   (Judg. 8:11)
48 Join
49 Market players
50 Set fire
51 Pilotess ___ Earhart

DOWN

1 Give impression
2 ___ Antoinette
3 Swelling
4 Trot
5 Chromosome chain
6 Neither vegetable nor
   mineral (Gen. 1:24)
7 Pig (Amos 9:13)
8 Therein
9 Necromancers
   (Lev. 19:31)
10 Nicaragua president
   Daniel ___
11 dBASE developer ___-
   Tate
13 Clay brick

19 Bul. bd. sys.: comp.
23 Lobe piercers
25 Taste liquid
26 Feeling dull pain
27 Org. of Amer. States:
   abbr.
28 A Sunday in May
   (Deut. 33:9)
30 Blood transfusion
31 Less lean
32 Head organ
33 Parcel (Acts 7:5)
34 Panamanian leader
   Guillermo ___
37 Tapered edge
38 Computer brand
39 Brilliant organization?
41 Therefore
43 Decline (Job 20:8)
45 Relaxation room
47 Hit hard

(Solution on p. 209)

BIBLICAL PARTS

ACROSS

1 Father of Rachel and Leah (Gen. 29:28)
6 Lamb's cry
9 Postal designation
12 Grossly overweight
13 Tablecloth shape: abbr.
14 Jesus' cry on cross (Matt. 27:46)
15 Tennis champ ___ Evert
16 Wager
17 Baseball tool
18 First part of the Bible (Rom. 1:2)
21 Fishing tools
22 Board game
23 Purim feast founder, in brief
26 Top cards
27 Litigate (Ezek. 7:25)
30 "Quintillionfold" prefix
31 Very angry
32 Spanish gentlewoman
33 Rile
35 Gather (1 Chron. 29:25)
37 Architectural band: var.
41 Second part of the Bible
44 Mont.'s neighbor
45 ___ carte
46 ___ Stevenson
48 Corn holder
49 Hat: slang
50 Bucks and does
51 Strong cleaner (Job 9:30)
52 Mineral spring
53 Excited

DOWN

1 Whereabouts, for short
2 Loathe (Lev. 20:23)
3 Entertainer Milton ___
4 Off the cuff remark
5 Snuggle (Isa. 34:15)
6 Ducks
7 Encourage
8 Wedding site (Gen. 8:20)
9 Isaac's wife (Rom. 9:10)
10 Surrounded
11 Copies
19 Satisfactory grades
20 Female address
24 Comp. document ext.
25 Israeli seaport
27 Mañana
28 Oblivious (Gen. 19:33)
29 Toward sunrise
32 Lions' den prophet (Ezek. 14:14)
34 Hotel chain
36 Tamperproofs (Rev. 5:5)
38 Acquiesces
39 Waterway
40 Computer maker
42 Piece of paper
43 Choices/Changes authoress
47 Hebrews' homeland, in short

(Solution on p. 209)

BIBLE GREENERY

ACROSS

1 First polygamist (Gen. 4:19)
7 Cluster fruit
12 Palestinian trees (Exod. 25:10)
14 King of Tyre (2 Sam. 5:11)
15 Ease
16 Big Blue computer
17 ___ Bombeck
18 Driving info. source
20 Cleanser
21 Chain of life
22 Tree Zacchaeus climbed (Luke 19:4)
25 ___ Shamra tablets
27 Early spring flower
28 Yak
30 Chests
31 Tranquil
33 Lincoln's nickname
34 Thorny prebloomers
36 Predecessor of MS-DOS
39 Solomon's great-grand-son (Matt. 1:7)
40 Nighttime insect eater
41 Isaac's mother (Heb. 11:11, KJV)
42 Small water-locked land
45 Stinging hairs
47 Firm
48 Shin guards (1 Sam. 17:6, KJV)
49 Rectify a text
50 Peaceful

DOWN

1 Tied a boot
2 Oak fruit
3 Baby's first words
4 Evangelical Council for Financial Accountability
5 AFL's counterpart
6 Pester (John 5:16)
7 Three before J
8 Eve's start
9 Stranglehold
10 Ancient paper (Exod. 2:3)
11 Program hosts
13 Command to dog
19 Supplemental equip.
23 Egyptian, Syrian, etc.
24 Encore
25 Subspecies
26 Baby's shirt protector: 2 wds. (Ezek. 3:14)
28 Flower (Gen. 40:10)
29 French explorer of Louisiana
31 Adulation
32 Replicate
33 Daisylike flowers
35 Frustration expression: slang
36 Birth a heifer (Deut. 28:51)
37 Beak clean
38 En ___ (all together)
41 Famous hero
43 Before zwei and drei
44 Terminal delay device
46 ___ off

(Solution on p. 209)

TONES

ACROSS

1 Injure
5 Tour vehicle
8 Nut's counterpart (Neh. 6:10)
12 Scheme
13 Swiss mt.
14 Computer operator
15 Repentant (Ps. 51:17)
17 Billy Graham's soloist
18 Major airline's code
19 Musical note
21 Beautify (1 Tim. 2:9, KJV)
24 Quote
25 Healthy-looking
26 Opp. of pride (Prov. 29:23)
30 ___pest meter
31 Birch's enemy
32 ___ volente
33 Happen
35 Mild (Prov. 11:2)
36 Fish food
37 English poet John ___
38 Fall (Joel 2:23)
41 Two N.T. letters
42 Experts
43 Trained (Rom. 1:14)
48 Beast
49 Place
50 Sea
51 Title
52 Prosecute
53 Meat and vegetable dish (Gen. 25:34)

DOWN

1 Here: Lat.
2 Useless activity
3 Chg. name cmd.: comp.
4 Fully developed (Phil. 3:15)
5 Remove water
6 Tops, for short
7 Sample (Prov. 24:10)
8 Basket type (Ruth 3:15)
9 Govt. safety agency
10 Suggestive look
11 Catch (Prov. 1:17)
16 Fled on foot
20 Mix around
21 Queen Jezebel's husband (1 Kings 19:1)
22 Dog or Scandinavian
23 King of Norway
24 Surgical scraper
26 Absolute purity (Rev. 22:11)
27 Same: abbr.
28 Bet. 12 and 20
29 Ox's necklace? (Matt. 11:28)
31 Explosive noise
34 Mistreated (Judg. 19:25)
35 Ethics (Dan. 7:25)
37 Supporting paper: slang
38 "Like peas in ___ ___"
39 Entreat
40 Ripped
41 Attractive
44 Moses' bk. of remembrance
45 Tit for ___
46 Barely muster
47 Natural watering (Judg. 6:40)

(Solution on p. 209)

ANIMAL BOAT

ACROSS

1 Male of 11-down (Prov. 7:22)
5 Dog sound
8 Norway's neighbor: abbr.
12 ___ sapiens
13 102
14 Rabbit resembler (Lev. 11:6)
15 Spotted cats (Heb. 1:8)
17 Irritate
18 Shade
19 Calf (Gen. 15:9)
21 Indicator
24 Pretense
25 Back
26 Tail-stinger (Luke 11:12)
30 Play part
31 Disarray
32 Pool stick
33 Where everyone in the world heard a rooster: 2 wds.
35 Toward sunset
36 Piercers (Exod. 21:6)
37 Bothersome animals
38 Alcohol type
41 Sheep sound
42 Rope ring (Exod. 36:11)
43 Animal lover St. Francis ___ ___
48 Wood-shaping tool
49 Archaeological mound (Ezek. 3:14)
50 Animals' first home (Gen. 2:8)
51 Youth
52 Look
53 Grassy place

DOWN

1 Outer covering, in brief
2 Foot part
3 O.T. sheepherding prophet
4 Burrowing rodent (Gen. 6:14, KJV)
5 State of Brazil (Isa. 5:10)
6 Make free
7 Angler's tool
8 Prawn
9 Stray animal
10 Perry Mason author
11 Fawn, for one (Deut. 14:5)
16 Suppl.
20 Corn's form
21 Shah's country
22 Egyptian pharaoh (2 Kings 23:33)
23 Facts
24 Wound marks (Gal. 6:17)
26 Onionlike plants
27 Freezes over
28 Put out
29 Trapping tools (Isa. 19:8)
31 Raised roadway, for short
34 Come about
35 Symbolically sneaky mammal
37 Faux ___
38 Braid
39 Traveled by donkey
40 Seep (Judg. 3:22)
41 Hay form
44 Charge (Isa. 52:3)
45 Ms. Tarbell or Wells-Barnett
46 Stitch
47 Lodge (Josh. 2:1)

(Solution on p. 209)

ON THE FARM

ACROSS

1 Dog's feet (Lev. 11:27)
5 Baby goat (1 Sam. 17:33)
8 Soothing ointment
12 Death notice
13 Master
14 Rainless
15 Cat sound
16 Church inscription
17 Umps
18 Cattle (2 Tim. 2:16)
20 Assets of deceased (Josh. 24:30)
22 Yes
23 Travel plan, for short
24 Livestock raiser (Gen. 4:2)
27 Slow-moving shell
31 Mil. entertainment org.
32 Hard water
33 Noisy shake (Job 39:23)
37 Open lands (Gen. 4:8)
40 Judge's addr.
41 Donkey
42 Bud or shoot (Ps. 65:10)
45 Cicada (Exod. 10:14)
49 Mammal's clothes?
50 Creed or faith: abbr.
52 St. pointing west
53 Image
54 In the past
55 Harvest (Gal. 6:7)
56 Animal companions (Job 41:5)
57 Captured soldier
58 Cook's meas.

DOWN

1 Snaps
2 Adjoin
3 Cable
4 Brook (Deut. 9:21)
5 Roll type
6 German I
7 Dry wasteland (Gen. 14:6)
8 Trade services (Ezek. 27:9)
9 Region
10 Raise (Exod. 14:14)
11 Goods
19 Cereal grass
21 Stewart Udall's nickname
24 Jacket
25 Film-speed rating (1 Kings 15:8)
26 Decay
28 Sesame plant
29 Liquid crystal display
30 Plural vowel
34 Woody spines (Gen. 3:18)
35 Groza or Wilke
36 Snare
37 Tilled but unseeded (Exod. 23:11)
38 Modernization of 25-down
39 Accompany (Gen. 12:20)
42 Large boat
43 Horse's gait (Gen. 33:14)
44 Extremely funny
46 Guitarlike insts.
47 Smack (Job 16:10)
48 Bugle call
51 Self

(Solution on p. 209)

JUDGMENTS

ACROSS

1 Coiffure
7 On hand (Gen. 1:22)
12 Penn. city
14 Mistake
15 First church martyr (Acts 6:12)
16 Benefit (Exod. 22:4)
17 Gentle
18 Picture studio
20 Red planet
21 Accum. age
22 Western state: abbr.
24 Badger
25 Prohibition #1: 3 wds. (Matt. 7:1, NIV)
27 Accomplishes
29 Woodwind
30 Prohibition #2: 3 wds. (Matt. 6:34, NIV)
34 ___ vs. *Wade*
35 Pimpled
36 Mideast sea: abbr. (Num. 13:29)
39 ___ Bombeck
41 Newspaper seg.: abbr.
42 ___ Canaveral
43 Mennonites
45 Monetary matters
47 Island near Italy (Acts 28:1)
48 Man's whole duty: 2 wds. (Eccles. 12:13)
49 Golfer Sam ___
50 Bedcovers (Exod. 26:1)

DOWN

1 Rashly (Prov. 21:5)
2 Sacrifice site (Gen. 13:4)
3 Enumerated things
4 Braided fastener
5 Play-___
6 Bringer of sin into the world: 2 wds. (1 Cor. 15:21)
7 Few, for short
8 London streetcar
9 Walt Disney World city
10 Valor (Josh. 1:18)
11 Variety store chain
13 A in acronym WASP
19 Mass. school
22 ___ Rica
23 Norwegian bay
25 God: Lat.
26 Preceded by *R* or *L* in Dallas
27 Gatekeeper (Ps. 84:10)
28 Distance soldier could command goods carried (Matt. 5:41, NIV)
30 What Joseph interpreted (Gen. 40:8)
31 Int'l liberal church assoc.
32 Switch positions: 2 wds.
33 Depends (2 Chron. 16:8)
36 Dog's skin disease
37 Fla. attraction
38 Actions (Josh. 24:31)
40 Travel agents' org.
42 Loving concern (Gen. 45:11)
44 Taken
46 Denial: slang

(Solution on p. 210)

THE E'S HAVE IT

ACROSS

1 Roof overhang
5 Hang downward
8 Yield
12 Terminated
13 Father of Solomon's tax officer (1 Kings 4:18)
14 Unusual
15 Vocalize music (Exod. 15:1)
16 Wind (Job 20:6)
17 Pitcher ___ Hershiser
18 Revered (Deut. 33:24)
20 Water sources: abbr.
21 Paralytic Peter healed (Acts 9:34)
23 Cast doubt
27 Small bite
31 Write letters (Gal. 3:1)
32 Horses
33 Marbles
35 Celebrities (Judg. 18:2)
36 Queen of Persia
38 The way in, briefly (Gen. 3:24)
41 Chick hatchery
46 Eight
47 ___ is on first?
48 Comply (Gen. 17:1)
49 ___ Domini
50 Esther time of arr.
51 Cripple (Gen. 49:6)
52 Malicious look
53 Summer schedule
54 Otherwise

DOWN

1 Relaxation (Gen. 27:39)
2 Central pivot
3 Release (Job 40:11)
4 Fringe (Luke 8:44)
5 Mariners
6 Foreigner (Jer. 22:3)
7 Vegetable site (Gen. 2:8)
8 Horizontal beam
9 Lawman Wyatt ___
10 Riffraff (Ps. 75:8)
11 Snakelike fish
19 Largest birds of prey (Isa. 40:31)
22 Aspirers
23 Longest O.T. prophetic bk.
24 Auto's economy rating
25 Pod dweller (Gen. 25:34)
26 Kind of motive
28 Sis's sibling (Gen. 4:2)
29 Shelter
30 Tee's predecessor
34 Fretted (Gen. 25:29)
35 Lecherous man? (Gen. 31:10)
37 Upper regions: abbr.
38 Weigh, for short
39 Number of ungrateful lepers (Luke 17:17)
40 Fork part
42 Where the heart is
43 Palestinian mount (Deut. 11:29)
44 Floral necklaces
45 Tick disease

(Solution on p. 210)

O HOLY NIGHT

ACROSS

1 D. L. Moody's school initials
4 Master (Gen. 2:4)
8 Right away
12 Impact crush (Gen. 15:9)
13 Before bellum or chamber
14 Pianist Kartsonakis
15 "God is with us" (Matt. 1:23)
17 Bet. *K* and *P*
18 Bow shapes
19 O.T. predictor of 15-across
21 Little Orphan ___
23 57 in Rome
24 Computer modem speed
25 Mixed, as a dorm
26 Steal (Gen. 49:19)
29 Prenight (Gen. 4:1)
30 *Treasure of Sierra* ___
31 Shortest O.T. bk.
32 East-coast state
33 Drinks
34 Flat boat
35 Periods
36 Pedaled
37 ___ Mary (Luke 1:34)
40 ___ mater
41 Thought
42 Jesus' birth month
46 Easy
47 Cry of sadness (Jer. 30:7)
48 Affirmative cry
49 Other
50 Unburdens
51 Before

DOWN

1 Advanced church pedagogical degree
2 Impact sound
3 "God is with us" (Isa. 7:14)
4 Spear
5 Blame
6 Circuit: abbr.
7 Frees (Deut. 7:2)
8 Mr. Stevenson
9 ___ Valley, Cal.
10 Follows *Santa* in Mexico
11 Winnie's one
16 Dry
20 One of coin's two
21 Sleep site (2 Kings 4:10)
22 Atrium to altar
23 Mineral veins
25 Date keeper (Job 3:6)
26 To lull baby to sleep
27 Woodwind
28 Streetwalker
30 Christ child's visitors (Matt. 2:7, NIV)
34 Computer RAM insert
35 Type size
36 Bestow good (Gen. 9:26)
37 Compressor
38 Worship object (Deut. 4:16)
39 Biblical citations, briefly
40 Mil. training sch.
43 Prophet Samuel's mentor (1 Sam. 1:3)
44 Head part (Exod. 21:6)
45 Flour or feed

(Solution on p. 210)

HEAVEN AND EARTH

ACROSS

1 Physical dimension
5 Officially prohibit
8 Mount of curses (Deut. 11:29)
12 Verbal
13 Lyric poem
14 Moniker
15 Heat
16 Mountainous district of Palestine (Josh. 11:2)
17 Small winged insect
18 Breaking
20 Wheels' round parts
21 Benjaminite general (2 Chron. 17:17)
23 Double-cross
27 Flattens
31 Forward
32 Cave of Mach-___ (Gen. 50:13)
33 Jewelled crown
35 Gait
36 Town of Zebulun (Josh. 19:15)
38 King of Edom (Gen. 36:32)
41 Relatives
46 Plain of Syria (Amos 1:5)
47 Evangelical Video Institute
48 Jewish captive (Neh. 7:20)
49 Plow wheel
50 Placed
51 Return
52 Additional
53 Attempt
54 ___ of Life (Rev. 2:7)

DOWN

1 Plants seeds
2 Clan of Edom (Gen. 36:43)
3 Son of Judah and Tamar (Matt. 1:3, KJV)
4 Shade trees
5 Physically (Lev. 9:2)
6 King ___-bezek (Judg. 1:6)
7 Asian idol (2 Kings 17:30)
8 Chiseler
9 Levite Rehum's father (Neh. 3:17)
10 Southern Judean city (Josh. 15:26)
11 Allows
19 Started out for
22 Uttermost parts of sea (Deut. 32:22)
23 Negative, as influence
24 Son of Benjamin (Gen. 46:21)
25 Divining leaf type
26 Emanating glow
28 Priest Hophni's father (1 Sam. 4:4)
29 Young man
30 Reference to a sister
34 Causeth (Ps. 39:11, KJV)
35 Rationality
37 Bile gland
38 Commanded
39 Wickedness
40 Smaller portion
42 Truth
43 Fragrance
44 Calcium oxide (Isa. 33:12)
45 What will bow at Jesus' name (Phil. 2:10)

(Solution on p. 210)

SAD AND GLAD

ACROSS

1 Melody
5 Neuter possessive
8 Esau's country (Gen. 32:3)
12 Canaanite city of giants (Josh. 11:21)
13 Meshed fabric trap
14 Trim
15 Settle
16 Ocean
17 Enoch's son (Gen. 4:18)
18 Immortality (Job 27:23)
20 Rolling valley
21 Hold to
23 Each
27 Injury or harm
31 Daughter of Asher (Gen. 46:17)
32 Animal's passenger
33 Penitentiary
35 Assume the position of (Gen. 12:2)
36 Skilled occupations
38 Sight
41 Appreciative
46 Son of Pahath-moab (Ezra 10:30)
47 Received
48 Valley of ___ ("weeping"; Ps. 84:6, KJV)
49 Rip
50 Fearful reverence
51 Rock where Samson captured (Judg. 15:11)
52 Beach turf
53 Hotel
54 City in Benjamin (Josh. 18:28)

DOWN

1 Story
2 Composite
3 Church's central part (Ezek. 41:1)
4 Father of Peleg and Joktan (Gen. 10:25)
5 Within
6 Escaped by the skin of my ___
7 Remained
8 Rapidly spreading disease
9 Brother of Ethan and Heman (1 Chron. 2:6)
10 By word of mouth
11 Darius the ___ (Dan. 5:31)
19 Father of Thara (Luke 3:34, KJV)
22 Most uncommon
23 Venomous snake (Isa. 11:8, KJV)
24 According to
25 Son of Bela (1 Chron. 7:7)
26 Toward sunrise
28 Fuss
29 Jewel
30 Before
34 Father of Esli (Luke 3:25)
35 Hammered
37 Suffocate in water
38 Cauldrons
39 Thought
40 Father of Naphtali leader Ahira (Num. 10:27)
42 City of Issachar (Josh. 19:20)
43 Destiny
44 Corecipient of Agur's messages (Prov. 30:1)
45 Jesus' dying cry (Matt. 27:46)

(Solution on p. 210)

THE REVEREND

ACROSS

1 Stringed instrument (Gen. 4:21)
5 Arrow shooter (Gen. 27:3)
8 Apple center
12 Done
13 Be in debt
14 So be it (Deut. 27:15)
15 Ordained clergyman
17 Fuzz
18 Greek past tense: abbr.
19 Highest earned degree (Col. 4:14)
21 Stars' home (Josh. 3:4)
24 Proposal
25 Go over
26 Clergy's indoor sport?
31 Amount to be paid
32 Exp. diff. opinions (2 Sam. 19:9)
33 "Water" prefix
34 Preliminary examinations
36 Clout
37 Bet. B and F
38 Rome's home (Acts 18:2)
39 Service bureau (Gal. 1:1)
43 ___-fi
44 Queen Anne's or curtains
45 Religious worker (Heb. 8:6)
50 Bog (Job 8:11)
51 Govt computer language
52 Dark region of moon
53 Framing timber
54 Henpeck (Judg. 16:16)
55 Slide

DOWN

1 Prefix to *net* and *stings* (Num. 20:21)
2 ___ Maria
3 Clergy address
4 Sermonizer (Eccles. 1:1)
5 Dutch So. African
6 Possess
7 Tying knots? (Matt. 24:37)
8 Before spar or tuff
9 Leave out (Lev. 5:16)
10 Nevada city
11 Way in, in brief
16 Small deer
20 Unusual
21 Iranian monarch
22 Window glass
23 Amer. Soc. of Travel Agents
24 Intrude
26 Fix-it person
27 Water sacraments (Matt. 3:16)
28 Water
29 Put to sleep (Judg. 16:19)
30 Easter plant
35 Transport regulator
38 Inner City Impact
39 Charitable contributions (Matt. 6:1, KJV)
40 Horse trot
41 Pale beige
42 Lack (Gen. 6:21)
43 Hidden obstacle
46 Potato state: abbr.
47 Rabbinical bk.
48 Before
49 Sea Hebrews crossed (Josh. 2:10)

(Solution on p. 210)

BEING NEIGHBORLY

ACROSS

1 Facts, for short
5 Goblin or fairy
8 Christian Business Men's Committee
12 Bound (Ps. 29:6)
13 Sticky substance
14 Cookie brand
15 Second great commandment (pt. 1; cont. in 42-across)
18 Sleeper's sounds
19 Jesus as divine and human
20 Sprinted
21 Skirt length
22 Raised platform
24 Green-eyed (Ps. 10:3, KJV)
28 Sternward
29 *Children of Crisis* author, Robert ___
30 Capture game
31 Gifts (Gen. 24:53)
33 Disrespectful
34 Adj. modifiers
35 Foot: Lat.
36 Female Shaker founder: 2 wds.
39 Baptist preacher ___ Rogers
42 Second great commandment (pt. 2; Lev. 19:18)
44 Taken back, in brief
45 O.T. bk.
46 Corporate name pt.
47 Cry of despair (Num. 24:23)

48 Cyclinder thickness: abbr.
49 Small amount: 2 wds. (Gen. 50:10)

DOWN

1 Afflictions (Ps. 35:13)
2 Lighted sign
3 Preferred (Gen. 25:28)
4 Dramatic musicals
5 Psyches
6 Costello or Gehrig
7 Pardons (Ps. 103:3)
8 Revise a manuscript together
9 Periphery (1 Kings 7:23)
10 Precedes *phone* or *polis*
11 Al, Ferdinand, or Mindy
16 Japanese currency
17 Computer network workstations
21 Sloughs
22 Skip
23 Cont. so. of Eur.
24 Transmitted (Esther 1:12)
25 Compliant (Deut. 13:18)
26 Egypt-Syria alliance
27 Pepper's prefix (Beatles title)
29 Relinquishes
32 Tossed or garden
33 Iran's ancient name (Ezra 1:2)
35 Drug compendium: abbr.
36 ___ cadabra
37 "The First ___," (carol)
38 ___/AARP Bulletin (magazine)

39 Ecuador Indian tribe: formerly
40 Opp. of baja
41 St. John's island
43 Overseas Crusades, Inc.

(Solution on p. 210)

CHURCH TALK

ACROSS

1 Dark spot (Gen. 6:7)
5 Total
8 Slightly open
12 Jesus' mother (Matt. 2:11)
13 Second letter
14 Broken
15 Follows "In Jesus' name"
16 "___, black sheep"
17 Author unknown: abbr.
18 The church: 3 wds. (Eph. 4:12)
21 Actor ___ Carney
22 Notice of 31-down
23 Sins (1 Pet. 1:24)
26 Bet. L and P
27 Eggs
30 Hillside: Scot.
31 Fellowship of Suffering
32 Intercede (Phil. 4:6)
33 Critical care area
34 Vase type
35 Termites, e.g.
36 Observed
38 Prohibition (1 Sam. 18:13)
39 Members of conservative
   churches
44 Obligate (Matt. 18:18)
45 Kid (Gen. 2:22)
46 Identify
48 Ruin
49 Totally
50 Key element

51 Snow ride
52 Potassium hydroxide (Jer. 2:22)
53 Brink (Luke 16:26)

DOWN

1 Bible Memory Assoc.
2 Sweet, innocent person
  (John 1:29)
3 Creme cookie
4 English Bible translator
  William ___
5 Monastery superior
6 Hard of hearing
7 Elected church leaders
  (1 Tim. 3:10)
8 Japanese graphical computer
9 Custodians (Esther 1:5)
10 O.T. prophet
11 Lease (Luke 20:16)
19 Long time, for short
20 Movie channel
23 Hoover's agency
24 Circular
25 Conference on World Evange-
   lism city
26 Contemporary: slang
28 European sales tax (1 Kings
   7:38)
29 Sailors' affirmations
31 Burial ceremony (Matt. 9:23)
32 Acts of contrition (Ps. 51:16)
34 Seek handout

35 ___-Man © (comp. game)
37 Stopped
38 Holy Scriptures (Ezra 7:10)
39 Wanes (Lev. 26:16)
40 Flask (1 Sam. 16:1)
41 Easter plant
42 Rendered fat
43 Conceited
47 Denotes runnable program:
   comp.

(Solution on p. 210)

DANIEL AND HIS FRIENDS

ACROSS

1 Cognizant: slang
4 Obscures
8 Cries
12 Lung food?
13 Palo ___ , Calif.
14 Can do
15 Daniel's famous place:
   2 wds. (Dan. 6:19)
17 Lymph, for one
18 Butter pieces
19 Directions (Dan. 2:12)
21 Upper regions: abbr.
23 Term of disgust: slang
24 Pitcher ___ Hershiser
25 Grapefruit pieces: abbr.
26 Portable sleeper
29 Pen brand
30 Rattled (Ezek. 19:7)
31 Term of disbelief: slang
32 Secret agent
33 Human grip
34 Chron. musician ___ Hess
35 Flower sites
36 Daniel's diet (Dan. 1:12, KJV)
37 Show up
40 Lifeless
41 Zorba the Greek actress ___
   Kedrova
42 One of Daniel's friends (Dan.
   1:7)
46 RCC's add'l Bible bks.
47 ___ Cola

48 Wedding date, in brief
49 Holland, for short
50 Emperor's greeting (Matt. 27:29)
51 A crazy _____

DOWN

1 Late Great Planet Earth author
   ___ Lindsey
2 Number of Daniel's companions: rom.
3 Daniel's book type (Dan. 4:33)
4 Food-avoidance periods
   (Dan. 10:12)
5 Buick's twin
6 Communications giant
7 Seen with Daniel's friends in
   furnace (Dan. 3:25, KJV)
8 Singer ___ Patti
9 Woodwind
10 House maker: abbr.
11 Cathedral towns
16 Nationwide
20 Secy. of State Dean ___
21 Elves
22 Handle
23 Underlings
25 Another of Daniel's friends
   (Dan. 1:7)
26 People holding Daniel and his
   friends (Dan. 1:4)
27 Acorn makers
28 "With this ring I ___ wed"
30 George Beverly ___

34 San ___ , PR
35 Seaside
36 Foot power
37 Author-preacher ___ Redpath
38 Conduit
39 Story line (Dan. 11:17)
40 "Ten" prefix
43 Big snake
44 Bearded antelope
45 Gr. lake: abbr.

(Solution on p. 210)

SOME OLD, SOME NEW

ACROSS

1 Grapes' support
5 Reference to Mary
8 Grandson of Esau (Gen. 36:15)
12 Divisible by two
13 Ancient liquid measure (Ezek. 45:14, KJV)
14 Valley
15 Valuable perfume (Song 4:14)
16 Abijam's son, king of Judah (1 Kings 15:8)
17 Man of Naphtali (Num. 7:78)
18 Prickly plants
20 Stationary position
21 Healed paralytic (Acts 9:33)
23 Pertaining to Aaron's son (Exod. 6:23)
27 Greatly fears
31 What Jesus did after his burial
32 Country joined with Persia (Dan. 8:20)
33 Source of Palestinian wheat (Ezek. 27:17)
35 Belted (Exod. 12:11, KJV)
36 Entice
38 Stumble
41 Converted runaway slave (Philem. 1:10)
46 "___ and Circumstance"
47 Compete
48 Pleasant
49 Empowered
50 And such like, in brief
51 Extended family line
52 Close to
53 Look at
54 Restrained

DOWN

1 Outlet
2 Babylonian district (Isa. 37:13, KJV)
3 Zerubbabel's grandfather (Luke 3:27)
4 Extremities
5 Balances
6 Trousers (Dan. 3:21, KJV)
7 Removed
8 Supervisor
9 Long horsehair
10 Despairing cry
11 Lease
19 Father of one desired as Judah's king (Isa. 7:6, KJV)
22 Organized military forces
23 Short sleep
24 Son of Ithran (1 Chron. 7:38)
25 Put on
26 Assyrian prince (Ezra 4:10, KJV)
28 Continue
29 Be killed
30 Deplorable
34 Hand covers
35 Country of Thessalonica (1 Thess. 1:7)
37 Join together
38 Period of time
39 Ear part
40 Father of prophet Micaiah (2 Chron. 18:7, KJV)
42 Foot part
43 Distance to carry Roman's gear (Matt. 5:41)
44 First reader of Proverbs 30 (Prov. 30:1)
45 Dispatch

(Solution on p. 210)

MIXED BAG

ACROSS

1 Sunset direction
5 Crowd
8 Secure
12 Fallow
13 Individual
14 Stomped
15 Cloth joint
16 Misery
17 Farmland measure
18 Caves where David hid
 (1 Sam. 23:29)
20 Wealthier
22 ___-professionals (Acts 4:13)
23 Deed
24 Large opening
27 Paid attention to
31 Song
32 "___ written you"
 (Philem. 1:21)
33 Woman Peter resurrected
 (Acts 9:40)
37 Celibate
40 Abraham's ally, ___col (Gen.
 14:13)
41 Three in Rome
42 Brother of Alvan and Ebal
 (Gen. 36:23)
45 Smoldering coals
49 Shove
50 Kneel
52 Brought first accepted offering
 (Gen. 4:4)

53 An Asherite with three sons
 (1 Chron. 7:39)
54 Respectful wonder
55 ___-Hamath (Num. 34:7)
56 Belonging to Hannah's priest
 (1 Sam. 2:20)
57 God ___ the people out of
 Egypt
58 To sketch

DOWN

1 Sagacious
2 Priest Kore's assistant
 (2 Chron. 31:15)
3 Glassy, molten mass
4 Ashhur's son by Naarah
 (1 Chron. 4:6)
5 Cutting
6 Where Nehemiah refused to
 go (Neh. 6:2)
7 Prince of the tribe of Reuben
 (1 Chron. 5:6)
8 Sweet spice
9 Doorway vault
10 ___ fathers (Lev. 26:45)
11 A descendant of Levi
 (1 Chron. 24:30)
19 Put on
21 Frozen water
24 The ever-living One
25 Commotion
26 Authorization, in brief
28 Unearth

29 Midianite king Moses killed
 (Josh. 13:21)
30 Haunt
34 Simon Peter (John 1:42)
35 Burning remains
36 Caleb's grandson (1 Chron.
 2:50)
37 Observed
38 Town in Judah's extreme
 south (Josh. 15:29)
39 Vulgar
42 Cast forth
43 Ship body
44 Ancestor of Jesus (Luke 3:25)
46 Leader of Amok clan
 (Neh. 12:20)
47 Midianite king Moses killed
 (Num. 31:8)
48 Leisurely
51 Have due

(Solution on p. 210)

PEOPLE AND PLACES

ACROSS

1 1,760 yards
5 Hang downward
8 "The Lord is my Shepherd; I shall not ___" (Ps. 23:1, KJV)
12 Grandfather of David (Ruth 4:18)
13 Father of Solomon's tax officer (1 Kings 4:18)
14 Stench
15 One-man band?
16 Artificial manner
17 Come alive again
18 Revered
20 Leg joint
21 Healed paralytic (Acts 9:34)
23 Blueprint
27 One of David's heroes (2 Sam. 23:37, KJV)
31 Levite ark mover (1 Chron. 15:11)
32 Caesar's empire
33 Feeds on
35 Top course of stone (1 Kings 7:9, KJV)
36 Son of Dishon (Gen. 36:26)
38 Endure
41 Joshua's grandfather (1 Chron. 7:26)
46 A priest who married foreign women (Ezra 10:26)
47 Outlaw
48 Jewish returnee from Babylon (Neh. 10:26)
49 Bushed
50 Son of Ithran (1 Chron. 7:38)
51 Encryption
52 ___-i, city of Bashan (Deut. 3:10)
53 Chicken
54 Realized

DOWN

1 "___ love to thee, O Christ" (hymn)
2 Large wading bird (Lev. 11:17)
3 Gave temporarily
4 Fringe
5 Mariners
6 Foreigner
7 Eden's description
8 "Idle hands are the devil's ___"
9 Jewish captive subclan (Ezra 2:15)
10 Snout
11 ___ of Conscience (Gen. 2:17)
19 High flyers
22 Miriam's brother's (Num. 12:1)
23 Excavated
24 Make mistake
25 Temple assistant (Neh. 7:47)
26 Clan descended from Gilead (Num. 26:30, NIV)
28 Popular Windows word processor: comp.
29 Left home
30 Present participle former
34 Well named by Jacob (Gen. 26:33, KJV)
35 Son of Arphaxad (Luke 3:36)
37 Sound loudly
38 ___ Ruth
39 Father of Gaal (Judg. 9:26)
40 Twelfth Hebrew month (Ezra 6:15)
42 Writer for hire
43 Soon: arch.
44 Fashioned
45 Once more

(Solution on p. 210)

WHAT TO DO

ACROSS

1 "My God shall supply all your
___" (Phil. 4:19, KJV)
5 Increase (Phil. 1:17)
8 Trepidation (Phil. 1:14)
12 Assistant
13 Cow's sound
14 "I ___ ___ glad that Jesus
loves me" (chorus)
15 Precept statement: 3 wds.
(Phil. 4:7)
18 Repeat verbatim
19 Device to achieve a goal
20 Related suffix?
21 "Fix your thoughts on what is
___" (Phil. 4:8)
22 Intense dislike
24 Characterized by long hard
work
28 First lady
29 Deliberately avoids
30 Small enclosed truck
31 Mentally ponder
33 Religious group
34 Roman tribe's basic unit
35 Passover mo. (Lev. 23:5)
36 Hebrews' first enemy after
the Exodus (Exod. 17:8)
39 Briers
42 Precept statement: 2 wds.
(Phil. 4:5)
44 "Keep putting ___ practice all
you learned from me" (Phil. 4:9)
45 Garment
46 "May it be" (Phil. 4:20)
47 Kiss
48 Single (Phil. 3:13)
49 For fear that

DOWN

1 Not artificial: abbr. (Lev. 17:15)
2 Ireland
3 Formally schooled
4 Urge
5 French friend
6 Spanish nobleman
7 Tenet
8 Mockeries
9 Give off
10 Small leaves
11 College military pgm.
16 Teletype device: comp. abbr.
17 Carries away
21 Acclaims loudly
22 Skirt bottom
23 ___ Maria
24 "Give___ ___ the Lord, for he
is so good!" (Ps. 118:29)
25 Prevailed over
26 Apple computer
27 "Inside" prefix
29 Reinforce against erosion
32 Eskimo estates
33 Helical coil
35 "All my prayers for you ___ full
of praise to God" (Phil. 1:3)
36 Baby food catcher? 2 wds.
37 Food selection
38 Fifth N.T. book
39 Perimeter
40 Follows *form* or *lamin*
41 "I am generously supplied
with the gifts you ___ me"
(Phil. 4:18)
43 Charged particle

(Solution on p. 211)

ROD AND STAFF

ACROSS

1 Common cooking meas.
5 Paper currency (Luke 16:7)
9 Honest ___
12 Author of this puzzle
13 Amazement expressions
14 Home or end, e.g.
15 Jesus' statement (cont. in 31-across)
18 Start of enumerated list
19 Damascus Road convert (Acts 9:27)
20 Rowers
21 Make uneasy
22 Legal corp. designation
24 "If you love me, ___ me" (John 14:15)
27 Opponent
28 Basic
31 Jesus' statement (cont. in 49-across)
35 Color
36 Short order?
37 Placed
38 Teachers' org.
39 Large keg, for short
41 Oil-price controller
44 Polio vaccine inventor
46 English ship registry
49 Jesus' statement (concluded; John 10:11)
52 Woman, for short
53 Average grades
54 Forearm bone
55 Resort
56 Weapons (John 4:45)
57 Twirled

DOWN

1 Bangkok language
2 Sacks (Mic. 6:11)
3 Coin entry
4 Yassir Arafat's org.
5 Twang type
6 Hawaiian island
7 ___ ___, the Witch, and the Wardrobe (C. S. Lewis bk.)
8 Mental telepathy
9 Vicinity
10 Am. politician Aaron ___
11 Stops (John 4:35)
16 Dots per inch
17 Ad ___
21 "The ___ have it" (motion passed)
23 O.T. wall bldr.
24 Venerable
25 Projecting window
26 Body's lamp
27 Opp. of rev.
28 Good Judean king
29 Bible Lit. Intl.
30 Massenet's composition "Le ___"
32 Dir. of Chron. Ed.
33 "___ ___ Let Me Walk with Thee" (hymn)
34 Chicago's state.
38 Noncom
39 Invoke divine favor (Luke 1:30)
40 66 in the Bible: abbr. (John 21:25)
41 Show-___ (exhibitionists)
42 Glance (Isa. 10:14)
43 Evang. For. Missions Assoc.
45 Pardon me
46 Cry in trouble
47 Choice list
48 Cross over (Job 14:5)
50 Radio Corp. of Amer.
51 English Reformer John ___

(Solution on p. 211)

NAME THE PREACHER

ACROSS

1 Robert ___ Chorale
5 Largest U.S. denom.
8 Wise___ (Isa. 5:10)
12 Mother of our Lord (Luke 1:42)
13 Largest on-line computer database: abbr.
14 Produced offspring (Eccles. 2:7)
15 Drug addict
16 Tablecloth size
17 Joshua's role to Moses (Exod. 24:13, NIV)
18 700 Club head
21 Between Hab. and Hag.
22 Relief!
23 Gospel singer Mrs. Waters
26 Between Jon. and Nah.
27 Ecology guardian
30 What God promised Abraham (Gen. 18:10)
31 Between Deut. and Judg.
32 Blueprint (Gen. 18:17)
33 Ump
34 ___ and flow
35 Mississippi outlet
36 Pet's itch-maker (1 Sam. 24:14)
38 Germany's loc.
39 Coral Ridge TV Minister
44 *Rubaiyat* author ___ Khayyam
45 Campground
46 Saline liquid (Gen. 21:16)
48 Between *k* and *p*

49 Frequent end to business letter
50 Soapstone
51 Urban Alternative head, Mr. Evans
52 Joins *q* and *u*
53 An ___ whose time has come (Num. 14:4)

DOWN

1 Dallas football team
2 Hinge part
3 Phone code (Gen. 12:6)
4 Christian musician Don ___
5 Reporter's goal
6 Lettuce type
7 *Mere Christianity* author
8 Relieve taxes
9 Dallas's First Baptist Church former pastor
10 Make over
11 First garden (Gen. 2:8)
19 Kin or faith, shortened
20 11's position, in brief
23 Cup part (1 Cor. 12:16)
24 Mao ___-tung
25 Lutheran Hour speaker
26 Many heads but no brains
28 Pres. Nixon's wife
29 Follows *Santa*
31 PTL former head
32 *This Present Darkness* author Frank ___

34 Dees's successors
35 Harass
37 In Croce's song, he was "big, bad"
38 Make bill law (2 Chron. 24:6)
39 Sudden shock
40 Comes in kegs or rounds
41 Ages
42 Out of play (Rev. 1:17)
43 George Bush's alma mater
47 David Sarnoff's corp.

(Solution on p. 211)

STRICTLY PERSONAL

ACROSS

1 Advantage
5 Go astray
8 Where wicked go
12 Oppress (Exod. 5:9)
13 Regret (Luke 11:42, KJV)
14 Ancient Turkey (1 Cor. 16:19)
15 Tender
16 Father of Shimei (1 Kings 4:18)
17 Son of Caleb (1 Chron. 4:15)
18 Hugged
20 Babylonian plain (Dan. 3:1)
21 The same
23 Intestines
27 Nahor's concubine (Gen. 22:24)
31 Salt water
32 Grass or sword part
33 Duration
35 Jupiter's son: myth. (Acts 28:11, KJV)
36 Giant of Hebron (Josh. 15:14)
38 Without a date
41 Team dialoguers (1 Cor. 1:20)
46 Jacob's priestly son (Gen. 35:23)
47 Heavy Hebrew judge (1 Sam. 4:18)
48 Tablecloth shape
49 "So be it" (Deut. 27:19)
50 X
51 Deep mud
52 Combines with *plank* or *way*
53 "___ Everything to Me" (chorus)
54 Sounded, as a bugle (Judg. 3:27)

DOWN

1 Otherwise
2 Terrible fate
3 Right-wing Prot. denom. (2 Kings 25:29)
4 Featherweight champ ___ Jofre (1 Chron. 23:23)
5 Sets up
6 Lines on paper
7 Verbal beholder
8 Small unspecified amounts (Deut. 23:25)
9 Isaac's favorite son (Gen. 25:28)
10 Fabricator
11 Buddhist monk (Mark 15:34)
19 Feeleth ill (Gen. 21:17, KJV)
22 Temple assistant (Neh. 7:48)
23 Closed cylindrical container, for short
24 Mineral-bearing rock
25 Gain victory
26 Starting a battle (Jer. 37:11)
28 Pallet
29 Bother
30 "___ name is 'woman'" (Gen. 2:23)
34 "He ___ my soul in the cleft of the rock" (hymn)
35 Bungalows
37 Brawl
38 Waste from smelting 24-down
39 Son of Ishmael (Gen. 25:15)
40 Part of street address (Hos. 10:8)
42 Jesus' resurrection site
43 "Deliver us from the ___ One" (Matt. 6:13)
44 Exquisite
45 Killed (2 Sam. 1:22)

(*Solution on p. 211*)

ON DEATH AND DOOM

ACROSS

1 Passover meat (Exod. 12:21)
5 Child of Ruth and Boaz (Ruth 4:22)
9 Trap of connected concentric circles (Job 27:18)
12 ___ and the Night Visitors, var. sp.
13 Beloved
14 Wonder
15 Smallest Greek letter (John 8:44)
16 Straight line on heart monitor
18 Gown
20 Pretense (Eph. 4:22)
21 Rained on Gomorrah (Gen. 19:24)
23 O.T. minor prophet book
27 New moon shape
32 Italian Fascist leaders' title
33 Chest protector
34 Posture to pray
36 Appendix-shaped state: abbr.
37 Name means "red" (O.T. char.)
39 Terrible (Ezek. 26:21)
41 Straight lines to the water
43 Game cube
44 O.T. prophet with herds of 1-across
47 Black-robed Hebrew teacher (Matt. 9:18)
51 Bright glow (Exod. 34:30)
55 Yellow/white kernels (Deut. 33:28)
56 Number of birthdays
57 Five-pointed guide (Matt. 2:7)
58 Norwegian king
59 Mssrs. Carlos or Cervantes
60 Sharpen
61 "That's a ___ - ___" (prohib.)

DOWN

1 Placed, as a wreath
2 Latin love affair
3 Counterpart (Exod. 36:11)
4 Loud trumpet calls (Rev. 8:6)
5 Uneven
6 Yellowjackets, e.g.
7 One
8 Night vision
9 Past presence
10 Mama sheep
11 Resting place
17 In the center
19 Overcome and pillage (Jer. 5:17)
22 Forcibly separate
24 Sleeve encircling wrist
25 Liberal lobby
26 Get better
27 Ship operators
28 Yeast's result (Exod. 12:39)
29 Mount opposite Gerizim (Deut. 11:29)
30 Abner's father (1 Sam. 14:50)
31 Placed golf ball
35 53-down for lions
38 River of Persia (Dan. 8:2)
40 Church servant (Phil. 1:1)
42 Break up
45 Upon
46 Read quickly
48 String tie
49 Fiber flakes
50 Data
51 Energy unit
52 Back then (Gal. 3:8)
53 Cub pack (Dan. 6:19)
54 Before

(Solution on p. 211)

GOING FISHIN'

ACROSS

1 Isaac's substitute sacrifice caught in a bush (Gen. 22:13)
4 Firmly bound
8 Masters
12 Years since birth
13 Ancient Ptolemais (Judg. 1:31)
14 Wolf cry
15 Ruminant's rechewed food
16 As a result
17 Carry out order
18 Desert climate
20 Edomite capital (1 Chron. 1:46)
22 Flat-topped bank
24 Gave food
27 ___-nekeb, city of Naphtali (Josh. 19:33)
29 Nimble
31 The devil, who will be caught and bound (Rev. 20:2)
32 King Lemuel of ___ "caught" wisdom (Prov. 31:1)
33 Wrinkle-catcher?
34 City assigned Judah (Josh. 15:42)
35 Unhappy
36 Son of Ephraim (1 Chron. 7:20)
40 Grown up
41 Greatest degree
44 Assigned job
47 Location
49 Jacob's youngest son, Ben-___ (Gen. 35:18)
50 Mental conception

51 Current
52 Relatives
53 Where God caught and killed the first animal (Gen. 3:21-23)
54 This kind
55 Secret-catcher

DOWN

1 Good-for-nothing (Matt. 5:22, KJV)
2 Author of Proverbs 30 (Prov. 30:1)
3 Mentally caught and pondered (Ps. 73:17)
4 Obese
5 "The troubler of Israel" (1 Chron. 2:7, KJV)
6 Jewish priest with seven sons (Acts 19:14)
7 Invigorating beverage
8 Zalmon's hometown (2 Sam. 23:28)
9 Corn core
10 Type of lamb
11 Crafty
19 Deserted Paul (2 Tim. 4:10)
21 Joined together
23 Washed lightly
24 Barbed-wire catchers? (Amos 4:2)
25 Other
26 Loved
27 Snakes (Deut. 32:33, KJV)

28 Brother of Zimri and Calcol (1 Chron. 2:6)
30 Grandson of Esau (Gen. 36:11)
37 Passions
38 Job's fourth visitor (Job 32:4)
39 "Lofty" junk catcher
40 Son of Ezer (Gen. 36:27)
42 Prune
43 Very small
44 Attach with rope
45 Interpose
46 Look
48 ___col, source of giant grapes (Num. 13:23)

(Solution on p. 211)

OLD TESTAMENT

¹	²	³	■	⁴	⁵	⁶	⁷	■	⁸	⁹	¹⁰	¹¹
¹²			■	¹³				■	¹⁴			
¹⁵			¹⁶				■	¹⁷				
■			¹⁸			■	¹⁹				■	■
²⁰	²¹	²²			■	²³				■	²⁴	²⁵
²⁶				■		²⁷			■	²⁸		
²⁹			■	³⁰	³¹			■	³²			
³³		■	³⁴				■	³⁵				
³⁶		³⁷				■	³⁸					
■		³⁹			■	⁴⁰			■	■	■	
⁴¹	⁴²			■	⁴³			■	⁴⁴	⁴⁵	⁴⁶	
⁴⁷			■	⁴⁸			■	⁴⁹				
⁵⁰			■	⁵¹			■	⁵²				

ACROSS

1 Ingest
4 Still
8 Foot
12 Pair
13 Shammah's father (2 Sam. 23:11)
14 Peleg's father (Gen. 10:25)
15 Freed from impurities
17 Multicolored marble
18 Cushion
19 Indication
20 "Place of confusion" (Gen. 11:9)
23 "Seventh year—the Year of
___" (Deut. 31:10)
26 Dreadful cry
27 Jonathan's son (Ezra 8:6)
28 Sigh
29 Son of Shem (Gen. 10:22)
30 City in Nimrod's empire
(Gen. 10:10)
32 Caleb's oldest son (1 Chron.
4:15)
33 For example
34 Chaldean place (Ezek. 23:23)
35 Southern Canaanite city
(Num. 33:40)
36 David's second son (2 Sam. 3:3)
38 Belonging to hot springs dis-
coverer (Gen. 36:24)
39 Pounded
40 To and ___
41 Idled (Zech. 1:15)
43 Flood sign

47 Catch
48 Predicament
49 A particular
50 Bottom borders
51 Ceremony
52 The Creator (Gen. 1:1)

DOWN

1 And other such, for short
2 Leather-worker's tool
3 From head to ___
4 Man-made waterway
5 Old
6 Directed
7 Personal reference
8 Pleaded
9 River of Syria (2 Kings 5:12)
10 Started
11 Until
16 Gorillas
17 Impaired or troubled
19 Son of Cush (Gen. 10:7)
20 Associate of Balaam (Rev.
2:14, KJV)
21 Israelite campsite (Num. 33:13)
22 Fouled
23 Ish-Bosheth's assassinator
(2 Sam. 4:6, NIV)
24 Abraham's wife (Gen. 17:15)
25 Pertaining to King Eglon's murderer (Judg. 3:20)
30 In front
31 Outer garment

32 Hebrew cdr. (1 Chron. 27:9)
34 Slumbers
35 By and by
37 Son of Tola (1 Chron. 7:2)
38 Come forth
40 Refrain from food
41 ___ Kazin (Canaanite city,
Josh. 19:13, NIV)
42 "We ___ [God's] friends"
(1 John 1:6)
43 Supporter of David (1 Kings 1:8)
44 Swamp
45 City Shemed built (1 Chron.
8:12)
46 Joined together
48 Male address

(Solution on p. 211)

STOCKS AND BONDS

ACROSS

1 Binding rule
4 Brother of Havilah (1 Chron. 1:9)
8 Waiter's tool
12 "Whatever is has been long ___" (Eccl. 3:15)
13 Plain in Syria (Amos 1:5)
14 Zoom
15 Temple gate (2 Kings 11:6, KJV)
16 Use as support
17 Insects in colonies
18 Home of prophet Amos (Amos 1:1)
20 Surprise attack
22 Which one
24 Approaches
28 Spare
31 Convert of Peter (1 Pet. 5:13)
34 Hat
35 Worked in winepress
36 Deplore
37 Son of Levite Abinadab (2 Sam. 6:3)
38 King Hezekiah's mother (2 Kings 18:2)
39 Heap
40 Tenant payment
41 Emblem
43 Blockade
45 Amalekite King Saul captured (1 Sam. 15:8)
48 King's forest manager (Neh. 2:8)

52 Sometimes-dry brook
55 Wild pig
57 Cove
58 Foundary material
59 To the form of
60 Befogged
61 ___, twenties, thirties, etc.
62 "Realize how kind the Lord has ___ to you" (1 Pet. 2:2)
63 Tavern

DOWN

1 Trailing
2 Fever (Lev. 26:16, KJV)
3 Labor
4 Eber's father (Gen. 10:24, KJV)
5 Between day and night
6 Tolerate
7 Widow recognizing infant Jesus as Messiah (Luke 2:36)
8 Exchange
9 Dashed
10 "An ___ of God" (calamity)
11 As you say
19 Was indebted
21 Pen and ___
23 King Ahab's father (1 Kings 16:28)
25 Dull hurt
26 For 40 days and nights (Gen. 7:4)
27 Area
28 Pierce

29 Hebron (Josh. 15:13)
30 Null
32 Like an ice pick
33 Strip of cane
37 Hugging instruments
39 Hook
42 Increases
44 Golden calf maker (Exod. 32:4)
46 Passover month (Deut. 16:1, KJV)
47 Departed
49 Levite from Merari clan (2 Chron. 29:12)
50 Penalty
51 Sacred song
52 Sanity
53 Plurality of being
54 Put on
56 Consumed

(Solution on p. 211)

IT'S CLEAR

ACROSS

1 Sick
4 Covered
8 Brother of Heman and Ethan
(1 Chron. 2:6)
12 Notice
13 Champion
14 Monkeys
15 Without relentment
17 Bars
18 One of David's valiant men
(1 Chron. 11:31)
19 Twenty-year-___ (1 Chron.
27:23)
21 Fodder trough
24 Consumed
27 Midianite king (Josh. 13:21)
30 Pinnacles
32 Source of deportees to
Samaria (2 Kings 17:24, KJV)
33 King of Judah (Matt. 1:7)
34 The Messiah
35 Ministerial training: abbr.
36 Irrational
37 Mayor of Samaria (1 Kings
22:26)
38 In harp family
39 Peas, beans, or lentils (Dan.
1:16, KJV)
41 Where Paul boarded ship for
Italy (Acts 27:5)
43 Troubles

45 Courtier of King Josiah
(2 Kings 22:14)
49 Female red deer
51 Come to recognize
54 Supporting worker
55 Site
56 English beverage
57 Overlook
58 Terebinth tree (Isa. 6:13, KJV)
59 Border

DOWN

1 Son of Asher (Gen. 46:17, KJV)
2 Forty days before Easter
3 Jacob's first wife (Gen. 29:23)
4 Seat
5 Causal command
6 "You ___ my witnesses"
(Isa. 44:8)
7 Judge Tola's grandfather (Judg.
10:1)
8 Famous wise man (1 Kings 4:31)
9 Abandonment of the faith
10 Color of Tabernacle's top
skins (Exod. 36:19)
11 Jackal
16 Valley of Weeping (Ps. 84:6, KJV)
20 A smaller amount
22 Thing
23 Heart
25 At any time
26 Designation
27 Sloping passageway

28 Isaac's son (Gen. 25:26)
29 Eroded ridges (Isa. 30:6)
31 Inconsequential
34 Slayer of Sisera (Judg. 4:21)
38 Cord pulled through eyelets
40 Vertical surfaces
42 A hideout of David (1 Sam.
30:29)
44 Spit
46 Snack
47 Hot spot
48 Narrated
49 Brother of Shem and Japheth
(Gen. 9:18)
50 After two, in Rome
52 Until
53 Ally of David's army chiefs
(1 Kings 1:8)

(Solution on p. 211)

AUTHORITIES

ACROSS

1 Whip
5 Uncooked
8 Freshwater fish (Ezek. 30:5, KJV)
12 As far as
13 First deceived person (1 Tim. 2:14)
14 Demolish
15 "___ on believing" (1 John 2:24)
16 Mediterranean ___
17 Evangelist ___ Roberts
18 Charlemagne and Constantine, e.g. (Esther 1:2)
20 Cruise
21 Modifies
23 Fearful
27 Birthing efforts
31 "Be ye ___ of the word, and not hearers only" (James 1:22, KJV)
32 Hebrew weight measure (Ezek. 45:12, KJV)
33 Expelled
35 Travesty (Mal. 2:8)
36 Where Noah's ark is (Gen. 8:4)
38 What Noah's ark made from (Gen. 6:14)
41 Place in Babylonia (Ezra 2:59, KJV)
46 Figurative name for Israel (Hos. 2:1)
47 At the drop of a ___
48 Paint crudely

49 "___ not thyself because of evildoers" (Ps. 37:1, KJV)
50 Broadcast
51 Land measurement
52 Wheel
53 Negative vote
54 Foot back

DOWN

1 Doctor disciple (Col. 4:14)
2 Levitical city (1 Chron. 6:73)
3 Dance move
4 "___ deferred makes the heart sick" (Prov. 13:12)
5 Marketed again
6 Turn away
7 "Pop Goes the ___"
8 Horizontal beam
9 Place in Assyria (1 Chron. 5:26)
10 Father of Palal (Neh. 3:25)
11 For Whom the ___ Tolls
19 Lifter
22 Home of Shimei (1 Chron. 27:27)
23 Extend
24 "___ he's a jolly good fellow"
25 Israelite loyal to David (1 Kings 1:8)
26 Canaanite clan (Gen. 10:18)
28 Surprised refusal: 2 wds. (Neh. 6:2)
29 Mainland China's "color"
30 Timid

34 Prophet to David (2 Sam. 7:2)
35 Meager
37 Son of Micah (1 Chron. 5:5, KJV)
38 Gently drift
39 Wicked king of Israel (1 Kings 16:16)
40 Manna measure (Exod. 16:36)
42 Wife of Esau (Gen. 36:10)
43 Division of humanity
44 Certain
45 First shepherd (Gen. 4:2)

(Solution on p. 211)

PEOPLE AND PLACES

```
 1  2  3  4  ▓  5  6  7  ▓  8  9  10 11
12        ▓  13       ▓  14
15        16          17
18              ▓  19
▓        20    ▓  21          ▓  ▓  ▓
22 23    ▓  24          25 26 27
28       ▓  29          30
31       32          33
▓        34          35          ▓
36 37 38    ▓  39          40 41
42             43
44       ▓  45    ▓  46
47       ▓  48    ▓  49
```

ACROSS

1 Painting and sculpture, for examples
5 Acquired
8 Place of business
12 Grumble
13 In current existence
14 Assyrian place Israelites taken (1 Chron. 5:26)
15 Palestinian group against returned Jews (Ezra 5:6, KJV)
18 Town of Sidonians (Josh. 13:4)
19 Dirge
20 Fisherman's tool
21 Founder of 60 cities (Josh. 13:30)
22 "Choose you ___ day whom ye will serve" (Josh. 24:15, KJV)
24 Experienced fighters (Exod. 17:8)
28 Strike
29 Swirls violently
30 Compete
31 Paul's first Asian convert (Rom. 16:5, NIV)
33 Express
34 Father of Hushim (1 Chron. 7:12)
35 Armed conflict
36 Temple governor who imprisoned Jeremiah (Jer. 20:1, KJV)
39 Cinnamon (Exod. 30:24)
42 Task finishers
44 Skin defect
45 Cereal grass
46 Beverages from steeping leaves
47 Convulsive cries
48 Nautical rope
49 "It ___ good for man to be alone" (Gen. 2:18)

DOWN

1 City assigned to Judah (Josh. 15:26)
2 Jericho spies' escape device (Josh. 2:15)
3 Family descended from Ephraim (Num. 26:35, NIV)
4 Booby traps
5 Maher-shalal-___-baz, Isaiah's son (Isa. 8:3)
6 Grandson of Zophah (1 Chron. 7:38)
7 Proclaims
8 A Levite in Hezekiah's time (2 Chron. 29:13)
9 Despise
10 Brother of Ram and Bunah (1 Chron. 2:25)
11 History
16 Tattle
17 What God has numbered about us (Matt. 10:30)
21 Judean border town (Josh. 15:21)
22 "___ Lord is my Shepherd" (Ps. 23:1)
23 Thigh
24 Where Jesus made wedding wine (John 2:6)
25 Job of elder or deacon
26 ___-Tin-Tin
27 Put
29 Hebrew governor (Ezra 4:8)
32 Belonging to Abraham's brother (Gen. 22:20)
33 Queen Esther's predecessor (Esther 1:9)
35 Has been
36 Decline
37 Canaanite city (Judg. 1:31)
38 Crust
39 Quote as proof
40 Shah's country
41 Second in charge
43 Not clergy

(Solution on p. 211)

OLD TESTAMENT PROPHETS

ACROSS

1 Just (Prov. 1:3)
5 Criticizes: slang
9 Dad's mate
12 Entreat
13 Reword
14 Eisenhower's nickname
15 Beach material
16 Hardened
17 35mm camera type
18 O.T. prophet who parted the Jordan River (2 Kings 2:14)
20 O.T. prophet who called down fire from heaven (1 Kings 18:36)
22 End of line
23 Intensive Care Unit
24 Supernatural signs (John 6:30)
29 Christian Scientist Mary Baker ___
32 Time frame
33 Id counterpart
34 Jehovah (Gen. 14:22)
35 Where Jesus restored a dead boy (Luke 7:11)
37 Plague on Egypt's light source (Exod. 10:21)
40 Capture
42 Third letter
43 Overcome (Exod. 23:31)
46 Inciters
50 Ms. Braun or Le Gallienne
51 Grizzly, for one (1 Sam. 17:34)
53 Fever
54 Trouble
55 Author Gardner
56 Joni Eareckson-___
57 Erase: comp. abbr.
58 Lion's home (Jer. 4:7)
59 God-planted garden (Gen. 2:8)

DOWN

1 Circuit protector
2 Large Russian sea
3 "Fire" prefix
4 Water parted by Moses (Exod. 15:22)
5 Summoned back (Ps. 77:11)
6 ___ Augusta, Countess of Lovelace
7 Wide toll road
8 Phonograph needles
9 Calculate wrongly
10 Tex. neighbor
11 Tool-related: abbr. (Rom. 7:6)
19 Ad ___ committee
21 Greenland's ground
24 Males
25 Irish Republican Army
26 Withheld several years by 20-across (1 Kings 17:1, 7)
27 Computer display type
28 Magic worker (Acts 13:6)
30 Opp. of don'ts
31 Dry gds. meas. (Gen. 21:16)
36 Natl. Assoc. of Evangelicals
38 Small barrel
39 Make void
41 Where different languages supernaturally began (Gen. 11:9)
43 Condition before resurrection (Mark 5:35)
44 Singer Tornquist
45 "Trillion" prefix
47 Mild oath of surprise
48 Discourteous (1 Cor. 13:5)
49 Actors Connery and Penn
52 Boxer Muhammad ___

(Solution on p. 211)

PLACES

ACROSS

1 Sponsors' times
4 Gifts to the poor (Matt. 6:1, KJV)
8 Foot support (Acts 4:11)
12 Beat (Exod. 35:7)
13 Outer garment (Luke 9:3)
14 Where David Koresh lived
15 Doctors' group
16 Mackerel "game"?
17 Praise song (Mark 14:26)
18 ___ -Cola
20 Chr. yth. org.
22 ___ Warner football
24 Prohibited (Mark 7:36)
28 ___ Braves
32 Boston ___
33 Pension plan
34 Scripture dist.: abbr.
36 "___ do!" attitude (Gen. 4:7)
37 Al Unser's vehicle
40 Jesus' death site (Luke 23:33, KJV)
43 Bootlace route
45 ___ Faggs, track and field "Starr"
46 Lie adjacent
48 Approaches (1 Cor. 10:11)
52 Track wager
55 Halftime marchers (Isa. 9:4)
57 Canon (Gal. 4:5)
58 "Ready, willing, and ___"
59 Love
60 Prot. denom. init.
61 LSD
62 Lively
63 Chicago's Soldier Field's "roof" (Gen. 1:9)

DOWN

1 "___ ___ on the shoulder"
2 Notre ___
3 Hike a football
4 "Where the ___ is" (Esther 3:7)
5 ___ Gehrig's disease
6 Indefinite number (Rev. 19:12)
7 Baton (Exod. 14:5)
8 Brief try: 2 wds.
9 Sugar ___ Robinson (Lam. 3:21)
10 Religious magazine: abbr.
11 Spouse name
19 Fashionable resort
21 Tooth
23 Home-school org.
25 Bibletown: ___ Raton
26 Single obstacle (Josh. 7:21)
27 Just say no (1 Cor. 9:25)
28 ___dale
29 Flat support (Mark 6:25)
30 Officer's braid
31 Super Bowl XIX network
35 PGA champ ___ Snead
38 Team spirit after win
39 Basketball stat.
41 Cowboys' Christian coach
42 After "you"?
44 Largest brasses
47 Pack bases
49 Skiers' paradise
50 Place the balls (Ps. 38:5)
51 Incline to change (Exod. 23:2)
52 Traveler's aid
53 Public television
54 Prophet Samuel's mentor (1 Sam. 2:11)
56 Computer logic circuit (Gen. 2:5)

(Solution on p. 212)

ALIVE AND WELL

ACROSS

1 Ardor
5 Humorous word twist
8 Wound crust
12 Solomon's biographer (2 Chron. 9:29)
13 Imitate
14 Head covering
15 Son of Jerahmeel (1 Chron. 2:25)
16 Mouth liner
17 Discourteous
18 Assyrian god (2 Kings 17:30)
20 Carried
22 Brother of Arodi and Areli (Gen. 46:16)
23 Waste away
24 Surrounded (Acts 27:17)
27 Leader of Temple workers (Neh. 11:21)
31 Bk. of the Hebrews' Egyptian exodus
32 Boat propeller
33 Tenth Hebrew month (Esther 2:16, KJV)
37 To the rear
40 Dead ___
41 Put
42 Jumped
45 Portland's state
49 "My God" (Mark 15:34, KJV)
50 Turmoil
52 Back of the neck
53 Town where children were slaughtered (Matt. 2:18, KJV)
54 Hurtful
55 Follows dow or teen
56 Flirtation devices
57 None in particular
58 "Lord, I'll go! ___ me" (Isa. 6:8)

DOWN

1 City of David (2 Sam. 5:7)
2 ___-i, city of Bashan (Deut. 3:10)
3 Son of Beriah (1 Chron. 8:15, KJV)
4 Yearned
5 Gaunt (Isa. 13:8)
6 News service
7 Son of David (2 Sam. 5:15)
8 Bushes
9 Membrane (Exod. 29:13, KJV)
10 Servant
11 Propagated
19 "Happy ___ the ... merciful" (Matt. 5:7)
21 Daughter of Zechariah (2 Kings 18:2)
24 Wagered
25 Hatchet
26 City of the priests (1 Sam. 22:19)
28 ___ polloi
29 Wash gravel for gold
30 Son of Benjamin (Gen. 46:22)
34 O.T. prophet most quoted in N.T. (Mark 7:6, KJV)
35 Number of Commandments (Gal. 4:24)
36 Temple worker (Neh. 7:48)
37 Gory (Ezek. 7:23)
38 Sound receptacle
39 Laughing scavengers
42 Withered (Ps. 129:6)
43 Sport
44 Israel's ruler in N.T. times (Acts 1:6)
46 Measuring instrument
47 "God has ___ ears to those who worship him" (John 9:31)
48 Socially inept person
51 Anchorman ___ Rather (Deut. 33:22)

(Solution on p. 212)

HEADY THINGS

ACROSS

1 Physical affection
5 Liable
8 Philistine giant (2 Sam. 21:18)
12 Son of Atarah (1 Chron. 2:26)
13 Feel remorse
14 Priestly duty course (Luke 1:5, KJV)
15 Opposed
16 "How powerful is [God's] mighty ___" (Luke 1:51)
17 Small
18 Jeremiah's second bk.
20 At least one
22 King Saul's general (1 Sam. 17:55)
25 Propositions
29 Remain
30 Philistine idol (1 Sam. 5:1)
34 Rodent
35 "There is only ___ God" (1 Cor. 8:6)
36 Milk source
37 Brother of Jephunneh (1 Chron. 7:38)
38 Nourished
39 Absolute
41 Traverse regularly
42 Savor
44 Conforms
46 Total
48 Number of each animal that came to Noah (Gen. 7:16)
49 Descendant of Ishmael
52 Employ
54 King against Elijah (1 Kings 21:20)
58 Hurl abuse
59 Cerebrate
60 "I am the ___ of Sharon" (Song 2:1)
61 Wood source for David's palace (2 Chron. 2:3)
62 Father of Canaan (Gen. 10:6)
63 Take action against

DOWN

1 Chaldean location (Ezek. 23:23)
2 No room there
3 Held court
4 Happy countenance
5 Balaam's homeland (Num. 23:7)
6 "Throwing dice": Pers. (Esther 9:26)
7 Region of Ishmael's descendants (Job 6:19)
8 Half man and half goat
9 Wife of King Ahaz (2 Kings 18:2)
10 Impale
11 Straw
19 Bela's brother (Gen. 46:21)
21 Fourteenth letter: Hebrew
22 In a high place
23 Descendant of King Saul (1 Chron. 8:37)
24 Requires
26 Fruit of the vine
27 Before usual time
28 Remains
31 Appear
32 Received
33 Have due
39 Jew who divorced a Gentile (Ezra 10:34)
40 Lineup
43 Tabernacle furniture
45 Plank
47 Extravagant
48 Swarm
49 Craft
50 Glimmer
51 Birds' habitat
53 Fishes' habitat
55 Garden tool
56 King to whom Azariah prophesied (2 Chron. 15:8)
57 ___ and the Dragon (apoc. bk.)

(Solution on p. 212)

AROUND THE HOUSE

ACROSS

1 Leaves for first clothes (Gen. 3:7)
4 May
7 Countenance
8 Charge against property
10 Hill in Jerusalem (Jer. 31:39)
11 Moses' father (Exod. 6:20)
13 Spoiled
14 Equip with weapons
16 Farewell
18 Exalted lyric poem
19 How dogs drink (Judg. 7:5)
20 Contrivance
21 Mounted messenger
24 Palestinian town Abel-___ (Judg. 7:22)
27 City of Simeon (Josh. 15:32)
29 Son of Jacob and Bilhah (Gen. 35:25)
30 Entered a ship
34 Transactions
38 From one ___ to the other
39 Divinity school: abbr.
41 Chaldean place (Ezek. 23:23)
42 Boy
43 Minimum witnesses needed (Heb. 10:28)
44 Youngster: slang
45 Levite son of Merari (Exod. 6:19)
48 Father of Leah and Rachel (Gen. 29:16)
51 Where Jesus resurrected a boy (Luke 7:11)
52 Cain's grandson (Gen. 4:18)
53 Stake
54 Light period

DOWN

1 Much more
2 Water to walk on
3 Syrian shipbuilding city (Ezek. 27:9)
4 Securely fastened
5 Ambition
6 Saul's grandfather (1 Chron. 9:39)
7 Lessened in intensity
9 Wealthy sheep rancher (1 Sam. 25:2)
10 Father of King Menahem (2 Kings 15:14)
12 Seaport of Lycia (Acts 27:5)
13 ___ashan, city of Canaan (1 Sam. 30:30)
15 Son of Hezron (1 Chron. 2:9)
17 King ___baal, Jezebel's father (1 Kings 16:31)
22 Corn crop
23 Dispose of
25 Exercised, such as mercy
26 "God, the Righteous ___" (Prov. 21:12)
28 Birds preparing a home
30 Babylonian idol (Isa. 46:1)
31 Son of Atarah (1 Chron. 2:26)
32 Persian city yielding Jews (Ezra 2:59)
33 Nighttime automatic watering
35 Nimrod's city (Gen. 10:10, NIV)
36 Flank
37 Dejected
40 Son of Abihail (1 Chron. 2:29)
46 Fortune
47 Rest
49 Brother of Jephunneh (1 Chron. 7:38)
50 Reddish brown

(Solution on p. 212)

MEN OF OLDE

ACROSS

1 Father of Cain and Abel (Gen. 4:1)
5 Gear tooth
8 Precious
12 Related to peninsula between Israel and Egypt
13 Black cuckoo
14 Payment for work
15 Fifth N.T. book
16 Sea Moses crossed (Num. 33:8)
17 Specific region
18 One of 12 apostles (Luke 6:14)
20 Merited (Rom. 11:6)
22 Swift-running Australian bird
23 Clumsy person
24 One of 12 apostles (John 20:24)
27 Boaz's grandfather (Ruth 4:18)
31 N.T. bk. bet. Philem. and James
32 Samuel's priestly mentor (1 Sam. 3:1)
33 Jehoshaphat's general (2 Chron. 17:17)
37 Joab's brother (2 Sam. 23:24)
40 Amer. Bible Soc.
41 Quickly snatch
42 Peter (John 1:42, KJV)
45 Edom's neighbor: poss. (Jer. 49:8)
49 River in Persia (Dan. 8:2)
50 Aaron's colleague (Exod. 17:10)
52 In the same place: Lat.
53 Complete destruction
54 "Don't ___ bad language" (Eph. 4:29)
55 ___ Fitzgerald
56 Edifice, for short
57 Uncooked
58 Onionlike vegetable

DOWN

1 Priority notation
2 You: Ger.
3 "Against" prefix
4 Adherent of Islam: var.
5 Paul's friend at Troas (2 Tim. 4:13)
6 Uno
7 Famous for his fleece (Judg. 6:39)
8 Makes small in comparison
9 Gain by effort
10 Father of Shammah (2 Sam. 23:11)
11 Verbalize text (1 Tim. 4:13)
19 ___ Hogg (heiress)
21 Amer. Auto. Assoc.
24 Particular
25 Lighter than air: abbr.
26 Kimono sash
28 Question expression
29 Bravo: Sp.
30 Nothing
34 Oohing and ___
35 Doing business as
36 Shem's son (Gen. 10:22)
37 Apostle Peter's brother (Matt. 4:18)
38 Motor oil grading
39 Father of Ahi (1 Chron. 5:15)
42 Roadway's raised edge
43 Sixth Hebrew month (Neh. 6:15, KJV)
44 "Jesus ___ It All" (hymn)
46 "God is ___ to keep you from slipping" (Jude 1:24)
47 Egypt's river (Gen. 41:1)
48 Southern northern state.
51 Country Washington governs

(Solution on p. 212)

CROSS TALK

ACROSS

1 Jesus' address to his Father (Mark 14:36, KJV)
5 Cat's foot
8 Dressed
12 Goof off
13 Nebraska's largest city: abbr.
14 Divinity school
15 Duty cycle
16 ___ King Cole
17 Where Paul was imprisoned
18 Formally charge (Ezek. 22:2)
20 World ruler in Jesus' time (Luke 2:1)
22 Illinois' largest city: abbr.
23 Liquid meas.: Heb. (Exod. 29:40, KJV)
24 Man Jesus resurrected (John 11:43)
28 End of life (Gen. 9:29)
32 Neighbor of Miss.
33 Perch
35 "Gloria in excelsis ___" (hymn)
36 Strength (Deut. 6:5)
39 Two crucified with Christ (Matt. 27:38, KJV)
42 Ingest
44 "Organized" suffix
45 Take chances (Luke 23:34)
48 Barabbas's occupation (John 18:40)
52 Repeat
53 *Want* or *personal* types
55 Plane related
56 Cathedral top
57 Op. ___ (thesis ref.)
58 Trails
59 White precipitation
60 Horse food (Prov. 10:5)
61 Ponder (Ps. 39:3)

DOWN

1 "High" prefix
2 Great help
3 Data transfer rate
4 Cross-carrier Simon's country (Matt. 27:32)
5 Christ's condemner (1 Tim. 6:13)
6 Oriental wet nurse
7 Tomb guard duty (Luke 21:36)
8 Cross-carrier Simon's city (Matt. 27:32)
9 Cambodia's neighbor
10 Before *mater*
11 Fawn, for one
19 Follower of Jesus: abbr. (Acts 6:5)
21 Help
24 Saddest O.T. bk.
25 ___ Baba ("Open, Sesame!")
26 Goes with *zig*
27 Command to dog
29 Promote, in brief
30 Ball holder
31 O.T. minor prophet (Rom. 9:25)
34 Jesus' condition on cross (John 19:28)
37 Jesus' race (John 19:17)
38 Good angel in Peretti's books
40 Intl. Stds. Org.
41 Prepare body for burial (Luke 23:56)
43 Jesus' role to disciples (Matt. 11:29)
45 Jehovah's
46 Part of Shakespeare's address
47 Short note
49 Suitor
50 Energy units
51 What Jesus did after his burial (Acts 2:32)
54 Precedes *gram* and *meter*

(Solution on p. 212)

BIBLE MEN

ACROSS

1 Weep
4 Two quarts: Heb. (Exod. 16:36)
8 Animal caught for food
12 Cultivate, as a garden
13 Stack
14 Infrequent
15 Apostle Paul's coworker (Philem. 1:23)
17 Sign of impending events
18 Iranian language
19 Meat/vegetable mixture
21 Boat Noah built
23 David's weapon against Goliath
27 Son of Joktan (1 Chron. 1:20)
30 Owl's home
33 Width of a circle, for short
34 Crop-raising site
35 Mamie's husband
36 Service tax
37 Month festival of shelters observed: abbr. (Ezek. 45:25)
38 Moving a foot forward
39 Kangaroo or oat grass
40 More timid or bashful
42 Ancient rabbinical writings, in brief
44 City of tribe of Benjamin (Neh. 11:31)
47 Use with power
51 "Jesus was ___ upon a wooden cross" (Gal. 3:13)
54 Assyrian King Ashurbanipal (Ezra 4:10)
56 Otherwise
57 How Judas identified Jesus (Luke 22:48)
58 Main public road: abbr.
59 Give birth
60 Individual
61 Short oral response?

DOWN

1 Head cook
2 Reserve Officers' Pension Act
3 Period of time
4 Ancient gold-mining site (1 Chron. 29:4)
5 Title of religious leader in India
6 Belonging to Shimei's father (1 Kings 4:18)
7 Sabbath schedule (Exod. 23:12)
8 Roam stealthily
9 Amminadab's father (1 Chron. 2:10)
10 Sooner than
11 Japanese currency
16 23rd, for example
20 Second O.T. bk. named for a woman
22 Woven together
24 Forbidden worship object
25 Refuse: arch.
26 Festive occasion
27 Unidentified Flying Objects
28 Father of John the Bapt. (Luke 3:1)
29 Ostentatiously skilled
31 ___ out a living
32 Ninth month
36 Famous Dutch flower
38 Respectful title of distinguished Indian
41 Anxiously anticipative
43 Flooded
45 Make light of
46 Province of Epaenetus (Rom. 16:5)
48 Hebrew half-bushel measure: var. (Ezek. 45:11)
49 Mowed, grassy area
50 Opposite of wets
51 People Moses led: abbr. (Exod. 9:13)
52 Tree yielding caucho
53 Numismatic Society of America
55 National Security Council

(Solution on p. 212)

HOLY MOSES

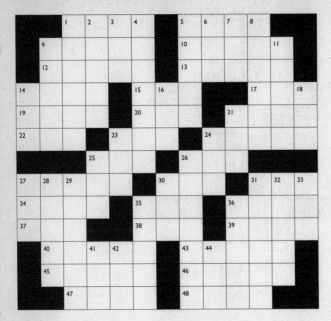

ACROSS

1 John's "water work," for short (Matt. 3:11)
5 Drop suddenly
9 Island near Sicily (Acts 28:1)
10 Barrier guards (1 Sam. 25:14)
12 Father of rebels Dathan and Abiram (Num. 16:12)
13 Jethro's relation to Moses (Exod. 3:1)
14 "Don't ___ about your plans for tomorrow" (Prov. 27:1)
15 Lunar Excursion Module
17 Chatter
19 The shah's country
20 Before
21 Irritating gas (Gen. 19:28)
22 Indoor sports spot
23 A get-together: abbr.
24 Slumbered (Judg. 4:21)
25 Printer speed: comp.
26 "___ to the world, the Lord has come" (hymn)
27 First Passover sacrifices (Exod. 12:6)
30 Nearly landlocked water body
31 One hundred and four, in roman
34 Gn. Idi ___ (Uganda)
35 Milk-maker (Lev. 3:1)
36 Produced
37 International fighting (Gen. 14:1)
38 35th O.T. bk.
39 Carved quartz (Exod. 25:7)
40 Mount where Moses received Ten Commandments (Exod. 19:20)
43 Base eight system: comp.
45 Cut, such as in two
46 Birth related
47 Ornamental staff
48 Thrifty, for short

DOWN

1 Prophet hired to curse Hebrews (Num. 22:5)
2 Straighten
3 School org.
4 Ten Commandment stones (Exod. 25:16)
5 Earliest or best part
6 Local Area network: comp.
7 Olive, for one (Exod. 27:20)
8 Disastrous evil (Exod. 9:3)
9 Full of high spirits
11 Wet spongy land
14 Large
16 Work measurement unit
18 Wager
21 Insect miraculously multiplied in Egypt (Exod. 8:21)
23 Data transfer speed: comp.
24 Chinese liquid condiment
25 Cable network
26 Samson's weapon to slay 1,000 (Judg. 15:15)
27 "The ___ was given by Moses, but grace and truth came by Jesus" (John 1:17, KJV)
28 Gather
29 Moses' sister (Exod. 15:20)
30 Coiling crushing snake
31 Hebrews' destination after the Exodus (Exod. 2:24)
32 Peaceful poem
33 Annoy
35 Scold (Col. 1:22)
36 Slogan
41 Minneapolis-based airline
42 Nuclear regulatory agency
44 Catholic Apostolic Church

(Solution on p. 212)

DESIRABLES

ACROSS

1 "Jehovah is our ___ , Jehovah alone" (Deut. 6:4)
4 Central African republic and lake
8 First child born (Gen. 4:1)
12 First name of *Arabian Nights* woodcutter
13 "In a ___ everyone runs" (1 Cor. 9:24)
14 Turkish or Syrian pound
15 Last courses of sweets
17 ___-Oberstein (German town)
18 Shed for small animals
19 Insult (Matt. 17:27)
21 Best part
23 Flat narrow strip
24 "There are three things that remain—faith, ___ , and love" (1 Cor. 13:13)
25 Type of leather (Num. 4:25)
29 Chicago-based airline: abbr.
30 Fill with joy
31 International Transport Association
32 "Wherever your ___ is, there your heart . . . will also be" (Luke 12:34)
34 Unforeseen obstacle
35 Delicate handmade laces
36 "The people are ___ in love with their idols" (Jer. 50:38)
37 Give off shoots
40 "You must be ___ again" (John 3:7)
41 Long period of time: var.
42 Cooperative (Luke 2:51)
46 Strong windstorm
47 Central part of church (Ezek. 41:1)
48 Observed
49 Made with difficulty
50 "Know what his Word ___ and means" (2 Tim. 2:15)
51 Small Business Administration

DOWN

1 Roam about (Gen. 30:11)
2 Bravo
3 Follower of Jesus (John 20:19-21)
4 Mediterranean island (Titus 1:5)
5 Large rabbit
6 Play part (Eph. 5:15)
7 Devoid of inhabitants (Acts 1:20)
8 Cracks in rocks
9 Assistant
10 Country east of Iraq
11 Geek
16 Part
20 Destiny
21 Grandson of Noah (Gen. 10:6, KJV)
22 Lion's prolonged sound
23 Glides high
25 Overeaters
26 "His ___ is meant to lead you to repentance" (Rom. 2:4)
27 Boot-shaped country, for short
28 Hungarian premier
30 Jacob's twin brother (Gen. 25:25)
33 "Iniquity is ___ for by mercy and truth" (Prov. 16:6)
34 Pakistani woman's garment
36 Manners
37 Wise person
38 Mountain's summit (Deut. 34:1)
39 Character played by an actor
40 Large group (Esther 2:19)
43 Sheep's sound
44 Pinch
45 St. Louis-based airline: abbr.

(Solution on p. 212)

AT THE RIGHT TIME

ACROSS

1 Also
4 "We cry, ___ , Father" (Rom. 8:15, KJV)
8 Affirmative rallying cry
11 Rahab's business (Josh. 2:1)
12 Buckets
14 Paddle
15 Large rodent
16 Untimely
18 Father of Methuselah (Gen. 5:21)
20 Govern
21 Help
23 Son of Jahdai (1 Chron. 2:47)
27 Ashteroth-___ , city of the Rephaim (Gen. 14:5)
31 Condition
32 David's chaplain (2 Sam. 20:26)
33 "It is water over the ___" (Eccles. 1:15)
35 Brook ___ed (Num. 21:12)
36 Venerable wise persons
39 Monthly cycles
42 Son of Judah (Gen. 38:11)
44 And moreover (1 Cor. 12:22, KJV)
45 One of David's famous warriors (1 Chron. 11:29)
47 Political leader signing Nehemiah's covenant (Neh. 10:19)
51 Ordered
55 Diminish
56 Ben-___ ("Son of my sorrow"; Gen. 35:18)
57 Greeting call
58 City of Syria (2 Kings 16:9)
59 Married
60 Joint
61 Mother of Hezekiah (2 Kings 18:2)

DOWN

1 Become weary
2 Tamar's second husband (Gen. 38:8)
3 Upon
4 Christian woman in Colosse (Philem. 1:2)
5 Jewish sorcerer, ___-Jesus (Acts 13:6)
6 Coffin (2 Sam. 3:31)
7 Cypress or sandalwood (1 Kings 10:12, KJV)
8 Direct address
9 Cereal head
10 Currently
13 Revenues from goods
17 Submit to proof
19 Be able
22 Accomplished
24 Son of Milcah and Nahor (Gen. 22:22)
25 Not much: 2 wds. (Gen. 50:10)
26 Belonging to Abner's father (1 Sam. 14:50)
27 Touch with lips
28 Son of Ulla (1 Chron. 7:39)
29 Violent anger
30 Diagram
34 Most troops
37 Campsite with 12 springs (Exod. 15:27)
38 Son of Arphaxad (Gen. 10:24, KJV)
40 Indiscriminate
41 ___abarim, wilderness site (Num. 21:11)
43 City in Egypt (Isa. 30:4)
46 Frivolous
48 ___h coin (half a shekel, Exod. 38:26, KJV)
49 Baby's eating attire: 2 wds. (Ezek. 3:14)
50 Brother of Zaccur (1 Chron. 24:26)
51 Calf
52 A single
53 In the center of
54 Shimei's father (1 Kings 4:18)

(Solution on p. 212)

BIG EVENTS

ACROSS

1 Hebrew Torah
4 Duplicate
8 Former caterpillar
12 Evangelical Literature Award
    (1 Kings 4:18)
13 Region
14 USS ___ (explosion site)
15 Possesses
16 Engagement (Song 8:6)
18 "Somewhat" suffix (2 Sam. 2:8)
19 Appropriate (Lev. 19:32)
20 John's "denomination"
25 In the past
28 Trees used for Tabernacle
    (Exod. 25:5)
30 Stir
31 Eucharistic bread
32 ___-cam modeling: comp.
34 Whitish complexion
35 ___ Pro word processor:
    comp. (Ezra 2:57)
36 Valley of Judah (Josh. 10:12)
38 Israeli statesman David ___
    Gurion
39 Die
41 Hepburn-Tracy movie
    Adam's ___
42 Young of beaver or fox
45 Looks back
51 Independent retirement
    income (1 Chron. 7:7)
52 Baking site

53 Jesus' cry from cross (Mark
    15:34, KJV)
54 From head to ___
55 Canvas shelter
56 ___ of Worms: ch. hist.
    (Dan. 1:12)
57 Eventuate

DOWN

1 Town in Utah and Judah
    (Judg. 15:9)
2 Cry of regret
3 Sink (Exod. 30:28)
4 Truck driver's "home"
5 Gold-bearing rock
6 Favorite or intimate
7 Near-meter measures
8 Penny's old equal
    (Luke 12:59, KJV)
9 Goes with aah
10 Major air carrier
11 Precedes low or yard
17 "Find ___ that I am God"
    (Exod. 7:17)
21 "Be careful how you ___"
    (Eph. 5:15)
22 3.1416
23 Sea-___ Intl. Airport
24 Sarah's only son (Gen. 17:19)
25 King Agag's nationality
    (1 Sam. 15:8)

26 Eliam's hometown (2 Sam.
    23:34)
27 Animals Jesus drove from
    Temple
28 Elijah's king (1 Kings 18:1)
29 "We ask that your kingdom
    will ___ now" (Matt. 6:10)
33 Gambling cube
34 Ballet dance (1 Chron.
    11:13, KJV)
37 Swedes' "yes"
39 Low light
40 Declined (Lev. 26:16)
41 Lease
43 Forging metal
44 Bound
45 Decay
46 Mother of all mankind
47 Wise ___ sought the new-
    born Christ
48 Cotton gin inventor
    (1 Sam. 1:3)
49 ___ v. Wade court decision
50 Remain inactive

(Solution on p. 212)

ARCHAEOLOGY

ACROSS

1 Circulate
5 Irene Dunne movie *I Remember ___*
9 Gold storage
12 River in Persia (Dan. 8:2)
13 Wife of Esau (Gen. 36:10)
14 Valuable rock
15 Light beams
16 Secured
18 Concentrated extract
20 Bridge move
21 Bereaved mother in Ramah (Jer. 31:15, KJV)
23 Father of prophet Micaiah (2 Chron. 18:7, KJV)
26 Deborah's military companion (Judg. 5:1)
29 Young man
31 Hole maker (Deut. 15:17, KJV)
32 Humbled (Phil. 4:12, KJV)
34 Temple porter (Ezra 2:42)
36 Hezekiah's mother (2 Kings 18:2)
37 Excavate
39 Carried over
40 Go ashore
42 Son of Ezra (1 Chron. 4:17)
44 Grain winnower
46 Patterns
50 Tribe descended from Mizraim (Gen. 10:13, NIV)
53 Ark builder

54 Higher learning place, for short
55 "The church should ___ for widows" (1 Tim. 5:5)
56 Prey
57 After *ho* and *mo*
58 Grandson of Ephraim (Num. 26:36)
59 Killed (2 Sam. 1:22)

DOWN

1 Undefiled
2 Expression of regret
3 Declares
4 Canaanite military leader's (Judg. 4:2)
5 Father of Achish (1 Sam. 27:2, KJV)
6 Son of Ishmael (Gen. 25:13, KJV)
7 First bk. of N.T.
8 King who sold himself to the devil (1 Kings 21:20)
9 Female servant (Gal. 4:22, KJV)
10 "Happy ___ the kind" (Matt. 5:7)
11 Sea Moses crossed (Num. 33:8)
17 N.T. book to Gaius: ___ John
19 Unclothed
22 Joktan's son Havi-___ (Gen. 10:29)
24 Pear-shaped stringed instrument (Ps. 150:3)
25 One young man

26 False god of Canaanites (1 Kings 18:40)
27 Endearing term for God as Father (Rom. 8:15, KJV)
28 Shower (Ezra 10:9)
30 Social engagements
33 Lackluster
35 "Good ___ we bring to you and your kin" (hymn)
38 Judean lowlands city (1 Chron. 27:28)
41 Waterway controller
43 Assyrian city Nimrod built (Gen. 10:8, 11)
45 Seacoast city of France
47 Hockey score
48 Personal designation
49 Display (Gen. 24:12, KJV)
50 Fifth N.T. bk.
51 Son of Lamech (Luke 3:36, KJV)
52 Rained on Sodom (Gen. 19:24)

(Solution on p. 212)

TRAVEL THINGS

ACROSS

1 Before *tree* or *tray*
4 Thin transparent mineral
8 Twelfth sacred Hebrew month (Esther 3:7, KJV)
12 Garden work
13 Dry
14 Uncovered
15 Constellation in So. Hemis. (1 Chron. 7:38)
16 Loathed
18 Flower place
19 Film speed (1 Kings 15:9)
20 Citizens of Macedonian city (Acts 17:10, KJV)
25 Taxi
28 Sapphira's husband (Acts 5:1)
30 Past
31 Curve
32 Slangy pop. music style
34 Son of Jerahmeel (1 Chron. 2:25)
35 Boy
36 Arizona desert
38 Economic Research Service of USDA (Gen. 38:8)
39 Manasseh family head (1 Chron. 5:24)
41 Difficult
42 Acorn bearer
45 Temple chorister (Neh. 12:42)
51 Son of Abdiel (1 Chron. 5:15)
52 Cry of despair

53 ___ in USA (label)
54 Put on
55 Wheel parts
56 X marks it
57 Woman's reference

DOWN

1 Queen Jezebel's husband (1 Kings 16:29)
2 Fester
3 Hair holders (Isa. 3:20)
4 Crazy
5 S. Korean train wreck site (1 Chron. 7:7)
6 Father of Saul (Acts 13:21, KJV)
7 Persian city (Ezra 2:59)
8 Son of Rehoboam (1 Chron. 3:10, KJV)
9 Tribe of Israel (Gen. 35:25)
10 "You ___ to be perfect" (Matt. 5:48)
11 Sea where Egyptians drowned (Josh. 24:6)
17 Animal who spoke to Balaam (Num. 22:28, KJV)
21 Conclude
22 New England state code
23 Kernel holder
24 Temple music leader (1 Chron. 15:17)
25 Big deliveries (Acts 14:13)
26 Thousand bucks: 2 wds. (2 Sam. 23:11)

27 Interest-bearing certificate
28 "He Is ___ to Deliver Thee" (hymn)
29 Close by
33 Mattress cover
34 Part of a series
37 ___ John, written to Cyria
39 Name of God: Heb. (Ps. 68:4, KJV)
40 "___ father was God" (Luke 3:38)
41 Former Chicago mayor Daley's nickname
43 Pause tones: 2 wds. (2 Sam. 23:28)
44 Cows (Gen. 32:15, KJV)
45 Cylindrical container
46 Inventors Whitney or Terry (1 Sam. 4:18)
47 Eat with eggs
48 Brief sleep
49 *Much ___ about Nothing*
50 Pay after deductions

(Solution on p. 218)

MEN AND WOMEN

ACROSS

1 Where Samson killed 1,000 men over a girl (Judg. 15:9)
5 Rachel wept for her children here
9 Paddle
12 Heating compartment
13 King Hezekiah's father (2 Kings 16:20)
14 Strive for superiority
15 Saul's uncle's (1 Sam. 14:50)
16 "Rime of the Ancient ___ "
18 Association of widows (1 Tim. 5:11)
20 Male ancestor of Jesus
21 God gave his Son so we might have everlasting ___ (John 3:16)
24 Canaanite city (Judg. 1:31)
27 Persian palace guard (Esther 6:2)
31 Mary said, "They ___ taken the Lord's body" (John 20:2)
32 Every kind
33 Non-Jewish Palestinians
35 Daytime repose
36 Insurrectionist Abimelech defeated (Judg. 9:39)
38 Time five bridesmaids missed the wedding (Matt. 25:5)
40 Queen Jezebel's hometown (1 Kings 16:31)
42 One Mesdames
43 Performs
45 Walking steps
49 Members of sex that bear young
52 Place near Jerusalem (Jer. 31:39)
53 Number of virgins in Jesus' parable
54 "O woman of ___ beauty" (Song 5:9)
55 Otherwise
56 "___ everything to me" (chorus)
57 Gush out in a stream
58 Flower holder?

DOWN

1 Drawn out (Gen. 13:10)
2 Always
3 Champion (Ps. 52:1)
4 Verbal disparagement
5 Male sheep
6 Gloating cry
7 Naomi's requested name (Ruth 1:20)
8 Son of Zattu (Ezra 10:27)
9 Projection
10 Where living believers will meet the Lord (1 Thess. 4:17)
11 Egyptian sun god
17 City of Egypt (Isa. 19:13, KJV)
19 ___-hiroth where Pharaoh overtook the Israelites (Exod. 14:9)
22 Groundwork place?
23 Where Tamar seduced Judah (Gen. 38:14)
25 Babylonian district conquered by Assyria (2 Kings 18:34, KJV)
26 Reserved
27 Pouches
28 Man from Ahoh (1 Chron. 11:29)
29 Brings joy (Prov. 15:20)
30 Father of Solomon's superintendent of public works (1 Kings 4:6)
34 Click
37 Weaver (Isa. 38:12)
39 Physical representations
41 Draws close
44 Crack (Ps. 3:7)
46 Young male horse
47 Freedom from work
48 Noah's oldest son
49 Amount charged
50 Until
51 Use needle and thread
53 "The 28___ of February"

(Solution on p. 213)

ANIMALS IN THE BIBLE

ACROSS

1 "Alligator Alley" state
4 Greenish blue color
8 Animal caught for food (Gen. 49:9)
12 Animal support
13 Fox residence (Luke 9:58, KJV)
14 Unusual
15 Female offspring of 41-down (Lev. 14:10)
17 Sign of impending events (Luke 21:25)
18 Poisonous snake (Prov. 23:32)
19 Meat and vegetable mixture
21 Makes sweetened beverage of lime or lemon
23 David's weapon against Goliath (1 Sam. 17:40)
27 Animals' main parts: slang
30 Scape___ (Lev. 16:10)
33 ___ Quixote (book)
34 Beehive state
35 Petrol
36 Very small amount (John 8:44)
37 Abbr. after British firm name
38 Jobs to do, for short
39 Part of venetian blind
40 Untied, as a dog
42 Gun lobby
44 Noggin (Gen. 3:15)
47 Bird on Great Seal of U.S. (Job 9:26)
51 Animal's "bar" room?
54 Sound causing Peter to weep bitterly (Matt. 26:75)
56 Ants' quality (Prov. 6:6)
57 Optimistic confidence
58 WWII flying ___
59 Animal catcher?
60 Oscar
61 Disk Operating System: comp.

DOWN

1 Dog's parasite (1 Sam. 24:14)
2 Salacious (Ezek. 23:8)
3 Old
4 Swiss ___ (leafy vegetable)
5 ___ Kippur (Day of Atonement)
6 Clerical robes
7 A home for the birds (Deut. 22:6)
8 Roam stealthily, as a lion (Ps. 59:14)
9 Dodge truck (1 Chron. 2:10)
10 Sooner than
11 Japanese currency
16 Pet line?
20 O.T. bk. with woman's name
22 Hard-shelled babies (Deut. 22:6)
24 Forbidden worship image (Deut. 7:26)
25 ___ bene
26 Small biting fly (Matt. 23:24)
27 Heifer's father (Exod. 29:1)
28 ___ I, "the Great" (Holy Roman emperor)
29 Rectangular groove cut in board
31 Chestnut tree
32 The A of YMCA
36 Boy almost sacrificed in place of 9-down (Gen. 22:9)
38 Golf ball holder
41 What David watched as youth (1 Sam. 17:20)
43 Type it again, Sam
45 Hurt
46 Judgment (Deut. 7:26)
48 Received academic degree
49 Plumb ___ (crazy)
50 Females of 41-down
51 Hundredweight, for short
52 Birds' domain
53 Feds' procurement dept.
55 Control Program for Microcomputers

(Solution on p. 213)

WAR AND PEACE

ACROSS

1 Quickly traveled
5 Misfortune (Matt. 26:24)
8 Men organized for war (Gen. 14:10)
12 Comfort (Luke 21:34)
13 Annex
14 Floral container (Job 13:12)
15 Bible bk. stating, "A time for war; a time for peace"
16 Body-supporting limb
17 Hard-shelled hatcheries
18 Hole-making tool (Deut. 15:17)
20 Hearing organ
22 North African terrorist country (Ezek. 30:5)
25 Nation (Lev. 15:19)
29 Marriage vow
30 Owed obligations
34 U.S. presidential election mo.
35 Title of Muhammad's descendants
36 Uncooked
37 Gross national income
38 ___ voyage
39 Where Saul consulted a medium (1 Sam. 28:7)
41 Snakelike fish
42 Refine, as metal (Ezek. 22:20)
44 Three-foot measurements
46 Make a law
48 Ask earnestly
49 Group with a common interest
52 Armed fighting between nations
54 Physician companion of Paul (Col. 4:14)
58 Irritate
59 O.T. auth. who said, "They shall beat their swords into plowshares"
60 Approved
61 Shout
62 Continually urge
63 Move on a course

DOWN

1 Bishop's jurisdiction
2 Political Action Committee
3 Get free, for short
4 Postpone
5 Upright enclosure
6 Solemn poem (Hab. 3:19)
7 Line of beginning or ending
8 Turn away (Jer. 11:15)
9 Waste cloth
10 Imparted info: abbr. (Gen. 50:17)
11 Not no
19 Form into a little mass
21 Ancient "truck" (Gen. 16:12)
22 Jointed appendages
23 Expression with a special meaning
24 Carried (Ps. 55:12)
26 Strong feeling of displeasure
27 Gave a particular inflection to
28 Crimes
31 White-tailed sea eagle
32 Not good
33 Between one and three
39 Additional persons or things
40 Cereal grain grass
43 Brand
45 Made bright, as if by fire (Exod. 34:35)
47 Born with another
48 Boast
49 War ___ (Salvation Army magazine)
50 Falsehood
51 Underwriters' Laboratories License
53 King whose heart was perfect before God (2 Chron. 15:17)
55 Small four-string guitar, for short
56 Extent of one's comprehension
57 Highest pedagogical degree

124

(Solution on p. 215)

BEAUTY AND THE BEAST

ACROSS

1 "___ am I in the hollow of his hand" (chorus)
5 Distribute in small portions (Lev. 26:26)
9 "___ the way my Savior leads me" (hymn)
12 President's office
13 Region
14 "___ from his head, his hands, his feet" (hymn)
15 "Perish every ___ ambition" (hymn)
16 Under two years old (Exod. 29:38)
18 "___ we have heard on high" (hymn)
20 Works dough
21 Battering weapon
22 "Deeper than the mighty rolling ___" (hymn)
23 Performance
26 Beaver's house
28 "No condemnation now I ___" (hymn)
32 Rhyming thoughts
34 Pen point
36 "There is a ___ I love to hear" (hymn)
37 Platters
39 "To write the love of God above would drain the ocean ___" (hymn)
41 Silvery metal
42 Largest religious body in USA
44 Awkward person
46 Key: two words
49 Crazy
53 Choral selection sources
55 Spanish lady
56 Computer monitor type
57 Sand hill
58 Between Lam. and Dan.
59 ___ Bo Peep
60 Potato
61 Colorants

DOWN

1 Couch
2 Stratford on ___
3 Sharp tooth
4 Church official (1 Pet. 5:1)
5 "Neither is there any ___ betwixt us" (Job 9:33, KJV)
6 Crater Lake state
7 Releases of classified data (Nah. 2:8)
8 Worked for
9 Turkish province (Acts 16:6)
10 "Mary, Joseph, ___ your aid, with us sing our Savior's birth" (hymn)
11 Broken on two crucified thieves (John 19:32)
17 "More about Jesus let me ___" (hymn)
19 Child
23 Fitting
24 Addressees of 7th N.T. letter: abbr.
25 Beverage from steeped leaves
27 "___ toil and tribulation and tumult of her war" (hymn)
29 "Give me to ___ and live with Thee above" (hymn)
30 Clan of Temple workers (Ezra 2:57)
31 Hangout (Jer. 7:11)
33 Christian singer ___ White
35 Casually perused 53-across
38 Criticizes severely (Matt. 19:13)
40 Informal OK
43 Childhood larynx disease
45 Diminished (Lev. 13:56)
46 O.T. bk. of vanity
47 Visited Christ child
48 Emphasis type
50 Snug and warm
51 "Come, adore on bended ___ Christ the Lord" (hymn)
52 Hairy Asian oxen
54 African antelope

(Solution on p. 213)

CRIME AND PUNISHMENT

(crossword puzzle grid)

ACROSS

1 Skin leak
4 Small swelling
8 Glow
12 Some or all
13 Computer operator
14 1/60,000 of a minute, for short
15 Helpful suggestion
16 Put inside
17 Apiece
18 Super bargain (Exod. 20:15)
20 Length of newborn
22 Neuter ownership
24 Good model
28 Mellowed
31 ___ mater
34 Delivery time
35 Stare
36 "___, foh, and fum"
37 Traveler's aid for 28-across
38 Douglas ___ (tree)
39 Young women entering society
40 ___ and crafts
41 Computer and game maker
43 Youngest child of Noah's wife
   (Gen. 9:24)
45 Mimicked mom
48 Sandcastle site
52 Light of God's Word
   (Ps. 119:105, NIV)
55 Prepare room for child
57 Wider lookout window
58 Contemporary Christian
   female singer
59 Shortened
60 Obscure
61 Care for child's needs (Gen. 2:15)
62 Quick!
63 Mary's preferred labor room
   (Luke 2:7)

DOWN

1 Garfield and Felix (Ps. 73:7)
2 Single-family ___ (Exod. 26:6)
3 Keyboard a report
4 Erected new house
5 Branch of service
6 New York ___ (baseball)
7 Bolster, as with pillows
8 32-down's goal for U.S. Consti-
   tution
9 "Made in ___" (label)
10 Child's play, for short
11 Before an or or (Gen. 36:38)
19 Volunteer as a teacher's ___
   (2 Chron. 34:20)
21 Athletes in Action
23 "___ sex" (monogamy or absti-
   nence)
25 Jacob's family camp site
   (Gen. 35:21, KJV)
26 Elizabeth's relation to Mary
   (Luke 1:36)
27 Settled sediment (Isa. 25:6, KJV)
28 German filmmaker
29 Canter or trot
30 O.T. family advocate (Neh. 8:9)
32 Women's ___ , movement for
   equal status
33 Hose type
37 Arrived
39 Scoop, such as of ice cream
42 Forced sexually (Gen. 34:2)
44 Prematurely terminate preg-
   nancy
46 Stages in development
47 Month left at the end of the
   money? (Deut. 24:17)
49 Father of Kish
   (2 Chron. 29:12)
50 Eve's first child (Gen. 4:1)
51 Sacred song (Matt. 26:30)
52 "Live and ___ live"
53 Broad st.
54 Lowest daily req.
56 Legal alias for home-based
   business

(Solution on p. 213)

YE MEN OF OLDE

ACROSS

1 ___ vs. Wade
4 Man's buddy
7 First Hebrew king (Acts 13:21)
8 Jericho's rebuilder (1 Kings 16:34)
10 King of Israel for seven days (1 Kings 16:10)
11 Rebel against King Pekah of Israel (2 Kings 15:25)
13 Yes: slang
14 Associate of Moses and Aaron (Exod. 17:10)
16 Precedes polloi
18 Chinese aborigines
19 Together: Lat.
20 Wane
21 Joab's chief enemy (2 Sam. 2:26)
24 Richest, wisest king (1 Kings 10:23)
27 ___ Dolorosa
29 Grandson of Shem (Gen. 10:22-23)
30 Palestinian king who almost converted (Acts 26:28)
34 David's high priest (2 Sam. 8:17)
38 Before quivocal or ventful
39 Single
41 Buz clan leader (1 Chron. 5:15)
42 Atlas name locator, for short
43 Not big: contr.
44 Translation, in brief

45 King of Goiim (Gen. 14:1)
48 Master of evil (James 4:7)
51 Fiddler emperor
52 Southpaw judge of Israel (Judg. 3:21)
53 Bound volumes, for short
54 Tractor-trailer combo

DOWN

1 Male sheep
2 "___ Father which art in heaven" (Matt. 6:9, KJV)
3 One of Job's "comforters" (Job 32:4)
4 King of Egypt (Gen. 39:1)
5 "His visits revived me like a breath of fresh ___" (2 Tim. 1:16)
6 Flower necklace
7 Og's kingly associate (Num. 32:33)
9 Saraph's home (Hebrew linen worker; 1 Chron. 4:22)
10 Midianite general with Oreb (Judg. 7:25)
12 Male tramp
13 Young Men's Association: abbr.
15 Young ___ (slang for children)
17 Intl. book num.
22 Midianite king in Moses' time (Josh. 13:21)
23 Tombstone inscription

25 Where Jacob saw the ladder (Gen. 28:19)
26 Wave: Sp.
28 "A Jew, a wonderful Bible teacher" (Acts 18:24)
30 Eighth mo.
31 Small biting fly
32 Syrian king (2 Kings 15:37)
33 Black cuckoo
35 Goliath's slayer (1 Sam. 17:57)
36 Child of Zerubbabel (1 Chron. 3:20)
37 Syrian resettlement city (2 Kings 16:9)
40 John's church leadership position (2 John 1:1)
46 Barak's female associate, for short (Judg. 4:10)
47 Captain Noah's boat
49 Brother of Muppim and Huppim (Gen. 46:21)
50 Ventura Users' Group

(Solution on p. 213)

VACATION DESTINATION

ACROSS

1 Explosion sound
4 South American coastal country
8 Move in a stream (John 7:38)
12 DOD-developed computer language
13 Ship's perimeter, "fence"
14 Niagara Falls' sound (1 Chron. 16:32)
15 Atlantic food fish
16 Rusts quickly in water (Gen. 4:22)
17 Grand Ole ___
18 Keep the head above water (Job 24:11)
20 Verbal dispute, for short
22 Valentine's Day mo.
24 Advantage resource
28 "Don't ___ and worry—it only leads to harm" (Ps. 37:8)
31 Devoid of water
34 Irish Republican Army
35 ___ Angeles, Calif.
36 Birth-control device: abbr.
37 Ad ___
38 In the style of: 2 wds.
39 Run away (Gen. 19:17)
40 Chicken cordon ___
41 Cemented
43 A drink
45 Insane
47 Upper story (Prov. 21:9)
51 Answerable for act: abbr. (Gen. 21:26)
54 Pair of antlers (Matt. 8:6)
57 Competitive card game
58 Discharge
59 Water-locked land (Isa. 23:2, KJV)
60 [, for short
61 "I Love ___ " (Ball)
62 Common levels
63 Hurricane's center (Exod. 21:24)

DOWN

1 Formal agreement (Gen. 21:27)
2 Aroma
3 Walk in water
4 "___ goes before destruction" (Prov. 16:18)
5 Sound sensor
6 ___ Grande River (U.S.–Mexican border)
7 Forearm bone
8 Water lily pad riders (Exod. 8:2)
9 Cut off
10 Ocean paddle (Ezek. 27:6)
11 Cleverly humorous
19 Ship's stern
21 Automobile water-cooler, for short
23 Remove water from boat
25 Window ledge
26 One of 44-down's Great ones
27 Social ban
28 Old Glory, for one
29 Wave action (Jer. 4:13)
30 Jacob's twin brother (Gen. 25:25)
32 Contrition
33 Thought (Num. 14:4)
39 Feds' food dept.
40 Wager
42 Dry well (Gen. 37:24)
44 Landlocked waters
46 Slow trickle of water (Amos 9:13)
48 Round air-filled water flotation device
49 Murky
50 Small shed
51 Organized faith, for short (James 3:1)
52 Ostrichlike Australian bird
53 Command dog to attack
55 Photo film-speed rating
56 Free from clouds: abbr.

(Solution on p. 213)

CHRISTIAN QUALITIES

ACROSS

1 "Christ the Morning ___ will shine in your hearts" (2 Pet. 1:19)
5 Building's grounds
9 "Be glad for ___ God is planning for you" (Rom. 12:12)
12 Give artificial quality to
13 Christian Hall of Fame state
14 Driver's compartment
15 Everywhere present, for short (Heb. 1:3)
16 Showing helpful concern (1 Tim. 5:4)
18 Where people repented at Jonah's preaching (Luke 11:32)
20 Pour on the sick with prayer (James 5:14)
21 Excavated again
23 Man bringing sin into human race (Rom. 5:12)
26 Trans-Jordan city Moses conquered (Num. 21:33)
29 A small amount
31 In the past
32 "Easier for a camel to go through the eye of a ___" (Luke 18:25)
34 What Jesus did to stormy sea (Mark 4:39)
36 Condensed water droplets
37 Add *ad*, then dressing
39 Burdens (Mark 11:16)
40 "So brief a ___ of life" (Job 14:15)
42 Adjust a lock again
44 Add *or* and shave
46 Story of Jesus (Matt. 13:35)
50 Savior (Job 19:25)
53 Guide
54 Dismiss from employment
55 Before *chute* or *clete*
56 Bring under control (James 3:8)
57 "Always give thanks for everything to our ___ and Father" (Eph. 5:20)
58 Heavenly ___ (Luke 2:13)
59 Taiwanese currency

DOWN

1 Steer clear
2 Novelist ___ Morrison (*Song of Solomon*)
3 Related by blood
4 Held in highest esteem (1 Pet. 1:17)
5 Joined, as oxen
6 Asher overseer (Num. 34:27)
7 Add *G* and answer
8 Stupid simpleton (2 Sam. 23:9)
9 Judas's burial plot (Acts 1:19, KJV)
10 Add *t* and be at the end (Matt. 18:34)
11 Weight measures, in brief
17 National Institute of Aviation
19 Head coverings
22 Governor's Advisory Council
24 Advanced in years
25 Alterations: slang
26 Testify about Christ "to the ___ of the earth" (Acts 1:8)
27 Far below surface
28 Honored for special service (Matt. 10:42)
30 Hay compressor
33 Kernel holder
35 Steadfast allegiance (Luke 16:13)
38 Jesus healed ten (Luke 17:12)
41 National Association of Evangelicals
43 Gold measure
45 36th O.T. bk.
47 Suitor
48 Tibetan Buddhist monk
49 Man's first home
50 Tease
51 Departure, for short
52 ___ Tse-tung

(Solution on p. 213)

WHAT DID THEY DO?

1	2	3	■	4	5	6	7	8
9			■	10				
11			12					
13				■	■	■	■	■
14				15	16	17	18	
■	■	■	■	19				
20	21	22	23					
24				■	25			
26				■	27			

ACROSS

1 Telegrapher: "dot"
4 Ball player's traction
9 Spud state, for short
10 Lower in dignity
11 Do-gooder (Luke 10:34)
13 Defender, as Goliath
14 Magicians (Exod. 7:11)
19 Pitcher ___ Ryan
20 All-powerful God:
   2 wds. (Ps. 89:8)
24 Examine closely
25 "Praise the Lord!"
   notation
26 Wanderer
27 English as a second language

DOWN

1 Floppies
2 Pacific NW state
3 Judah's daughter-in-law
   (Gen. 38:6)
4 Jesus' trade (Mark 6:3)
5 Living Bibles, Intl.
6 Consume
7 Old film-speed indica-
   tion
8 Number of lepers Jesus
   healed (Luke 17:17)
12 Carmaker
15 ___ Rogers
16 Run away to marry
17 Scolds vehemently
18 Fishhook connector
20 Relayed info, for short
   (Gen. 22:20)
21 Covered with frozen
   water
22 Republican moniker
23 Reformation leader
   Jan ___

(Solution on p. 219)

WARNING SIGNS

¹	²	³	⁴	■	⁵	⁶	⁷	■	⁸	⁹	¹⁰	¹¹

(crossword grid)

ACROSS

1 Cry aloud
5 Turf
8 Infrequent (1 Sam. 3:1)
12 Reflected sound (Jer. 6:7)
13 Recompense (Gen. 23:9)
14 Mount Gerizim's twin (Deut. 11:30)
15 Once again (Ps. 78:7)
16 Hard water (Job 6:16)
17 First Hebrew month (Exod. 12:2, KJV)
18 Repudiated (Luke 22:57)
20 Pointed pierce (Gen. 40:19)
22 Am. humorist Edgar ___
23 Maiden name
24 Peril (Gen. 13:7)
27 Jesus' prayer place (Matt. 26:36)
31 Tenth N.T. bk.
32 Debt ack.
33 Cancelled (Gen. 41:31)
37 Pressing (Gen. 19:3)
40 Reverence (Ps. 33:8)
41 Father of Abner (1 Sam. 14:51)
42 Easter flowers (Matt. 6:28)
45 Works dough (Hos. 7:4)
49 Adam's home (Gen. 2:8)
50 The third (1 Chron. 5:26)
52 Light tan
53 Birds' home (Ps. 104:12)
54 Fast footwork, past tense (Gen. 18:7)
55 Chieftain
56 Makes lace
57 Conclusion (Gen. 9:13)
58 Mends (Prov. 31:19)

DOWN

1 Necklace part (Song 4:9)
2 Pimples
3 Though
4 Mooing (1 Sam. 15:14)
5 Web maker (Job 27:18)
6 Open Air Campaigners, for short
7 Changing color (2 Chron. 2:14)
8 Harvester (John 4:36)
9 Dear Daddy: Gr.
10 Scold abusively (1 Sam. 25:14)
11 German river
19 Loop (Matt. 19:24)
21 ___ culpa: law
24 Bet. c and e
25 Loan computation
26 Nat. Housing Auth.
28 Perish (Gen. 9:5)
29 Two or more eras
30 Hard-shelled fruit (Song 6:11)
34 Paul and Peter, e.g. (Prov. 2:7)
35 Ram's mate (Gen. 21:28)
36 Crave (Eccles. 12:5)
37 Uncomplimentary (1 Pet. 3:9)
38 Computer command: change filename
39 Between Italians and Turks (Acts 19:10)
42 40 days before Easter
43 Thoughtful plan (Deut. 1:23)
44 For fear (Gen. 14:23)
46 Yearn (2 Cor. 6:10)
47 Pull out (Exod. 2:10)
48 Basks (Dan. 12:3)
51 ___ Thomas, Keswick leader

(Solution on p. 215)

NOURISHMENT AND RAIMENT

ACROSS

1 Tall shade tree
4 Scorch a steak
8 Detergent (2 Chron. 13:15)
12 Weed killer (Isa. 5:6)
13 Less-calorie version
14 "What's the big ___?"
15 One prefix
16 One ungentlemanly person: 2 wds.
17 Collapsible shelter
18 Bowler hat
20 Winnie the ___
22 Coca-Cola founder ___ Candler (1 Kings 22:41)
24 Interlace threads
28 "___ on first?"
31 Give a handle to
34 Beaver's abode
35 "My nourishment comes from doing the will of God and finishing his ___" (John 4:34)
36 Cotton gin inventor ___ Whitney (1 Sam. 1:3)
37 Prepared-food shop
38 Anger
39 Female sheep
40 Putter into practice (Rev. 14:15)
41 "___ ___ we trust"
43 N.T. bk. between Phil. and 1 Thess.
45 Girl

48 Wood in Solomon's Temple (1 Kings 10:12)
52 Violently tear apart, as a garment (Lev. 10:6, KJV)
55 Imitates (2 Chron. 9:21)
57 ___ in the hole
58 River of Germany
59 Come together as a pair
60 Price label
61 Mexican custard dessert
62 Making ___ meet
63 The father of Shimei (1 Kings 4:18)

DOWN

1 First Hebrew judge (Judg. 3:31)
2 The ___ Ranger
3 Golda ___ , former Israeli prime minister
4 Filters through earthy material (Lev. 6:28)
5 Precedes *cough* or *cup*
6 Faucet: 2 wds.
7 Make over
8 Ten percent donation
9 Middle of month: arch.
10 Daniel in the lions' ___
11 "He who does not [35-across] shall not ___" (2 Thess. 3:10)
19 Soak up sun (Jer. 9:23)
21 Be indebted
23 Over again

25 Drinks, such as lemon or lime
26 Valley (Gen. 14:3, KJV)
27 Mideastern prince
28 Global conflict in 1940
29 Cornucopia
30 Marjoram herb seasoning, for short
32 Add to ginger and drink
33 Assorted collection
37 Blunt
39 Evangelical Drama Awards
42 Ancient, as in ___ times (Jer. 21:2)
44 Desert watering holes (Hos. 13:15)
46 "Jesus Christ is the ___ yesterday, today, and forever" (Heb. 13:8)
47 Distance between supports
49 Fenced garden entrance
50 Corecipient of Agur's messages (Prov. 30:1)
51 One million, such as bytes
52 Before *ill* or *rain* (Exod. 16:23)
53 Building wing
54 Sports league
56 Esther Time of Dep.

(Solution on p. 215)

DENOMINATION INFORMATION

ACROSS

1 Regal bird (Ezek. 17:7)
6 Affection expression (Eccl 3:5)
9 "To thine own ___ be true" (Exod. 32:13)
13 Condescend to help (Ps. 31:10)
14 Distinctive period
15 S. Pacific islands
16 Nashville-based denomination
19 Diligent workers (Prov. 30:25)
20 Avoirdupois: abbr.
21 Unrefined (Prov. 7:11)
22 Affirmative vote
23 Publication preparers
24 Notice
25 Something to grind (Deut. 19:5)
26 Iacocca model
27 Church councils: abbr.
30 Strategized in detail (Exod. 39:5)
34 Harvest (2 Cor. 9:6)
35 Diminished (Dan. 1:10)
36 40th U.S. President: fam.
37 Indian religion
38 Indir. expressed
39 Last battle (Rev. 16:16)
41 Major network
42 O.T. prophet
43 Drink
44 "Go with the ___"
45 Body extension (Job 31:22)
46 ___ Dolorosa
49 Re. Jewish Torah (John 7:22)
52 Pop. Bible version
53 Groups over nines (Deut. 1:15)
54 Anglican communion in U.S.
57 *Divine Comedy* author
58 Ecology watchdog
59 Succeed (Job 41:8)
60 B.P.O.E.
61 O.T. bk. (Ezra 2:2)
62 Christian educator, Henrietta ___

DOWN

1 Short composition
2 Cover sin (Lev. 4:28)
3 Masses of fluid
4 Earthly divisions (John 19:24)
5 Tenth N.T. bk. (Acts 19:28)
6 Medicinal plants (Gen. 37:25)
7 Tea servers
8 Yak
9 The Evil One (Matt. 4:10)
10 Middle East prince
11 Setback (Gen. 24:67)
12 Chance
15 Leopard's distinctive (Jer. 13:23)
17 Church leader
18 Played the part
23 Second Bible bk. (Mark 12:26)
24 Sphere of influence
25 Son of Adam and Eve (Gen. 4:2)
26 Irreducible units
27 Yield (Dan. 9:18)
28 Base ornament
29 Extended, as a story
30 Narrative poem
31 Sin sacrifice (John 1:29)
32 Swiss mountains
33 "Straight as an ___" (1 Sam. 20:36)
34 Travel on
37 Leadership control
39 Big gas
40 Right-wing denomination
42 In Wonderland
44 Religious disciplines (Zech. 8:19)
45 Muslim God
46 Vice ___
47 Take liability
48 Lenten starter (Jon. 3:6)
49 Ally of Persian (Dan. 5:31)
50 A gem
51 Drop
52 Measure (2 Sam. 8:2)
53 Melody
55 After *pig*; before *knife*
56 ___ and haw

(Solution on p. 214)

133

NAMESAKE EVANGELIST

ACROSS

1 College disease
5 Org. mgr.
8 Outdoor evangelistic meeting (Gen. 12:6)
12 Manna measure (2 qts; Exod. 16:36)
13 Santa ___
15 Butter substitute
16 China, Korea, Japan, etc.
17 Most conservative Mennonites
18 Follows *Alexander Graham* and *Liberty*
19 Famous contemporary evangelist
22 Pod (Gen. 25:34)
23 Sought election (John 20:3)
24 German Reformation leader
26 Fraudulent (Ps. 36:3)
30 ___-de-camp
31 Arm or leg (Dan. 2:5)
32 St. Pete's neighbor
34 Traded for Esau's birthright (Gen. 25:34)
38 Adolescent facial disorder
39 GE's $6.3 bil. purchase
40 Biblical weed (Matt. 13:25, KJV)
41 Former Israeli prime minister Golda ___
42 Human source of good or evil (Luke 6:45)
44 Eye part
45 Pair of N.T. bks.
47 Last call (Rev. 11:15)
49 Foreign diplomat
52 Armed forces social supplier
53 Lawyers' org.
54 Namesake evangelist preceding 19-across
61 "Watch yourself ___ you be indiscreet" (Prov. 5:2)
63 Supreme or county (Exod. 10:7)
64 "There is not an ___ of truth in [the devil]" (John 8:44)
65 Isaac's oldest son (Gen. 25:25)
66 Out of order (Ps. 17:3)
67 The shortened way in
68 Waist wrapper (Lev. 8:7)
69 Weight meas.
70 Transport with delight (Mal. 3:1)

DOWN

1 Israel's O.T. eastern neighbor (Num. 21:11)
2 Oriental Missionary Society, Intl.
3 Astronaut Armstrong
4 Charismatic TV evangelist
5 Opera solo
6 Broadcast receptor (Jer. 22:28)
7 Gospel singer ___ Jackson
8 Kernel holder
9 First Hebrew letter
10 Free-for-all
11 Bear or circle
13 Attractive metal
14 Western Hemisphere, for short
20 Continual chatter
21 Wet earth (John 9:11)
25 Declaring religious experiences (Exod. 23:2)
26 Uncommunicative person
27 Evangelist John R. ___
28 All-encompassing prefix
29 Challenges (Num. 24:9)
30 Separate (Gen. 15:10)
33 Universal City studio
35 Canvas cover
36 Great Lake
37 Beyond the Mississippi (Gen. 12:8)
42 Type of curve or coil
43 Places faith in, such as Jesus (Matt. 18:6)
46 Spoke holder
48 Freq.
49 Joshua's companion (Num. 14:6)
50 Corpulent
51 Kind of twang
55 Bausch & ___
56 Evangelist ___ Palau
57 Age: abbr.
58 Salvation is what Christ has ___ (Eph. 3:6)
59 Drill sgt's shout: abbr.
60 Scotland ___ (Ezek. 42:1)
62 Egyptian king famous for treasure

(Solution on p. 214)

COMMANDS TO OBEY

A crossword grid with numbered squares (1–63).

ACROSS

1 Disobeyed at Jericho (Josh. 7:1)
6 Charge, for short (Ezra 4:6)
9 Johann Sebastian ___
13 Guilt (Gen. 43:9)
14 Constrictor
15 Hide
16 Fifth commandment beginning
19 Associates (Rev. 17:14)
20 Hired hand: abbr. (Ezra 8:20)
21 Remain loyal (Acts 15:1)
22 Accountable: abbr. (Gen. 21:26)
23 Retriever
24 Father
25 W. Hemisphere org.
26 Heap (Gen. 31:48)
27 Speed
30 Fifth commandment ending
   (Exod. 20:12)
34 Neophyte
35 Feels concern (1 Pet. 5:7)
36 Barely gain
37 Dead realm (Num. 16:30)
38 "So be it" (Deut. 27:15)
39 Tenth commandment
   (Prov. 24:1)
41 Ph.D., e.g. (Isa. 38:8)
42 Enclose (Ezek. 19:9)
44 Dreaded Windows 3.0 message
45 Syrian seaport (Josh. 15:47)
46 Rep. (Luke 10:22)
47 Printer's capability
50 Testify (Exod. 23:1)

53 Disgusting! (Isa. 30:22)
54 Betrayed (Acts 5:1)
55 Eighth commandment
   (Exod. 20:15)
58 Relieves (Gen. 27:39)
59 Disobey God (Rom. 3:6)
60 Endured (Ps. 55:12)
61 Runner vehicle
62 Accomplice, for short
   (Gen. 49:6)
63 Arched roofs

DOWN

1 Loathe (Ps. 101:3)
2 Make copy
3 Ancient Egyptian city (Isa. 30:4)
4 O.T. book
5 King Saul's uncle (1 Sam. 14:51)
6 Terrorist weapon: 2 wds.
7 Overthrow government
8 Elevator (1 Sam. 7:11)
9 Swim (Exod. 2:5)
10 Follows head and heart (2 Cor.
   6:10)
11 Actress Sarkisian
12 Roll call answer (Gen. 2:4)
15 Trained nucleus
17 Fermented froth (Exod. 12:15)
18 "[God] will never ___ you"
   (1 Pet. 4:19)
23 Cambodia's neighbor
24 Warning whistle
25 Portent (Luke 21:25)
26 Black tea
27 Appearance

28 O.T. wisdom bk.
29 ___ Spirit (Eph. 5:18)
30 One bounder: 2 wds.
31 Reputation (1 Thess. 4:1)
32 Worthless part
33 Evade commitment (Matt.
   21:33)
34 "My country 'tis of ___"
37 Quick!
40 Should (John 13:14)
42 King of Persia (Ezra 1:1)
43 Defenses (Exod. 17:9)
45 Preset
46 Passion (Heb. 5:7)
47 Not just hearers (James 1:22)
48 Anti-gravity device
49 "A fool ___ away his time"
   (Prov. 12:11)
50 Affirmative votes
51 Young horse (Zech. 9:9)
52 Melt together
53 Single part
54 "___ being mean" (Eph. 4:31)
56 Cook's measure
57 Govt. agency

(Solution on p. 214)

ALL GOD'S CREATURES

(Solution on p. 214)

ACROSS

1 Cold sea mammal (Gen. 9:12)
5 Heartthrob: 2 wds
10 First creatures God made (Gen. 1:20)
14 Pharaoh's dream animals (Gen. 41:2-3, KJV)
15 Samson's censure for burning foxes (Judg. 15:3-5)
16 "Bring a pair of every animal ___ the boat" (Gen. 6:19)
17 Solomon's biographer (2 Chron. 9:29)
18 Hebrew frog plaguer (Exod. 8:5)
19 Variant of czar
20 Craftiest creature (Gen. 3:1)
22 Symbolic horned horse (Num. 24:8, KJV)
24 One flying mammal (Lev. 11:19)
25 20th Hebrew letter
26 Greek marketplace
29 German preposition
31 Never-satisfied sucker (Prov. 30:15)
35 Horse harnessers (Prov. 26:3)
37 Settle snugly (Isa. 34:15)
38 Account's "bottom line"
39 Customary practice
41 O.T. minor prophetic bk.
42 King David's labor leader (2 Sam. 20:24)
45 Horned, hoofed animal (Deut. 14:5)
48 Sympathetic efferent nerve activity limit: acron.
49 Canadian Cattlemen's Association
50 Dividing offerings: abbr. (2 Chron. 31:14)
51 Hebrew priests' town (1 Chron. 6:60)
53 Long journey
55 Burrowers (Lev. 11:4-5)
58 Number of lines of printed material
62 Single stinging insect
63 Royal murder, for short (2 Kings 12:20)
65 Fibrous plant
66 Falsified (Gen. 18:15)
67 Worm-produced fibers (Ezek. 16:9)
68 Dead (Luke 23:54)
69 Mother who delivered in a stable (Luke 2:5-7)
70 Declarer
71 First and necessary: abbr.

DOWN

1 Boot runners
2 Platonic ideas
3 Man: pref.
4 Can "a ___ take away his spots?" (Jer. 13:23)
5 Syrian river (2 Kings 5:12)
6 Cryers like a sheep
7 Peter cut one off (John 18:10)
8 Love affairs
9 Tawny leather color
10 Polecat pelts
11 ___ far as
12 Led astrologers to Christ (Matt. 2:1-2)
13 Male sheep noisemaker (Exod. 19:13)
21 Mount of cursing
23 Patmos or Samos (Rev. 1:9, KJV)
26 Endearing term for fathers: Gr.
27 Slope
28 Anointing by pouring ___ the head: 2 words (2 Kings 9:6, KJV)
30 Deceived by goatskin-clad son (Gen. 27:21)
32 Culture's character
33 Applauded
34 Jael's husband (Judg. 5:24)
36 European-Mediterranean: mil.
37 Trap for 10-across (Matt. 4:18)
40 Resembling a tiny, winged insect (Matt. 23:24)
43 ___ Ann
44 Away from the wind
46 Animals' first home (Gen. 2:8)
47 Pleasing
49 Anointing spice (Exod. 30:24)
52 Copper and zinc alloy (Job 40:18)
54 Light washing (Lev. 6:28)
55 Aromatic resin (Gen. 43:11)
56 King Rehoboam's son (1 Chron. 3:10, KJV)
57 Antlered animal (Ps. 42:1)
59 Conspirator against Abimelech (Judg. 9:28)
60 Inheritance, for short (Luke 16:12)
61 Plant support (Jon. 4:7)
64 Stealthily clever

FIRMLY PLANTED

ACROSS

1 Thorn (Isa. 55:13, KJV)
6 Matures
10 Increased in size (Matt. 13:26)
14 Before active or fit
15 Greater
16 Prickly-stemmed flower (Song 2:1)
17 Prevent (Jer. 11:15)
18 "Help me never to tell ___": 2 wds. (Prov. 30:8)
19 ___ fescue: forage grass
20 ___ son, Abner (1 Sam. 14:50)
21 "The ___ ways are best" (Luke 5:39)
22 Mating rod source tree (Gen. 30:37)
24 French vineyard
25 "We are all parts of ___ body" (Eph. 4:4)
26 Cause of ruin
27 Poisonous plant
29 Self
30 Plant fluid
33 Solomon's imported animal (1 Kings 10:22)
34 National Ass'n of Evangelicals
35 Frog's floats
36 Bitter ___ for Passover (Exod. 12:8)
39 Sweet bread
40 Baby Moses' boat material (Exod. 2:3)
41 O.T. fruit-gathering prophet
42 Night flyer (Lev. 11:19)
43 Tall Australian tree
44 Blossom beginning (Isa. 27:6)
45 ___ and void: law
46 Hebrew's temple paneling (2 Chron. 3:5)
50 Judges' qualification (Exod. 18:25)
51 Previous: arch.
52 Nevadan ___ So La Lee
53 Hebrews' wilderness guide (Exod. 13:21)
56 Praise poem (Hab. 3:19)
57 Liver liquid
58 Forbidden image (Deut. 27:15)
59 Priest killed for a touch (1 Chron. 13:10)
61 Shady shelter
62 Mount to view Promised Land (Deut. 34:1)
63 Predictor (1 Sam. 9:11)
64 After musk (Num. 11:5)
65 Direction to first garden (Gen. 2:8)
66 ___ and haws (Num. 15:38)
67 Belonging to first garden (Ezek. 36:35)

DOWN

1 Stem division (John 15:4)
2 Show honor (Lev. 22:32)
3 Forum: Lat.
4 Makes mistake
5 Plant decomposition (Isa. 5:24)
6 Eliphaz's son (Gen. 36:12)
7 Heaven's pavement (Rev. 21:21)
8 God's Son (Gen. 46:16)
9 Oozing
10 Juicy berry (James 3:12)
11 Scripture parchment
12 Founded: abbr.
13 "___ my yoke—for it fits perfectly" (Matt. 11:29)
21 Formerly
23 Where Nehemiah refused to go (Neh. 6:2)
25 Surprise expression after 4-down
26 Precedes bag or ball (Ezek. 4:9)
28 Drug creation sites
30 Oil rating
31 Total (Rev. 22:18)
32 Letter addendum
34 Hard-shelled fruit (Song 6:11)
35 Fruit and its shape
36 Prophet in watchtower, for short
37 Flightless feathered friend
38 Aaron's budded (Num. 17:8)
39 Hay package
40 Fiber cords (Judg. 16:12)
42 Grasslike marsh plant (Exod. 2:3, KJV)
43 Town whose timbers were thrown into sea (Ezek. 26:7)
45 L.A. Lakers', etc. assoc.
46 Lebanon's largest trees (1 Kings 4:33)
47 Fit for food (Matt. 13:48)
48 Ship's lounge
49 Boats' backs (Acts 27:29)
50 Distribute (2 Chron. 31:18)
53 "Yearn for" this tree? (Isa. 41:19)
54 Suggestion (Deut. 1:23)
55 Arc throws
56 David's brother (1 Chron. 2:15)
57 Propagated (Eccles. 2:7)
60 Last letter
61 African Methodist Episcopal

(Solution on p. 214)

ACTS OF THE APOSTLES

ACROSS

1 Synagogue seat (Matt. 23:6)
4 Square's leftover
8 "The grass withers, the flowers ___" (Isa. 40:8)
12 Jewish captive (Neh. 7:20)
14 Ancient commemorative pillar
15 Hebrew race founder (Gen. 10:21)
16 God brought Jesus back to ___ (Acts 5:30)
17 Acts was written to one who ___ God (Acts 1:1)
18 At the back (Matt. 26:58)
19 First Christian martyr (Acts 7:59)
21 Waiters (Acts 27:23)
23 Shaped or cut (Deut. 10:3)
25 Stroke site
26 King Saul's grandfather (1 Chron. 8:33)
27 What Jesus dipped and handed Judas (John 13:26, KJV)
29 Kings' action against Christ (Acts 4:26)
33 Ancient farm tractor (Jer. 27:2)
36 Gulf needing people (Ezek. 22:30)
38 What Pharisees set for Jesus (Matt. 19:3)
39 O.T. questioning prophet: abbr.
40 Paul was willing to ___ for Jesus (Acts 21:13)
42 Has been
44 What church did with Lord's Supper (Acts 20:12)
45 Feels sick
47 Solemn oath by Paul (Acts 18:18)
49 One-of-a-kind (1 Chron. 17:21)
51 Walk on (Ps. 44:5)
53 Paul's "road" to Rome (Acts 27:1)
55 Returned Hebrew exile (Ezra 2:57)
56 Dull resounding noise
58 Steep slope
60 Christ "___ himself . . . to die" (Phil. 2:8)
64 Jewish insurrectionist (Acts 5:36)
68 Region stirred by God's message (Acts 19:20)
69 Converted saleswoman (Acts 16:14)
71 Jewish or Gentile (Acts 3:25)
72 "In the ___ days I will pour out my Holy Spirit" (Acts 2:17)
73 Giant Ishbi-___ (2 Sam. 21:16)
74 ___themum (tropical shrub)
75 David and Goliath's meeting place (1 Sam. 17:19)
76 Dishan's son (Gen. 36:28)
77 Conclude (Acts 5:24)

DOWN

1 Chums
2 Massage a manuscript
3 Sapphira's relation to Ananias (Acts 5:1)
4 How 19-across died (Acts 7:59)
5 Third bk. of Moses
6 Fermented, bitter beverages
7 Attack from all sides
8 Ardent nature of Paul's preaching (Acts 9:22)
9 One nectar gatherer: 2 wds. (Judg. 14:8)
10 Luke addressed Acts to a ___ friend (Acts 1:1)
11 Wrongs
13 Paul's ___ spared him from a plot (Acts 23:16)
14 What Jews did to Jesus (Acts 10:39, KJV)
20 King killed for accepting worship (Acts 20:23)
22 Peleg's son (Gen. 11:18)
24 Track like a hound (1 Sam. 17:43)
26 Outstanding character of Berean believers (Acts 17:11, KJV)
28 Clawed foot (Job 28:8)
30 Saddam Hussein subject (Isa. 19:23)
31 Giant armadillo
32 Dueling sword
33 Jumpin' Jehosha__! (1 Kings 15:24)
34 Lion's home (Jer. 4:7)
35 Fourteen
37 Ancient city of Edom (Gen. 36:39)
41 End of statement
43 Drum or noose (Ps. 124:7)
46 Jewish weekly holy day (Acts 13:14)
48 Unseld or Hopkins
50 Not moral (Gal. 5:19)
52 Decaliter, for short
54 Legal suit (Acts 18:12)
57 Toast type
59 Jezebel's husband (1 Kings 16:31)
60 Sound in health
61 Boundary range between Europe and Asia
62 Flat-topped hill
63 Fabric coloring user
65 Have courage (Acts 5:13)
66 One metal container
67 Dispatch (Acts 2:33)
70 Chromosome constituent

(Solution on p. 214)

JUDGES AND SAMUEL

ACROSS

1 Amalekite king (1 Sam. 15:8)
5 Conspirator against Abime-lech (Judg. 9:28)
9 Caesar's headquarters (Acts 18:2)
13 Descendant of Merari (1 Chron. 24:26)
14 High priest with Caiaphas (Luke 3:2)
16 O.T. author and sheepherder
17 Mount of antiphonal response (Josh. 8:33)
18 Leafy: arch.
19 Widow's ___ (Luke 21:2, KJV)
20 O.T. dream expert
22 City of Moab (Jer. 48:24)
24 Levite oxcart driver (2 Sam. 6:3)
26 Public uproar (Matt. 14:5)
27 Well-defended position
30 Bebai's son (Ezra 10:28)
34 Esau's in-law (Gen. 36:2)
35 One of David's heroes (1 Chron. 11:42)
37 "Round ___ virgin, mother and child"
38 Dodge truck (Ruth 4:18)
39 City Joshua conquered by ambush (Josh. 8:22-23)
40 To the same degree
41 Annoy
42 Upward: pref.
43 Sarai's husband (Gen. 11:29; 12:1-3)
44 Amount to be paid: slang
45 Belonging to Ethan's father (1 Chron. 6:44)
47 A deliverer of Israel (Judg. 3:31; 5:6)
50 Dutch pressed cheese
52 Model railroad scale
53 Elidad's father (Num. 34:21)
56 Twelves (Prov. 10:20)
60 Edomite priest-slayer (1 Sam. 22:18)
61 Oil to anoint kings (1 Sam. 10:1)
63 "Here ___ ___ in sackcloth" (Job 16:15)
64 Make lines with acid
65 King of Egypt about 3100 B.C.
66 Small cobras
67 Gideon's "angel food" con-tainer: abbr. (Judg. 6:19)
68 Eve's third son (Gen. 4:25)
69 Armies of heaven (Luke 2:13)

DOWN

1 What Samuel was in when God called him: 2 wds. (1 Sam. 3:9)
2 Philistine place Jonathan cap-tured (1 Sam. 13:3)
3 Signer of Nehemiah's cove-nant (Neh. 10:26)
4 Giant David defeated (1 Sam. 17:4)
5 Governor of Achaia (Acts 18:12)
6 One: Scot.
7 Giants' patriarch (Judg. 1:20)
8 Priests' washbasin (Exod. 31:9)
9 City rewarded for helping David (1 Sam. 30:27)
10 Leave out (2 Chron. 21:19)
11 Enemy of earthly treasure (Luke 12:33)
12 Compass direction at 5 o'clock
15 Israelites' northern enemies (2 Sam. 10:17)
21 Son of Benjamin (Gen. 46:21)
23 Smallest Greek letter (John 8:44)
25 "Walking ___ ___"
27 Hebrew codeliverer with 60-down (Judg. 4:14-16)
28 Son of Elioenai (1 Chron. 3:24)
29 Aegean island Paul visited (Acts 20:15)
31 Prevaricating (Lev. 6:3)
32 Main circulatory trunk
33 Textile retoucher
36 Ephraim boasts, "___ ___ ___ rich!" (Hos. 12:8)
39 David's most handsome son (2 Sam. 14:25)
43 Deadly disease
44 Judean king (2 Kings 14:1)
46 Giant's distinctive (Exod. 36:21)
48 Shaharaim's wife (1 Chron. 8:9)
49 In the past
51 Syndicate infiltrators (Isa. 2:20)
53 Small sleeping sites
54 Hell
55 4-down was over ___ feet tall! (1 Sam. 17:4)
57 It was this before Exxon
58 Tangs
59 Chicago's State Street: abbrv.
60 Female prophet and deliverer, for short (Judg. 4:4)
62 Animal doctor

(Solution on p. 213)

PLANTS IN GOD'S PLAN

ACROSS

1 Develop (Lev. 27:3)
4 Mature (Gen. 25:7)
8 Base (Gen. 20:10)
12 Lithuanian, for one
14 Moses' brother (Exod. 4:14)
15 Object of devotion (Deut. 27:15)
16 Dull; humdrum
17 Greek goddess with silver shrines (Acts 19:24)
18 Fish catchers (Tim. 21:11)
19 Oval, soft-shelled nuts (Gen. 43:11)
21 Ailment (Lev. 7:24)
23 Viscous plant substance
25 Light, silvery element, for short
26 Electrical or mechanical, e.g.: abbr.
27 Current time
29 Cooker
33 Bent over in a breeze (Ps. 29:9)
36 Babylonian god
38 Swell, such as bread (Exod. 12:39)
39 Off kosher diet (2 Pet. 2:22)
40 Extra large (1 Cor. 12:17)
42 Draw (Acts 27:16)
44 Local area network
45 Applied (Gen. 47:24)
47 Breach (Ezek. 22:30)
49 Hard, dark-brown wood
51 London___

53 Adhesive from plants (Gen. 37:25)
55 Short pipe connectors: var. pl.
56 Cereal grass with edible seed
58 Crowlike bird (Gen. 8:7)
60 Full-grown (Deut. 28:40)
64 Church foyer
68 One computer program defect
69 Steeply projecting rocks (Jer. 16:16)
71 Atoll (Isa. 20:6, KJV)
72 Close
73 Eating board (Gen. 43:32)
74 A fraud (1 John 2:22)
75 Asia and the Orient (Rev. 16:12)
76 Shammah's father (2 Sam. 23:11)
77 Single negative response: 2 wds.

DOWN

1 Eastern church father
2 Bitter drink (Ps. 69:21)
3 Ancient Persia (Dan. 8:2)
4 Sweet dried grape (1 Sam. 25:18)
5 Shielded savings
6 Duck's delight
7 Where Tamar seduced Judah (Gen. 38:13-14)
8 Offered to Christ on cross (Ps. 69:21)
9 Concept (Gen. 34:19)
10 Decision-making objects (Lev. 16:8)
11 Other (Gen. 15:4)

13 Spiny (Mark 4:18)
14 Appends (Prov. 10:22)
20 Arid region between Egypt and Israel (Gen. 13:1)
22 Hebrew holy day: abbr. (John 19:31)
24 Home of Ahimelech the priest (1 Sam. 21:1)
26 Zealous (Eph. 6:5)
28 Damp (Lev. 11:38)
30 Hardening ovens (Exod. 9:8)
31 Traded his birthright for peas (Gen. 25:30-34)
32 Lease (Luke 20:16)
33 Potato
34 Astute (Deut. 1:13)
35 Excavate (Deut. 6:11)
37 Down (Gen. 23:7)
41 Choke (Job 6:7)
43 "Drink the ___ of Life without charge" (Rev. 22:17)
46 Dry spell (Hag. 1:11)
48 Throwing dice: Per. (Esther 9:26)
50 Edible Old World legume (2 Sam. 17:28)
52 Nimble
54 Maim (Isa. 14:19)
57 Dorsal parts of midbrain
59 Flower container (Job 13:12)
60 Horse's hair (Job 39:19)
61 Solomon's grandson (1 Chron. 3:10, KJV)
62 Pulls (Acts 23:10)
63 Yank along ground (Exod. 21:14)
65 First Chinese dynasty
66 Esprit de corps
67 Dry copy process: pref.
70 Isaac's father: nickname (Gen. 21:3)

(Solution on p. 213)

BELIEVERS' NAMES

ACROSS

1 Cheese type
5 Thick and spreading
10 Inflamed swelling near eyelid
14 Mastered
15 "___ his courts with praise" (Ps. 100:4)
16 Think; suppose: arch.
17 Followers of Jesus (Acts 11:26)
19 Scrape smooth
20 Large metric measure
21 Female believer: informal (Rom. 16:1)
22 Earth hollows (Rev. 6:15)
23 Protective cover (Eph. 6:11)
25 Sleeveless hanging garment (Isa. 3:22)
26 Place of citizenship: abbr. (Eph. 2:19)
29 Enclosed truck
30 Work of aesthetic value
31 Law School Admission
34 Free (Ezek. 3:27)
36 Twelve disciples, e.g. (Luke 9:1)
38 Ancient Hebrew chests (Exod. 25:21)
39 Appointed times (Acts 1:7)
41 Belonging to a woman (Prov. 14:1)
42 Managers of another's property (2 Chron. 9:4)
44 Turn aside (Ps. 119:157)
46 Pounds per square foot
47 Before *orthodox* or *plasm*

48 Stinger (Isa. 7:18)
49 Drunkard
50 "Deliver us from the ___ One" (Matt. 6:13)
52 One who fails
54 Town near Jordan River (John 3:23)
56 Rural Youth Association
57 Tropical skin disease
61 Capital of Norway
62 Owners
64 Study of living organisms, for short
65 Friendly relations
66 Vanish: abbr.
67 Woodcutters (2 Sam. 12:31)
68 Nervous (Ps. 62:2)
69 Declares (Rev. 14:13)

DOWN

1 Certain truth (Jude 1:5)
2 Repeat (Jer. 6:7)
3 Bird resembling sea gull
4 Reubenite leader (1 Chron. 11:42)
5 Wager (2 Kings 18:23)
6 Simultaneous speaking (Exod. 19:8)
7 Riser (Gen. 28:13)
8 Female fowls (Matt. 23:37)
9 Age, for short (2 Pet. 3:8)
10 Long, narrow fastener (Jer. 27:2)
11 Pilgrims (3 John 1:10)
12 Oxen connector (Matt. 11:29)
13 Female sheep (Gen. 30:40)

18 "___ each other with humble spirits" (1 Pet. 5:5)
22 Siamese and tabby (Ps. 73:7)
24 Core or axle
25 Crucifixion instruments (Mark 15:27)
26 Fastener (Exod. 39:33)
27 Wrongful acts liable for civil suits
28 Close companion (Phil. 4:3, KJV)
30 Chimpanzee or gorilla (2 Chron. 9:21)
32 Type of motor
33 Valuable resource
35 Compass direction at 7 o'clock
36 Asian Theological Seminary
37 Particular adjective
40 *Much ___ about Nothing*
43 City of Judah (Josh. 15:50)
45 Sheds tears (Gen. 27:38)
48 Brags (Gal. 6:14)
51 Old stringed instruments
52 Specific antibody against blood cells, etc.
53 Comes back to life (Luke 16:31)
54 Weeps aloud (Gen. 45:2)
55 ___ Minor about Nothing (Obad. 1:20)
56 Apostle Paul's final destination (Acts 28:16)
58 Star of increased brightness
59 Where John's head was placed (Mark 6:25)
60 Venomous snakes (Rom. 3:13, KJV)
62 Congratulatory stroke (2 Cor. 5:12)
63 Hebrews are "the apple of God's ___" (Deut. 32:10)

(Solution on p. 213)

JESUS OUR LORD

ACROSS

1 Sorrowful (Mark 2:19)
4 Risk-free (Matt. 6:20)
8 ___ song
12 Stepped on repeatedly (Rev. 19:15)
14 Presented freely (Matt. 5:3)
15 Mexican "sandwich"
16 Slender woodwind instrument
17 Signs of future (Luke 21:25)
18 Anger
19 Illustrative story (Matt. 13:35)
21 Careful to obey (Mal. 3:17)
23 English royal house in Middle Ages
25 End of paragraph
26 Seminarian's wife's degree
27 Brief sleep (Luke 8:23)
29 Apostle called a stone (Matt. 16:18)
33 Hospitality recipients (Mark 2:15)
36 Before *night* and *way* (John 7:14)
38 City in Edom (2 Kings 14:7)
39 Advanced in years (Luke 1:7)
40 Indefinitely long time
42 Neither solid nor liquid
44 Poisonous snake (Rom. 3:13, KJV)
45 Abraham's Canaanite ally (Gen. 14:13)
47 Fisherman's tool (John 21:8)
49 Embalming ointments (Luke 23:56)
51 City of Crete (Acts 27:8)
53 Uncooked (Exod. 12:9)
55 Combustion residue (Exod. 27:3)
56 Exclamation of surprise (Ps. 35:21)
58 Main evil spirit (John 13:2)
60 Zabdi's hometown (1 Chron. 27:27)
64 Contributed (Ezek. 44:30)
68 Free from worry (Luke 21:34)
69 Son of Gad (Gen. 46:16)
71 Time of Jesus' crucifixion (Mark 15:25)
72 Cattle-breeding African people
73 "Believe on the Lord Jesus and you will be ___" (Acts 16:31)
74 Dull
75 Cuts off quickly (John 15:2)
76 "They were indeed in ___ ___ situation" (Exod. 5:19)
77 Inner: pref.

DOWN

1 Cease (Luke 8:52)
2 Hebron (Josh. 15:13)
3 "Knock, and the ___ will be opened" (Matt. 7:7)
4 Devout man who held Jesus (Luke 2:25)
5 "___ Maria"
6 Ward off
7 Follow as result (Job 41:8)
8 By Jesus' ___ we are healed (Isa. 53:5)
9 Homeless child
10 Liberal lobby
11 "The first ___ the angels did say"
13 Expirations (Matt. 10:21)
14 Gift to Christ child (Matt. 2:11)
20 Sharply-rising flattop
22 Uppermost part (Matt. 17:1)
24 Sacrificial sheep (Gen. 22:13)
26 Feet
28 What Prodigal Son fed (Luke 15:15)
30 "Lord, ___ us a prayer" (Luke 11:1)
31 "Only God is truly good, and no one ___" (Luke 18:19)
32 Knocks
33 Objective (1 Cor. 9:26)
34 Forearm bone
35 God "gave his only ___" (John 3:16)
37 ___ Kapital
41 King Saul's grandfather (1 Chron. 9:35)
43 Mediterranean country (Rom. 15:28)
46 Harvesters (John 4:36)
48 Somewhat
50 Cyprus, for one (Acts 21:3)
52 Lengthened expression
54 Married (Hos. 4:17)
57 Hebrew military general (2 Sam. 17:25)
59 Without legal force (Num. 30:12)
60 Confirmation of accuracy (Mark 14:3)
61 Ring of light (Ezek. 1:27)
62 "His time ___ ___" (Dan. 11:36)
63 Middle Eastern race (Neh. 2:19)
65 "Never ___ of loyalty and kindness" (Prov. 3:3)
66 Ahira's father (Num. 7:78)
67 Something owed (Matt. 18:27)
70 Eggs

(Solution on p. 214)

GOSPEL QUOTES

A crossword puzzle grid with numbered cells.

ACROSS

1 "You ___ me 'Master' and 'Lord'" (John 13:13)
5 Story of heroic deeds
9 "Praise God with the ___s" (Ps. 150:4)
13 Woodwind
14 "Be merciful unto me, as thou ___ to do" (Ps. 119:132, KJV)
16 Careless attitude when Christ returns (Matt. 24:37)
17 Dross (Ezek. 22:18)
18 Persian city Tel-___ (Ezra 2:59)
19 Idolatrous site in Israel (Hos. 10:8)
20 State of weariness
22 End-time critic (Jude 1:18)
24 Var. of Hosea (Rom. 9:25, KJV)
26 "At the name of Jesus every ___ shall bow" (Phil. 2:10)
27 "All men alike are ___" (Rom. 3:9)
30 "Be ___ and ready to forgive" (Col. 3:13)
34 Between Joel and Obadiah
35 Lengthy books
38 "___ there, Messiah!" (Mark 15:32)
39 Tit for ___
40 Hadad's father (Gen. 36:35)
41 "He will ___ the gates of heaven"
42 "Sarah had faith to become a mother despite her old ___" (Heb. 11:11)
43 Cattle clusters (Jer. 5:17)
44 Hebrew tribe: var. (Luke 2:36, KJV)
45 Snugly retreated (Ezek. 31:6)
47 "Buyers and ___" (Isa. 24:2)
50 "If you have ___, listen!" (Mark 4:9)
52 Nicodemus's spice-gift to Christ (John 19:39)
53 Opens, such as deaf ears (Isa. 35:5)
56 Woman Peter restored to life (Acts 9:40)
60 Hot to ___
61 "I will ___ my anger on you for your worshiping of idols" (Ezek. 7:3)
63 Fairy ___ (Luke 24:11)
64 Shammah's father (2 Sam. 23:11)
65 "I will put splints . . . upon their broken ___" (Ezek. 34:16)
66 Ephraimite patriarch (Num. 26:35)
67 Fuse together (Gen. 11:4)
68 Period before Good Friday
69 Where going, for short

DOWN

1 "Stay close to the Lord, whatever the ___" (Acts 11:23)
2 "God is ___ to keep you from slipping" (Jude 1:24)
3 "He personally carried the ___ of our sins" (1 Pet. 2:24)
4 Roman divisions (Luke 8:30)
5 Season of most direct sun (Gen. 8:22)
6 Enzyme suffix
7 Sets
8 One bag: 2 wds. (2 Kings 4:42)
9 Cause hearing loss
10 Rant and ___ (1 Sam. 18:10)
11 Consumer
12 "Be earnest, thoughtful ___ of prayer" (1 Pet. 4:7)
15 Type of whip used on Jesus (Luke 23:16)
21 "Be sure to ___ the abilities God has given you" (1 Tim. 4:14)
23 Stated charges (Isa. 52:3)
25 Organic chemical compound
27 "The God of peace will soon crush ___ under your feet" (Rom 16:20)
28 "God's glory is man made in his ___" (1 Cor. 11:7)
29 Musical tones (1 Cor. 14:8)
31 Ones farther away
32 One returned to thank Jesus (Luke 17:14)
33 Watchers
36 Strange (1 Cor. 12:23)
37 King Lemuel's home (Prov. 31:1)
40 Sleeping bag
43 High temperature (Rev. 16:9)
44 Notified (Judg. 16:2)
46 "I have thoroughly ___ your promises" (Ps. 119:140)
48 Who died in tenth Egyptian plague (Ps. 78:51)
49 Follows *water*
51 "Don't let others ___ your faith" (Col. 2:8)
53 "I have come to ___ sinners back to God" (Matt. 9:13)
54 "___, born is the King of Israel"
55 Part (Acts 2:15)
57 "God will take ___ of your tomorrow too" (Matt. 6:34)
58 Cry of despair (Num. 24:23)
59 Commissioned (John 20:21)
60 Marble shooter
62 Southern Baptist Network

BOOKS OF THE BIBLE

ACROSS

1 Christ child's visitors (Matt. 2:16, NIV)
5 Non-Jewish Palestinian (Neh. 6:1)
9 Established truths
14 Death notice
15 *Reader's Digest* cofounder ____ Wallace
16 Man who stole from God at Jericho (Josh. 7:1)
17 Bible book about priests and sacrifices
19 Actress ____ Garr
20 Tissue swelling
21 Follows *be* and *co*
22 Preacher and author John R. ____
23 Add to *gen* and breathe
25 Female superstars
27 Rite of anointing
31 Computer "plain text" file
32 Winnie the ____
33 Division of the U.K.
36 Piston power, in brief
39 Jesus is God's ____ begotten Son (John 3:16, KJV)
40 Promissory note
41 Medicine from lily plant (Num. 24:6)
42 *Recent* prefix
43 Short publicity notice
45 Photographic films
46 Complex whole, for short (Acts 24:14)
49 Bible book of beginnings
51 Bible book about David
55 Fond du ____, Wis.
56 ____ *Mutiny*
57 Letter between *o* and *q*
59 Boise's state
63 Japanese city
64 Christian composer and conductor ____ ____
66 Earth extractor
67 Migrant farm worker
68 Camping cover
69 Before tees
70 Phoenician city (Josh. 15:47)
71 Corrodes (John 6:50)

DOWN

1 Burrower
2 Resting place: 2 wds.
3 Donate (Rev. 21:6)
4 Bible book to a young pastor
5 Muhammad ____
6 Costa ____
7 Drunkard: 2 wds.
8 Sew temporarily
9 Heavyweights: infor.
10 Recluse
11 Bible books about kings
12 Tawdry dress in England
13 Irritations: infor.
18 Car for hire
24 Cry of alarm or pain
26 Cheer
27 Once ____ a time
28 Without exception (Gal. 6:5)
29 Bible book to early church
30 Astronaut ____ Armstrong
34 Actor ____ Costello
35 Hospital med-____ ward
37 ____ Bear
38 Minus (Exod. 30:15)
41 Brief personal tale
43 Br. thermal unit
44 ____ and the Dragon
47 Northerner: infor.
48 Slanders (Jude 1:12)
50 Horny sheath (John 20:25)
51 "O Lamb of God, ____ ____" (hymn)
52 Pathological suffix
53 Disney's Fla. center
54 Permitting escape
58 Middle Eastern prince
60 Region (Josh. 9:1)
61 Clue (1 Cor. 9:15)
62 Horse food
65 Charge (Exod. 22:15)

(Solution on p. 215)

WHOSE RESPONSIBILITY?

ACROSS

1 Part of United Kingdom west of England
6 Not yet disclosed
9 Drive away
13 Higher place
14 Common Market area: abbr.
15 Wm. Tyndale's death site (Isa. 55:3)
16 Our responsibility to God: 4 wds. (Ps. 100:4)
19 Lyric poems
20 Admit as true, in brief
21 Chariot "engines"
22 After *cor* and *part* (1 Sam. 14:51)
23 ___ Wednesday
24 Not even one
25 "Accidental" ___ of God (Exod. 21:13)
26 High-capacity storage drive: comp.
27 Wares, for short
30 Jesus' responsibility: 4 wds. (John 10:7)
34 Bargain
35 Large amount
36 Large West Coast school
37 Too much leads to poverty
38 After chow
39 Successfully opposes (Acts 9:22)
41 Get by one and keep beyond death: abbr.
42 In one—good; in roof—bad
43 ___ ton soup
44 Salvation or goodness, e.g. (Rom. 4:4)
45 Connect into
46 Precedes *cara* or *sacred*
49 Brother of Hezron and Carmi (Gen. 46:9, KJV)
52 Precedes *pass* or *plus*
53 Senior citizens' org.
54 God's responsibility: 4 wds. (Prov. 3:6)
57 Grounds
58 Rahab's business (Josh. 2:1)
59 One painted metalwork: 2 wds.
60 Eyelid inflammation
61 Fill up
62 Rose on hind legs

DOWN

1 Before *train* or *wheel*
2 "If my words ___ in you, ye shall ask what ye will" (John 15:7, KJV)
3 "Jesus, ___ of My Soul" (hymn)
4 Nights before Christmas (1 Tim. 2:13)
5 Do it to stage or table
6 Systematically impart truth
7 Nonsense
8 Sacred ___ of the Covenant
9 "Tell Me the ___ of Jesus" (hymn)
10 Laughs
11 Migrant farm worker: slang
12 Computer system vendors
15 Operation Desert ___
17 Makes 26-down (Nah. 2:5)
18 Stock interest
23 Long
24 A degree or level
25 Now hear this, for short
26 Result of 17-down
27 Valley
28 Transfer property
29 Drains
30 Distinctive doctrines
31 Mimics
32 Central street
33 Conscience prick (Hab. 10:3)
34 Blueprint
37 Before *light* or *page* (Rev. 5:5)
39 Pitiable
40 Promised (Gen. 26:3, KJV)
42 Alive with the sound of music
44 Smooth descent
45 Rotates
46 Chief city official
47 Single function: 2 wds.
48 Gushed out (Lev. 18:28, KJV)
49 Required ___ ed class
50 Take it or turn it up
51 Wrong
52 Burning bush loc. (Acts 7:30, KJV)
53 "___ boy! Way to go!"
55 Cutting remark
56 Elevator compartment

(Solution on p. 214)

CIVIL RIGHTS

ACROSS

1 Long-napped rug
5 Heavy blow
9 Nut palm fruit
10 People group (Acts 3:25)
11 Neighborhood (Acts 16:3)
12 Slippery fluids (2 Kings 20:13)
13 Black U.S. civil rights leader (name cont. in 16-across)
15 Special-interest group
16 Rest of 13-across
22 Et ___ (and others: Lat.)
23 Penn. port
24 State where 13-across was killed
25 Droops
26 Heart checkups
27 Network, for short

DOWN

1 Fraudulent scheme
2 Israeli round dance
3 Maple family
4 Animal hides (Exod. 26:14)
5 Unfairness
6 Greet (Matt. 27:29)
7 U.S. rights protection org.
8 Annoying person
14 Between 2 and 4 in Rome (1 Chron. 5:26)
16 Loathe (Luke 6:22)
17 Charged with emotion, in brief
18 Cartel (1 Sam. 26:5)
19 Senior's hair color (Gen. 44:31)
20 Lively dances
21 Leisure (Gen. 16:12)

(Solution on p. 214)

ANIMAL, VEGETABLE, OR . . .

ACROSS

1 Christians' status with God (Gal. 4:5)
5 Consumer agency
8 Harsh criticism (Ps. 77:9)
12 Available (Isa. 55:3)
13 Corn part (Lev. 2:14)
14 ___ hoop
15 Ten- (Mark 7:31, KJV)
16 Computer language
17 Having wings
18 Oak fruits
20 Exempt
22 Take nourishment (Gen. 2:16)
23 Christian consortium: abbr.
24 Gaping gulfs (Luke 16:26)
27 Small food seeds
31 Before drug names
32 Follows *bottle* or *snow* (Ezek. 27:10)
33 Honey ingredient
37 Pine type
40 Tulsa Christian college
41 Minors' gov't. support
42 Complete poise
45 Fly
49 Decline in strength (Heb. 13:5)
50 Reddish brown animal (Zech. 1:8)
52 Side squared (Gen. 19:31)
53 Amer. author, James ___
54 Go astray (Ps. 95:10, KJV)
55 Draft team's left side (Gen. 25:9)
56 Tear apart (Exod. 39:23, KJV)
57 Conseq.
58 Promote (Gen. 34:19)

DOWN

1 Carbonated water
2 Oil price council
3 O.T. Egyptian king (2 Kings 23:29)
4 Nooses for the unwary (Ps. 141:10)
5 Burden bearers (Eccles. 3:19)
6 Spoiled (Gen. 2:9)
7 Supreme planners (Hos. 4:11)
8 Thoroughly outdoes (Josh. 5:8)
9 Remarkable event
10 Cranston or Greenspan
11 "Old ___ ain't what she used to be"
19 Viet ___
21 After *Ginnie* but before *West*
24 Ted Turner enterprise
25 Gardener's implement (Isa. 5:6)
26 Circle part
28 "Caught in the ___" (John 8:4)
29 Apple computer
30 N.T. bk.
34 Ornamented leather (Exod. 32:4)
35 Take weapons (Num. 32:20)
36 Rolling stock
37 Brown-winged butterflies
38 Modern "records"
39 Majority of earth's surface (Gen. 1:6)
42 Opp. of 55-across (Isa. 30:27)
43 One side of a leaf
44 Debtor security
46 Something only God can make (Gen. 2:9)
47 Torpedo-like creature (Rev. 6:12)
48 Between viscount and marquis
51 .025 acre

(Solution on p. 214)

WOMEN NAMESAKES

ACROSS

1 Benefactions (Luke 11:41, KJV)
5 Apostle James's mother (Luke 24:10)
9 Deprive
12 Rachel's sister (Gen. 29:16)
13 Singer Tornquist
14 Employ
15 Lazarus' sisters: 3 wds. (John 11:19)
18 Some
19 Cooking measure
20 Ms. Bronte, Gilman, or Ray: fam.
21 Jaycees: abbr.
22 Female service div.
24 Tolstoy's ___ Karenina
27 Taxi
28 Not good
31 Woman Jesus cast seven demons from: 2 wds. (Luke 8:2)
35 Surprise!
36 Actress Gardner
37 Join
38 Humorist George ___
39 Lobe site
41 Eve's mate (Gen. 4:1)
44 Finish
45 Apple computer
48 Jesus' parents: 3 wds. (Luke 2:16)
52 Kind
53 "Extremely small" prefix
54 Concept
55 ___ Moines, Iowa
56 Neuter
57 Printed words

DOWN

1 Actress ___ Gluck
2 Trim
3 Wiped Jesus' feet with her hair (John 12:3)
4 Bashful
5 Choices lists
6 Wt. meas.
7 Edge (Exod. 37.12)
8 Cheer
9 King David's great-grandmother (Matt. 1:5)
10 Workplace watchdog
11 Cub's mother
16 Add-on, in brief
17 Pope's church's initials
21 Crow's relative
22 Crumple (Isa. 22:18)
23 Lawyers' union
24 Doctors' union
25 Slangy refusal
26 Hunters' lobby
27 Computer display type
28 Honey maker (Ps. 118:12)
29 Santa ___ , Cal.
30 Donkey's pty.
32 Crazy (Eccles. 9:3)
33 ___ Maria
34 8.5 x 11 sz.
38 Singer Ms. Grant
39 Like a lot (Lev. 17:5)
40 Fuss
41 Surrounded by
42 Mrs. Roy Rogers
43 Noah's boat and covenant chest (Gen. 8:18; Exod. 16:34)
44 ___ St. Vincent Milay
45 King Darius, for one (Dan. 9:1)
46 Peak
47 Converse
49 Shortened reply
50 Brief repose
51 Pose

(Solution on p. 214)

CREATOR'S CHARACTER

ACROSS

1 Droop
4 Mexican food
8 Foxy
12 L's three followers
13 Man God made (Gen. 2:23)
14 Scent (Exod. 16:20)
15 Competitive card game
16 Italy's capital
17 Social elites: slang
18 Divine character statement: 3 wds. (1 John 1:5)
21 ___ wiedersehen
22 Oxygenize
26 Molecule parts
29 Righteous (Prov. 28:2)
30 Soda fountain drink
31 Italian currency
32 Nebraska's capital
34 Of yesteryear (Jer. 21:2)
35 Fail to keep a promise
37 Solid state
38 Divine character statement: 3 wds. (John 3:33)
43 Father: Aram. (Mark 14:36, KJV)

46 Standby mode (Prov. 16:27)
47 Before chow in Chinese city
48 Baffled: slang
49 Great achievement
50 Anointing fluid (Gen. 28:18)
51 Bible translator Venerable, the ___
52 Sweet potatoes
53 Quietly clever

DOWN

1 Self-satisfied
2 Year: Lat.
3 God's benevolent character (Ps. 11:7)
4 Apostle Paul's hometown (Acts 9:11)
5 Mr. Hitler
6 Central Amer. Mission's new name
7 Alpha's other end (Rev. 1:8, KJV)
8 Sovereign One (Exod. 9:29)

9 Trouble
10 Lump (2 Sam. 21:18)
11 Annual events, for short
19 Christ's claim: 4 wds. (John 10:7)
20 Robe's edge
23 Quite dry
24 Wheatfield weed (Matt. 13:25, KJV)
25 Well-being
26 Takes en before or al after
27 Domesticated (James 3:8)
28 Photographer ___ Mills
33 Back then
34 Eights (1 Chron. 15:20)
36 Build up (Rom. 14:19, KJV)
37 Muslim religion
39 Mental conception
40 Celestial sightings
41 Labor
42 God's sacred character (1 Pet. 1:15)
43 Shortened form
44 Hive dweller
45 Opp. of 3-down (Gen. 2:9)

(Solution on p. 214)

FOUR OF A KIND

The crossword grid with numbered cells:

1	2	3		4	5	6	7	8		9	10	11
12				13						14		
15				16						17		
18			19				20		21			
		22					23					
24	25	26				27		28		29	30	31
32					33		34			35		
36			37	38		39		40	41			
		42			43		44					
45	46	47					48			49	50	51
52				53		54				55		
56				57						58		
59				60						61		

ACROSS

1 Deborah and Gideon, e.g.: abbr. (Ruth 1:1)
4 New insect
9 Spaceship foot (Luke 15:16)
12 Lubricate
13 Once more
14 Amy Grant song "___ to ___"
15 Medical insurance pgm.
16 Persians' allies (Esther 1:19)
17 Pottery vessel
18 Seaman turned hymnwriter John ___
20 Methodist John ___
22 Sprout
23 Type of camera
24 Jesus' resurrected friend (John 11:43)
28 Florida coastal city
32 Computer programming language
33 Truck or computer
35 Physician's address
36 Creed
39 Bible teacher and author Warren ___
42 Hunters' org.
44 Ohio city airline code
45 Pilgrim's Progress author John ___
48 Institutes of the Christian Religion author John ___
52 Now is

53 Religiously prejudiced person
55 Two's predecessor
56 Golfers' org.
57 Cover sin (Lev. 4:28)
58 Dynamite
59 ___ Aviv (Ezek. 3:14)
60 Despised
61 A letter

DOWN

1 Author of fourth Gospel (Rev. 1:1)
2 Ten to a dollar
3 Radiate
4 Western novelist Louis ___
5 Meeting plan
6 X-ray amount
7 Opinions (Matt. 16:23)
8 Scholasticism founder Saint ___
9 Apostle to the Gentiles (Acts 21:19)
10 Mean person
11 Repudiate
19 Forthcoming message
21 Exper. knowledge
24 Boy
25 Bother
26 Zig___
27 Woodcutting tool
29 Sale notices
30 Unruly crowd
31 Cold keeper
34 Madonna ___
37 Spring month
38 Palestinian southland (Deut. 1:1)
40 Overjoyed
41 Belief and ritual sys.
43 Crusader ___ Bryant
45 Jesus cousin, the ___ :abbr. (Matt. 3:1)
46 Plead
47 Astronaut ___ Armstrong
49 Cast ballot
50 Hotels (Josh. 2:1)
51 Animal traps
54 Secured

(Solution on p. 219)

MISSIONS

ACROSS

1 Go ___-free
5 Cape ___ , Mass.
8 Policeman
11 Book part
12 O.T. farmer prophet: abbr. (Luke 3:25)
13 Oil of ___
15 Small offshore land
16 Hallucinogenic drug
17 Socially inept person
18 Dawson Trotman's organization
21 One hundred and two
22 Needle hole
23 Waif (Job 6:27)
26 U.S.'s southern neighbor
30 College sports org.
31 Affirmative
32 Upland, Ind., Christian college
35 Entertainer
37 Falsify
38 Gun group
39 Preparing people for the gospel
46 "You must be ___ again" (John 3:7)
47 "The Raven" author Edgar Allan ___
48 Mental image
49 Gulp
50 English as a Second Language
51 Last letters
52 Understand
53 Concl.
54 Football team members

DOWN

1 Expectorate
2 Cold, hard ___
3 Gawk
4 David Wilkerson's org.
5 Geneva Reformer John ___
6 Oriental Mission Soc., Intl.
7 Bumper cars game
8 Adapting church to culture
9 Margarine
10 TV entertainer Jack ___
14 Football team's gain
19 Athletes in Action
20 "___ , matey"
23 Gr. Lake
24 Communications giant
25 Wages
27 Uncle Sam's collector
28 Signal
29 "Jesus Calls Us ___ the Tumult" (hymn)
33 Overhead injection valves
34 Follows sower and waterer (John 4:36)
35 Guardian ___ (Heb. 1:14)
36 Master of Relig. Educ.
39 TV channel
40 Columns' counterparts
41 Great Lake
42 Scent sensor
43 Same, for short
44 God's Word planted (1 Cor. 3:6)
45 Catholic celebration of Christ's sacrifice

(Solution on p. 215)

AT THE CROSS

ACROSS

1 Chooses
5 Large African lake
9 Lummox: slang
13 Inconsequential
14 Horse and dog are two kinds (Isa. 21:4)
16 Ready to eat
17 Quickly
18 Big Blue's small computer
19 Flying service
20 Pay for sin (John 6:51)
22 Morally right
24 Hit golf ball
26 Jesus' grandfather (Luke 3:23)
27 Drink offered Christ on cross (Ps. 69:21)
30 Organized crime syndicate
34 State with conviction
35 River in Germany
38 Sweet potatoes
39 Physician: fam.
40 Diseased animal
41 Water source
42 Greatly annoys
44 Revise a manuscript
45 Bank teller's workplace
46 Organized (Acts 24:14)
48 Bloated (Deut. 8:4)
51 Housetop
53 Fear expression: slang
54 Crooks (Luke 19:46)
57 Evenly separated (Josh. 3:4)
61 Hack away

62 Cognizant
64 Author of large topical Bible, Orville ___
65 Asked
66 Horizontal
67 Pennsylvania's northern seaport
68 Stockholm's lang.
69 Depend on
70 Old writing tool (Isa. 42:3)

DOWN

1 ___ Khayyam
2 Stance
3 Horned hopper
4 First pope? 2 wds.
5 Sevastopol's region
6 O.T. minor prophet
7 Peak
8 Sound result
9 Mob's cry to Pilate re. Christ (Matt. 27:22)
10 *Mona* ___
11 October birthstone
12 Meaning, in brief
15 Plotted (Judg. 9:3)
21 Brainwave test
23 Intl. Lit. Award
25 Great fear
27 *Quo* ___
28 Tusk material
29 Head holders? (Ps. 18:38)
31 Deadly
32 Man was made in God's ___ (Gen. 5:3)

33 Col. ski resort
36 Jerry Falwell's school init.
37 Itsy-___
40 Taking away (Lev. 14:40)
43 Lined (Deut. 25:1)
45 Vacuum or street, for example
47 End of entry: comp.
49 Intelligently
50 On the other side, in brief
52 Lesser number
54 Defrost
55 ___ and seek
56 "[Jesus] will ___ his people from their sins" (Matt. 1:21)
58 Special solicitude
59 Popular Christian female vocalist
60 Property title
61 Major network
63 Connected in some way: abbr.

(Solution on p. 215)

WHAT THEY DID THEN

ACROSS

1 Quartzlike gem
5 Jesus' first public miracle (John 2:3)
9 Sex seller (Judg. 11:2)
14 Rabbit fur
15 Worship object
16 Unverified news
17 Nashville's state.
18 Colorants
19 Incensed
20 Matthew and his ilk (Matt. 10:3)
23 Wise bird
24 Egg layer
25 Rechargeable batteries
29 From a distance
31 Rural address
34 Skunk's distinctive
35 Contrary to: slang
36 C. S. Lewis's ___ Christianity
37 Ezra's occupation (Ezra 7:10)
39 Oh, nuts!
40 Left, right, passing, etc.
41 IX
42 "Female" suffix
43 Musicians ___ and CeCe Winans
44 Clumsy
46 Powder and beer are two
47 Richard Helms's agency
48 Temple merchants (Matt. 21:12)
55 Boneless
56 Solid
57 Church head
59 Model of perfection (1 Thess. 4:2)
60 Environmental rel.
61 Mountain goat
62 Two-electrode tube
63 Every seven days
64 Relinquish

DOWN

1 Columbus Day mo.
2 Burns and frost, for example
3 Mexican ruler Santa ___
4 Tufted-eared cat
5 Leftover lines (Exod. 22:22)
6 Romantic interlude
7 "The First ___ the Angels Did Say" (hymn)
8 Do this or ___
9 Hemingway or Melville, for ex. (Ps. 45:1)
10 Great Lake
11 ___ of Khayyam
12 Decays
13 "Lo, How a Rose ___ Blooming" (hymn)
21 Pay on receipt
22 Gregorian ___
25 Cathedral at ___ Dame
26 Concepts
27 Paint layers (Lev. 10:5)
28 Jumps gap
29 In the past: arch.
30 Played with bugle and drum
31 Turned on again
32 Haydn or Liszt
33 Decimal system maker
35 Yassir Arafat is one (Neh. 6:1)
36 Waiter's tool?
38 Belated tribute
43 Horny-winged insect
44 Helpful and friendly (Gen. 50:21)
45 Delay
46 Work dough (Jer. 7:18)
47 Christmas sing
48 Multimedia std: comp.
49 Bread spread
50 Masticate
51 Cabby
52 Monumental saga
53 J. D. Douglas novel, The ___ (Gen. 37:23)
54 Drove fast
55 Topmast support
58 Binary code designation: comp.

(Solution on p. 215)

CATHOLIC CHURCH

ACROSS

1 ___ Presley
6 Ticketed
11 Jewish title of respect
14 The ___ Mutiny
15 Sneeze sound
16 Pindar's or Horace's type of poetry
17 Catholic order of educators and missionaries
19 Mama ___: Ital.
20 Supplement
21 Choose by ballot (2 Sam. 3:21)
22 Taken ___ (shocked)
24 Strangely
26 Instruments (Matt. 21:34)
27 What's most important (Prov. 22:5)
29 Fix in the midst
31 Golf clubs
32 Irregular splotches
33 Suction, for short
36 Animal's father
37 Expensive
38 Circular band of light (Ezek. 1:28)
39 S and P's highest bond rating
40 Largest blood vessel
41 Necessary for life
42 Twenty years
43 Specify distinctly
44 Body of Christ (Eph. 4:12)
47 Anticeptic acid
48 Spooky
49 Port-au-Prince's country
51 Athletes in Action
54 Seize
55 Reformation denominations
58 Tenn. Valley Auth.
59 Judah's daughter-in-law (Gen. 38:6)
60 Assumed name
61 Words meaning the same: abbr.
62 Gives off
63 Don't cry over ___ milk

DOWN

1 Evangelical Council on Financial Accountability
2 Edible blubber
3 Jesus' route to Calvary: var.
4 Where there was no room for Mary (Luke 2:7)
5 Withdraws from union
6 "___ at the Bat"
7 Carl McIntyre's fundamentalist group
8 The one indicated
9 Long time
10 Prescribed drug amounts
11 Pilate's and Paul's nationality (Matt. 27:2)
12 Royal decree
13 Birds' mouths (Gen. 8:11)
18 Troubles
23 Foundation
25 Sandpile
26 Art patron ___ Aldrich Rockefeller
27 Charge card
28 Vocal solo with instr. acc.
29 Above the rest
30 Puerto Rican city
32 Chilled sound
33 Catholic reformation council
34 Senator ___ Cranston
35 Amer. composer ___ Porter
37 Winnie-the-___
38 Stereo system
40 Receives (Deut. 20:11)
41 Truth: Lat.
42 ___ Lanka
43 Domino markings
44 Pennies
45 Weighty
46 Metropolitan
47 Coffin stands
49 ___ sweet ___
50 Jacob's funeral site (Gen. 50:10)
52 Denotes slanted type
53 Helper, for short (Gen. 42:30)
56 Cheerleaders' cry
57 Swiss mt.

(Solution on p. 215)

SPECIAL DAYS

ACROSS

1 Take hold suddenly (Exod. 4:4)
5 Eucharist celebration
9 Study for final exams
13 Crazy: slang
14 Catastrophe in Noah's time (Gen. 6:17)
16 Stun
17 Part of 50th state
18 Shotgun or .22
19 Incentive
20 Small brownish birds with upright tails
22 Headquartered
24 Hebrews' homeland: abbr. (Gen. 32:32)
25 December 25: 2 wds.
28 Automobile pioneers Charles and James ___
31 "Beautiful ___ of Somewhere"
32 Geologic era
33 Formal. org. grp.
36 Top Boy Scout rank (Ezek. 17:3)
40 Cole___ (salad)
42 Chopped (Gen. 27:40)
44 Roman historian Titus ___
45 Sales-pitched
47 Hemmed in
49 Compete
50 Pocket bread
52 Virgil's epic The ___
54 Christ's resurrection celebration: 2 wds.
59 Organization's executives: abbr.
60 Ownership proof
61 Poorly matched components: comp.
65 Meter maker? (Acts 17:28)
67 Waterproofing material (Isa. 34:9)
69 Verbal
70 Genealogy
71 Hooded coat
72 Aswan Dam's river (Gen. 41:1)
73 Ivy League seminary
74 Author Ogden ___
75 Bilk or scheme

DOWN

1 "Let your good deeds ___ for all to see" (Matt. 5:16)
2 Sound of Niagara Falls
3 Deep yearning
4 Overly lively
5 Mass maker, for short?
6 Excuse
7 Couches
8 Seasons of the sun
9 Smaller "records"
10 ___ transit (public)
11 Free Methodists' ___-Pacific College
12 Happy (Ps. 68:3)
15 Considers
21 N.Y. Mets' ___ Stadium
23 ___ Evans Rogers
26 Diaper disease
27 Anti-leaker
28 Short, fast run
29 Hideous
30 Harvest crop (Exod. 23:10)
34 Johann ___ Bach
35 Be indebted
37 Present
38 57
39 Spotted (Mark 16:10)
41 Bibles shortest verse, "Jesus ___" (John 11:35, KJV)
43 Inoperative (Gen. 20:3)
46 Eating plan
48 Malaysian hardwood
51 S. Dakota county
53 Woman's leg coverings
54 Void of contents (Gen. 8:18)
55 Jewish currency unit
56 Brace for action
57 Extremist
58 Makes out: slang (Josh. 10:24)
62 Waste acid
63 Fete affair
64 Grades K-6: abbr.
66 Pipe connector
68 Ridicule expression: slang

(Solution on p. 215)

BOOK OF BOOKS

The crossword grid (numbered cells as shown).

ACROSS

1 Eve's husband (Gen. 4:1)
5 Water-based resorts
9 Wash the deck
13 Sound sheep made
15 Three o'clock on compass (Gen. 2:8)
16 Jumping ___ stick
17 Numbered reference
19 Sphere
20 Jerry Pournelle's type of novel: abbr.
21 Piston chamber
23 Swindle
25 TV's predecessor
26 Threatening
30 Coral shelves
32 Lover; friend: Fr.
33 Where Saul consulted a medium
35 Islam's supreme being
37 Radio personality ___ Hutchcraft
38 Sure loser
40 Anger
41 Boils inside (Gen. 25:29)
44 Carried on, as a battle
46 Plane crash investigator
47 Group psyche
49 Stock payments
51 Saudi Arabia's southern neighbor
53 Venerated wise man (Gen. 41:8)
54 Cushioned (Ps. 65:10)
57 Turned all to gold
60 Death notice, for short
61 God's Word (2 Chron. 17:9)
64 "God is ___" (1 John 4:8)
65 Lust: Gr.
66 Burn with water
67 Buck or doe (Deut. 12:15)
68 Second year college, for short
69 Look-up lists, in brief

DOWN

1 Shortened form, for short
2 Speaker's platform
3 Accrediting Assoc. of Bible Colleges
4 Small island near Sicily (Acts 28:1, KJV)
5 Visualize
6 Palo Alto Research Center: comp.
7 Nineveh's country: abbr. (2 Kings 15:29)
8 Outstanding, as a performance
9 Cocker, for one
10 Jack Wyrtzen's organization (Phil. 2:16)
11 Let Us Now Praise Famous Men author James ___
12 Wild pig
14 Maliciously mar
18 Norwegian seafarer
22 Brainstorm
24 Establish a perpetual fund
26 Red planet
27 Express theatrically
28 Number of theses Luther nailed to door
29 Reproductive gland
31 Plastic wrap brand
34 Colleges in Denver, Col., and Weston, Maine
36 Company CEO
39 Overhaul
42 Appetite enhancer
43 Not all
45 Fingers
48 People have five
50 Subtract
52 "Death-related" prefix
54 Auctioneer's final shout (Gen. 37:28)
55 Woodwind instrument
56 Let loose
58 Descendants of Abraham through Ishmael (Neh. 6:1)
59 Market
62 "Related" suffix
63 Students for a Democratic Society

(Solution on p. 215)

BEST-SELLER

ACROSS

1 Gentle (James 3:8)
5 Talk to God (James 5:16)
9 Traveled in water
13 Company official, for short
14 Certain
15 Greek fatalist
16 Classic English Bible: 2 wds.
18 ___-cotta, as tile
19 Org. of Amer. States
20 Mass officiants' robes
21 Blatantly
22 Huntsville's state
24 Violin's lower relative
25 Tax collector
26 English Bible translator, John
    ___
29 Miracles (Heb. 2:4)
32 Supports (Gen. 44:11)
33 Chat casually
34 Stigma
35 Train tracks
36 Puerto Rican territory
37 Tenth mo.
38 Set of connected
    rooms
39 Mr. Castro
40 God's book: 2 wds.
42 Yearly remembrance: abbr.
43 Christmas carols
44 Ordinance (Exod. 15:25, KJV)
48 Humble
49 Fraud scheme
50 ___ Shamra tablets
51 Favored by God (Luke 1:48)
52 Speech sound science
54 Main blood artery
55 Suitable
56 Gather leaves
57 Pedestals
58 Scheduled mtg. (1 Sam. 18:5)
59 Reasons

DOWN

1 Prophet Amos's hometown
   (Neh. 3:5)
2 Centerline related
3 High IQ org.
4 Heart rhythm strip
5 Bible's longest book (Luke
   20:42)
6 Cuban dance
7 Mars
8 True
9 "Latin star" prefix
10 Scriptures: 3 wds. (Isa. 8:20)
11 Light and cheery
12 Communications giant
15 Bogs down (Dan. 2:8)
17 Jungle Aviation and Radio Service
21 English Bible popular with
   Lutherans
23 Storage receptacles
24 Come around again
26 Anglican Mideast envoy
   Terry ___
27 Countenance
28 Mt. Gerizim's twin (Deut. 11:30)
29 Chimney dirt (Lam. 4:8)
30 Foot part
31 Movable type inventor
   Johann ___
32 Gets out on guarantee
35 Russian currency
36 Coin maker
38 Spaniard's repose
39 Picture border
41 Crows
42 Phone giant
44 Dip
45 Bathsheba's husband (2 Sam.
   11:3)
46 Quite outmoded
47 Satisfactory report marks
48 Healing plant
49 Woodworking class
51 Remainder, for short
52 Golf org.
53 Communications giant

(Solution on p. 216)

SECOND PERSON

ACROSS

1 Safety agency
5 Army rank: abbr. (Gen. 37:36)
9 ___ du lieber: Ger.
13 Hint
14 Colors
15 Woodwinds
16 Relief bringer (John 15:26)
18 Hen sound
19 News service
20 Stringed instr.
21 Reeked
22 Correct, as a grievance
24 Silky fiber
25 Actor Mr. Carney
26 17 O.T. books (2 Pet. 3:2)
29 Denom. grps.
32 Caribbean island
33 Once around the track
34 Cambodia's neighbor
35 One of 26-across (Judg. 17:1)
36 Dalmatian cold wind
37 Service branch
38 After ocean or shelf
39 Concerns
40 Discloser (Dan. 2:47)
42 Clear, in brief
43 Rustic life poems
44 Billy Graham meeting
48 ___ and Me! video series
49 Fatless
50 Hem in
51 Provide what's wished
52 Third person of the Trinity
   (Matt. 1:18, KJV)
54 Casket stands (Luke 7:14, KJV)
55 Hay form
56 State with conviction
57 Totals
58 Scent
59 Flattop

DOWN

1 Happen
2 Hill
3 Damp
4 African Evangelical Fellowship
5 Second Person of the Trinity
   (Ps. 2:2)
6 Cars
7 Fruit skin
8 Ready-to-run pgm.: comp.
9 Embarrassment sign: 2 wds.
10 Adviser (Rom. 11:34)
11 Euphemism for Satan's abode
12 Chore, for short
15 Eight-tentacled creatures
17 Follows left or turn
21 Indolence
23 Mice relatives
24 Monk
26 Floor walker
27 Ripped (2 Sam. 13:31, KJV)
28 Resorts
29 Disparage
30 Relieve
31 Proven guilty (Mark 15:7)
32 Oregon city
35 ___ Bornes
36 Forbids
38 Cake sections
39 Hung on
41 Border trimmers
42 Intercession (Phil. 1:9)
44 Stringed instrument
45 On top
46 Drug amounts
47 Additional
48 Household helper
49 Burden
51 Bookstore org.
52 Movie channel
53 Noah's son

(Solution on p. 216)

CHRISTIAN SERVICE

ACROSS

1 "___ a story to tell to the nations" (hymn)
5 Extended family
9 King Saul's family name (1 Sam. 10:21, KJV)
14 Ice-ball precipitation
15 Jesus' new commandment to his disciples (John 13:34)
16 "Help me to ___ all crooked deals" (Ps. 101:3)
17 Therefore
18 "The good man returns what he ___" (Ps. 37:21)
19 Excite to activity
20 Apply consecrated oil and prayer (2 Kings 9:6)
22 Pig pen
24 "God . . . ___ sorrow in our lives" (2 Cor. 7:10)
25 "Pop-up" program: comp.
26 Surprise discovery expression
28 Planted seed
30 Regions
32 Where 12 spies reported on Canaan (Num. 13:26)
36 The man after God's own heart (Acts 13:22)
39 Parts to play
41 Female deer
42 Always
43 Regally attired
44 Punishment place
45 Bartok or Le Gallienne
46 "They that wait upon the Lord shall ___ their strength (Isa. 40:31)
47 Harmonized
48 Conservative seminary named for Texas city
50 Tigris, for one
52 Insects displaying wisdom and discipline (Prov. 6:6)
54 Male or female
55 O.T. praise bk.
58 Animal name given Jesus (John 1:36)
61 "Joint heirs with Jesus as we travel this ___" (chorus)
63 "Be ___ in the Lord, and in the power of his might" (Eph. 6:10, KJV)
65 Two to one
67 Brief reposes
69 Unauthorized breach of duty: mil.
70 Severe and solid (Matt. 1:19)
71 Adhere
72 Follows am or Point-au-
73 Nervous and uptight
74 Market
75 ___ of Knowledge or of Life

DOWN

1 Whole or cracked (Acts 27:38)
2 Merits
3 Intensity
4 One of Jesus' "seven last words" (Mark 15:34, KJV)
5 Dress
6 Moo (1 Sam. 6:12)
7 Suburban sts.
8 Straw hatcheries?
9 Damage or deface (Ruth 4:6, KJV)
10 Be plentiful
11 Consequently
12 "Jesus ___ from the dead" (Acts 2:32)
13 Indignations
21 What Mary poured on Jesus' feet (John 12:3)
23 Pulled together (1 Sam. 6:7)
27 Golden calf maker (Exod. 32:4)
29 "In the beginning ___ the Word" (John 1:1, KJV)
30 Ventilate
31 Earnest and temperate
33 Where work began (Gen. 2:8)
34 Dover flatfish
35 Contained
36 Exploit
37 Assoc. of Vocal and Video Artists
38 Young calf meat
40 C. S. or Carroll
43 Depends confidently on
44 Ben ___
46 Operated
47 Sermon starter
49 Efforts
51 Ship or tube
53 Psalms, hymns, and ___ (Eph. 5:19)
55 "Pray in the ___ and strength of the Holy Spirit" (Jude 1:20)
56 Night sound
57 One song for male voices: 2 wds. (Lam. 3:63)
58 Intense longing
59 Before lope or meridian
60 Appearance
62 Mr. Carnegie or ___ Evans
64 Engrossed
66 Compass direction (about one o'clock)
68 Assyrian king (1 Chron. 5:26)

(Solution on p. 216)

MATCH MATES

ACROSS

1 Emerge from egg (1 Kings 20:11)
6 Raised
11 Tire pressure
14 Marketplace: Gr.
15 Artists Uccello or Veronese
16 One: Ger.
17 Jacob's daughter (Gen. 46:15)
18 Embellished with needlework (Exod. 28:4, KJV)
20 Mary's aunt (Luke 1:36)
22 Palestinian fruit tree (Rom. 11:17)
23 Scribe, for short
24 "I ___ do all things through Christ" (Phil. 4:13, KJV)
25 Contract a muscle
26 Withered
30 Magna ___
34 Glow (Exod. 34:30)
39 Something in common
42 O.T. hymnbook
43 Eating surface
45 Weaker
46 Relies
49 Eye shutter
53 Teachers' org.
54 Habitually carry
58 Tractor-trailer rigs
60 Uriah's wife (2 Sam. 11:3)
62 Job hopeful
64 Gold weight
65 Pub drink
66 Quietness (Exod. 18:23)
67 ___ in Wonderland
68 Papyrus storage jar, for short
69 Sandaled, for ex.
70 Stinks

DOWN

1 Place of the dead (Matt. 16:18, NIV)
2 Nimble
3 Elixir (1 Tim. 4:8)
4 Loony
5 Laughter
6 Cheerful
7 Co-owner (John 13:8)
8 Disdain expression
9 Cotton gin inventor ___ Whitney (1 Sam. 1:3)
10 Stupid person: slang
11 Danger
12 Strainer (Amos 9:9)
13 Subject locator
19 Bad fairy
21 Before Christian era
26 Faded (Dan. 1:10)
27 Talk freely
28 Educator's adv. deg.
29 Calls a number
30 Portable bed
31 Samoa's national plant
32 Johnny ___ (Confederate soldier)
33 Path, in brief
35 ___ carte menu
36 N.T. manuscript: abbr.
37 Bee's follower
38 "To ___ is human"
40 Consumed
41 Soda
44 Act of contrition (Isa. 58:3)
47 Grossed
48 Morse code dash
49 Rebekah's husband (Gen. 25:20)
50 Answer
51 Spur forward
52 Summer Institute of Linguistics
54 Jonah's "submarine" (Ps. 104:26)
55 Spooky
56 Without adequate preparation; taken ___
57 Tariffs (Ps. 15:5)
59 Small drinks
60 Jezebel's god
61 Lingering damage sign
63 Company head

(Solution on p. 216)

DOUBLE SON

ACROSS

1 Heart sounds (Ps. 38:10)
6 Grassy cloistered quadrangle
11 Number cruncher
14 Journey: 2 wds.
15 Wary
16 Chop
17 Title of Jesus: 4 wds. (Matt. 14:33)
19 Seed-bearing spike
20 Egg layer
21 Bill
22 Witchcraft (Rev. 18:23)
24 Time frame
25 Falsified (Gen. 18:15)
27 Acne scar
28 ___ and the Dragon (apoc. book)
29 Honest ___ Lincoln
31 Same: Latin citation
34 Sheep pens
37 In among
38 Optical character recognition: comp.
39 Pinnacles: abbr.
40 Emergency measure
41 Slender rowboat
43 Anger
44 Peeved
45 Alter
46 Christian singer ___ Winans
48 Multiple compilers, for short
49 News service
50 Latin hour
52 Cookie containers, for ex.
54 Everyone
57 Flawless title of Jesus (Heb. 7:28)
60 Write quickly
61 ___ volente (God willing)
62 Overseas Crusades, Inc.
63 Title of Jesus: 4 wds. (John 5:27)
66 Hesitation expressions
67 Stretch
68 Simple (Prov. 8:4)
69 Small child
70 Penn. senator ___ Hatch
71 Go in

DOWN

1 Go swimming (Exod. 2:5)
2 Airwaves
3 Stadium, for one
4 "___ the season to be jolly" (carol)
5 Unblemished title of Jesus (1 Tim. 3:16)
6 Earth
7 African Evangelical Fellowship
8 From ___ to riches
9 Marched (Josh. 11:8)
10 "Water" prefix
11 Face part
12 Fruit and shape
13 Wrong
18 Crucifixion tool (John 20:25)
23 Christian Camping Intl.
26 Most moist
28 Wager
30 Cardinal, for ex.
32 Religious image
33 ___ Scott case
34 Fashionable
35 Mean monster
36 Title of Jesus: 2 wds. (Matt. 16:16)
37 Mastered
41 Title of Jesus (Acts 4:11)
42 Doctors' org.
44 Title of Jesus (John 8:4)
47 End of file: comp.
49 Soon
51 "Back" prefix
53 N.T. book: 2 wds.
54 Confess (Job 6:30)
55 Absent without ___ (AWOL)
56 Isolationist
57 Mope (Ps. 106:25)
58 Reflect back
59 Eye water
64 Empirical study, in brief
65 Air stirrer

(Solution on p. 216)

BIBLE PEOPLE

ACROSS

1 Fuss
4 Face off
8 Egyptian fertility goddess
12 *My ___* by Nancy Reagan
14 Chart
15 Hex. sign
16 Subject specialty
17 Walking pole
18 Surrounds saints (Ezek. 1:27)
19 O.T. judge, poet, and prophetess (Judg. 4:4)
21 Killed 600 Philistines with an ox goad (Judg. 3:31)
23 The ___ of the story
25 Shimei's father (1 Kings 4:18)
26 ___ *accompli*
28 At this time
30 The big fisherman (Matt. 4:18)
34 Bible's strongest man (Judg. 16:12)
36 Precedes *ter* or *too* (Lev. 19:28)
38 Jesus' cry from cross (Mark 15:34)
39 All human blood types
40 Smuggled
42 Computer's volatile memory
44 Mutual Broadcasting Sys.
45 Officers' hangout
47 Extra car rental coverage (1 Chron. 1:50)
49 Concubine of King Saul (2 Sam. 3:7)
51 Daughter of Asher (Gen. 46:17)

53 Priest in Samuel's time (1 Sam. 1:9)
55 Devil's name and character (John 8:44, KJV)
56 Boone or Robertson
58 Bell stroke
60 Governor who condemned Christ (Acts 4:27)
64 Christian stoned to death (Acts 7:59)
68 Jai ___ (game)
69 Common computer language
71 Helper
72 Usu. four to a table
73 Drunkard: 2 wds.
74 Esther's palace caretaker (Esther 2:3, KJV)
75 ___ and found dept.
76 40-day penitence period
77 Circuit indicator light: acron.

DOWN

1 Small amount, such as seasoning: 2 wds. (Gen. 50:10)
2 Last (Matt. 13:21, KJV)
3 Zeeb's Midianite cogeneral (Judg. 7:25)
4 Abiram's co-conspirator against Moses (Num. 16:12)
5 Before *quitous*
6 Building extensions to sides
7 Memory's "bottomless pit"
8 Abraham's first son (Gen. 16:15)
9 For males only
10 Allen, Kan., county seat

11 "Single-celled" prefix
13 Boaz was a relative of ___ husband (Ruth 2:3)
14 Nicholas of Russia, for one
20 What disk brake grabs
22 Before *ha* and *habet*
24 Fate
26 Aesop story
27 Love affair
29 Tolstoy's ___ *and Peace*
31 Central Florida city
32 Cause self-consciousness: abbr.
33 Foolishly hasty
34 Cysts
35 Soft fuzzy surface
37 Noah's ship sealant (Gen. 6:14)
41 Scot's denial
43 Cecil B. de___ (Greatest Show on Earth)
46 John the ___
48 Kind
50 Mothered two of Jacob's sons (Gen. 35:26)
52 Abraham's second altar site (Gen. 12:8, KJV)
54 Firmly demand
57 Foundry founder ___-cain (Gen. 4:22)
59 Impress deeply
60 Type of bearer (Isa. 25:7)
61 Margarine
62 Old horses
63 Bargain
65 Jericho's rebuilder (1 Kings 16:34)
66 Advantage
67 Require
70 Minicomputer maker ___ Microsystems

(Solution on p. 216)

MINOR PROPHETS

ACROSS

1 "Do ____ ____ about these things; disgrace will not overtake us" (Mic. 2:6, NIV)
10 Cheer
11 Age
12 Compete
13 Invent
15 A denomination
16 Bro's sib.
17 Shakes
18 Rind
20 Clay
22 Sound booster, for short
23 Corn bearer
24 Proper
26 Obadiah's target
28 Where Tibet and Taiwan are
29 Former surgeon general
30 A sandwich (abbr.)
31 Rends
32 "Daniel resolved not to ____ himself with the royal food and wine" (Dan. 1:8, NIV)
35 Leatherworker's tool
36 "But you brought my life up from the ____" (Jon. 2:6, NIV)
37 U.S. teachers' org. (abbr.)
38 "Who knows? God may yet relent and ... turn from his ____ ____" (Jon. 3:9)

DOWN

1 Nuclear watchdog (abbr.)
2 Paddle
3 "____ ____ say, 'The time has not yet come for the Lord's house to be built'" (Hag. 1:2)
4 Soaks
5 Where Salem, Sisters, and Bend are (abbr.)
6 His day's in June
7 "O Lord, are you not from ____?" (Hab. 1:12, NIV)
8 "For I know how many are your offenses and how great your ____" (Amos 5:12, NIV)
9 Aye
14 Suffer
15 Asphalt
17 Punch
18 Average
19 Dorothy's aunt
20 Her day's in May
21 When you think they'll get there: abbr.
23 Robber's nemesis
25 Magnum was one: abbr.
27 They're more positive than don'ts
28 TV critter from space
29 New Zealander
30 Greek letter
31 Org. for British fliers (abbr.)
32 "Jeroboam will ____ by the sword" (Amos 7:11, NIV)
33 Confederate general
34 The part that gives audience
36 An IBM-compatible 386 or a Macintosh: abbr.

(Solution on p. 216)

1 & 2 TIMOTHY

ACROSS

1 Talk back
5 FBI Agents
9 Monogram for famed circus man
12 Actor Baldwin or Guinness
13 Individual
14 Regret
15 "Some people, eager for money, have wandered from the faith and ____ themselves with many griefs" (1 Tim. 6:10, NIV)
17 The love of money, acc. to 1 Tim. 6:10 and others
19 What Exxon and Shell sell
20 An opinion, when voiced
21 "Thou ____ not . . ."
24 One who is doomed
26 This bird gets the worm
27 Fall behind
28 Little demon
31 Semis
32 Each
33 To make fast or make official
34 Winter bug
35 Teflon wearer
36 First lines
37 Posts
39 Played (with)
40 Neat-o
42 Scripture: abbr.
43 A kind of music foreign to Schönberg
44 Where Timothy served
48 What the Rijks, Tate, or MOMA show
49 Church hall
51 Trick
52 What apts. have
53 Woodwind
54 Have a ____

DOWN

1 Tree blood
2 Champ boxer
3 Espy
4 "When you come, bring the cloak . . . and my ____, especially the parchments" (2 Tim. 4:13, NIV)
5 What a guzzler needs
6 Last word
7 Charles's lady
8 Violin or cello
9 "If they continue in faith, love and holiness with ____" (1 Tim. 2:15, NIV)
10 Attire for Martha Graham's students
11 "Do your ____ to present yourself to God as one approved" (2 Tim. 2:15, NIV)
16 Madison, Lincoln, or Cleveland
18 "A deacon must be the husband of but ____ wife" (1 Tim. 3:12, NIV)
21 Medieval underling
22 Greet
23 "Don't have anything to do with foolish and stupid ____" (2 Tim. 2:23, NIV)
24 Wooded alcoves
25 Paddle
29 Stallion's mate
30 Go slowly
32 Buddy
33 Those who sleep loudly
35 "The church of the living God, the ____ and foundation of the truth" (1 Tim. 3:15, NIV)
36 Yen
38 In the fashion of (2 wds.)
40 Famous performer
41 Bait, sometimes
42 Went 75 mph
44 Direction from Rome to Jerusalem: abbr.
45 Litigate
46 Country that owns Guam: abbr.
47 TV or dining room ensemble
50 Gym class: abbr.

(Solution on p. 216)

JUDE

ACROSS

1 Attend
5 Gist
8 Spur
12 Much (2 wds.)
13 Best-selling Christian novelist Janette ____
14 At a time
15 "...for whom blackest darkness has been ____ forever" (Jude 1:13, NIV)
17 Burner
18 Threesome
19 "They have ____ for profit into Balaam's error" (Jude 1:11, NIV)
21 Actress Madeleine and her namesakes
23 French math man Auguste
24 In the tub?
25 Alley's pal
26 Lump
29 Tablet
30 Every American's uncle
31 A Guthrie
32 It's for horses
33 What an RN offers: abbr.
34 A look of contempt
35 Rise to the top
37 Maxim
38 Wax marker
40 Pinball error message
41 Samson's strength supply
42 Get out of the way
46 Before, prefix
47 A Gabor
48 Spanish unit of length
49 Cheers
50 The rich young ruler: abbr.
51 One who examines

DOWN

1 Colt or Mustang
2 Matador's cheer
3 "Build yourselves up in your ____ ____ ____" (Jude 1:20, NIV)
4 "The punishment of ____ fire" (Jude 1:7, NIV)
5 New, prefix
6 Hawaiian instrument, for short
7 Boudoir
8 "Whither thou ____ , I will go" (Ruth 1:16, KJV)
9 "Bound with everlasting chains for judgment ____ ____ ____ ____" (Jude 1:6, NIV)
10 Skin disease
11 Having kicked the bucket
16 Danger
20 He calls strikes
21 Hebrew letter
22 Continent
23 Work along with another agent
27 Designer Cassini
28 Carried
30 "These dreamers ... reject authority and ____ celestial beings" (Jude 1:8, NIV)
31 "Mercy, peace ____ ____ be yours in abundance" (Jude 1:2, NIV)
33 As well
34 Ride the wind
36 Stringed instruments
38 Burn
39 Indian princess
40 Peter or Nicholas
43 Vine
44 Grad. school test: abbr.
45 Lend an ____

(Solution on p. 216)

PHILEMON

ACROSS

1 In rectangles, it's height times width
5 Chimp and orangutan
9 He throws flags
12 Units of time
13 Channing musical
14 Direction Onesimus traveled from Rome to Colosse
15 Philemon's runaway slave
17 Distant
18 Object of worship
19 Summer TV fare
20 Rub out
23 Wonderland tourist
25 Crucial artery
26 No ____ intended
27 Writer of a personal ad: abbr.
30 Fluid-bearing pouches
31 Unit of work
32 Where Columbus, Springfield, and Lima are
33 Icelandic letter
34 Hawaiian dish
35 Become tumescent
36 Presses
38 Came to a close
39 Eve's bane, some say
41 Promise
43 Boston orchestra
44 "Onesimus . . . became my son while I was ____ ____"
(Philem. 10, NIV)
48 A bit of money
49 Debtor
50 First sea captain?
51 City trains
52 Golf cry
53 Fool

DOWN

1 Fuss
2 Hied
3 Place for a pupil
4 Gives a hand to
5 Bullets, for short
6 First three words of this epistle (NIV)
7 Type measures
8 Per ____
9 "You, brother, have ____ the hearts of the saints" (Philem. 7, NIV)
10 Abraham's grandson
11 A houseplant
16 Brainstorm
17 Predecessor of NRC
19 First name of TV dog
20 Relaxation
21 Word in Hope-Crosby films
22 "Fellow soldier" (Philem. 2, NIV)
24 Tote
28 Shady wit
29 Lose a game you were winning
31 A period of time
32 "I, Paul, am writing this with my ____ ____" (Philem. 19, NIV)
34 "The Raven" writer
35 A son of Adam
37 Monogram for Kidnapped author
39 Church part
40 Siloam, for one
42 4,840 square yards
44 ____ Jima
45 Promissory note
46 Snooze
47 That lady
49 ____ Mice and Men

166

(Solution on p. 216)

EVANGELISTIC TRIO

ACROSS

1 "____ is unto me, if I preach not the gospel!" (1 Cor. 9:16, KJV)
4 Wicked (Gen. 2:9)
7 Humans' homes: slang
11 Top off
12 Musician ____ Winans
13 Leave out (Lev. 5:16)
14 Evangelist #1 (2 wds., same first name)
17 Matchmakers
18 Arouse
19 Postal code
20 Cotton or hay form
21 Trim skin
23 Nevada city
24 Federal regulator
27 Evangelist #2 (2 wds., same first name)
30 Bachelor of Applied Science
31 Author James ____ (2 Sam. 23:11)
32 Hard and unyielding (Gen. 4:22)
33 Roasting skewer
34 Follows *chick* or *sweet*
35 Value highly (Prov. 22:1)
38 Warning devices
41 Evangelist #3 (2 wds., same first name)
43 Church body: abbr.
44 Not far
45 Intl. Bible Soc.
46 Move sideways
47 Mark
48 Drunkard

DOWN

1 Hybels's church: abbr.
2 Hawaiian island
3 Apostle Paul's coworker (Col. 1:7)
4 Honey makers (Deut. 1:44)
5 Amer. Bible Soc.
6 Bold disregard (2 Kings 19:16)
7 French maidservant
8 All: prefix
9 Food plan
10 Pigpen
12 Contractor, for short
15 Food press
16 Eskimo's home
20 Hem in
21 Toxic benzene compound
22 Surprise expression
23 Military unit (Acts 10:1)
24 Inhabitants of modern Jewish state
25 Dove sound
26 Turner's network
28 Garment's folded front
29 Falsifiers
33 Worsted suit fabric
34 Ship's home
35 ____ *Homo* (Behold the Man)
36 Plated horse feet
37 Strong flavor
38 Festoon
39 Mount where Moses viewed Promised Land (Deut. 32:49)
40 Complete computer: abbr.
42 Salt waters

(Solution on p. 217)

PHILIPPIANS

ACROSS

1 Did the descant
5 ____ Alto
9 Watchdog for community business: abbr.
12 Apple additive
13 Last word
14 Meadow
15 What happens after hurricanes
17 Poetic foot
18 Peddle
19 Cosmetic soap
20 Fruit of the vine
23 Alpine trill (var.)
25 Lubed
26 Cash's "A Boy Named ____"
27 League of Concerned Americans (abbr.)
30 A type of type
31 Big ____, California
32 Prison room
33 Telephone company
34 "And when he had dipped the ____, he gave it to Judas Iscariot" (John 13:26, KJV)
35 Late *TV Guide* writer ____ Stewart
36 Excited (2 wds., slang)
38 Tries
39 Luminous
41 Appear in the future
43 Hang
44 Machinations
48 Newspaper, informally
49 Jacques ____ is alive and well. . . .
50 Alcove
51 They are made of ft.: abbr.
52 Assistant
53 Helen's home

DOWN

1 Pouch
2 Every bit
3 Evangelical organization in the U.S. (abbr.)
4 "[Jesus] . . . did not consider equality with God something to be ____" (Phil. 2:6, NIV)
5 Author of previous epistle
6 "I am ____ ____, now that I have received . . . the gifts you sent" (Phil. 4:18, NIV)
7 ____ *Miserables*
8 "Even death ____ a cross!" (Phil. 2:8, NIV)
9 "So that you may become ____ and pure" (Phil. 2:15, NIV)
10 Judgment seat in Corinth
11 Infant
16 "I know what it is to be in ____" (Phil. 4:12, NIV)
17 Under the weather
19 Drink
20 Mongolian desert
21 Uprising
22 "Christ Jesus . . . for whose sake I have lost ____ ____" (Phil. 3:8, NIV)
24 "But ____ citizenship is in heaven" (Phil. 3:20, NIV)
28 Blood coagulation
29 Swiss peaks
31 Tiny amount
32 A fellow worker (Phil. 4:3)
34 Pigpen
35 It has electrons
37 Ultimate
39 Lively
40 Jesus' place vis-à-vis the church (Col. 1:18)
42 Eye lecherously
44 Follows Thurs: abbr.
45 Or not
46 To an inappropriate degree
47 Heavens
49 College degree

(Solution on p. 217)

GOING PLACES

ACROSS

1 Israel's O.T. neighbor (Gen. 19:37)
5 Miscellaneous information collection
8 Not fem.
12 Precedes *dextrous* and *valence*
13 Hastened
14 Boot-shaped country: abbr.
15 Ship bottom
16 Auto maker
17 French novelist Emile _____
18 Bury securely
20 Barked sharply
22 Number of Hebrew tribes
23 Communications giant
24 Continent S. of Europe (Matt. 27:32)
27 N.T. region N. of Greece (Acts 18:12)
31 Recline
32 Music Television
33 Noah's ark's mount (Gen. 8:4)
37 St. Francis's city
40 Follows *paj* or *Pan*
41 New Year in SE Asia
42 Tropic of _____
45 God's eternal home (Rev. 21:2)
49 Et _____ (and others)
50 File charges against
52 Floor covering
53 Book code
54 Service branch: abbr.
55 At _____! (mil. cmd.)
56 Meddle or pry
57 Distress call
58 Snow glider

DOWN

1 Create
2 Portent (Luke 21:25)
3 Wager (2 wds.)
4 Miss. Gulf city
5 Peninsula in SW Asia
6 Asian–U.S. war site
7 Ancient city of Turkey
8 O.T. benediction site (Gen. 31:49)
9 At uppermost (2 wds.)
10 Reduced price
11 Dressed
19 O.T. prophet: abbr. (Matt. 2:5)
21 Number cruncher, for short
24 Precedes *carte* or *mode*
25 Evergreen tree
26 Rural Electrification Assoc.
28 Lotus's word processor, _____ Pro
29 "You want to sing, _____ fresh like spring" (chorus)
30 Bird, prefix
34 Johnson Wax city
35 Black denomination
36 Saul/Paul's hometown
37 Greek capital
38 Bishop's territory
39 Illinois and Iowa are two
42 Eve's wayward son (Gen. 4:5)
43 Moreover
44 Pen points
46 Flask (1 Sam. 16:1)
47 Otherwise
48 "But my God shall supply all your _____" (Phil. 4:19, KJV)
51 Social service to military

(Solution on p. 217)

ACTS OF THE APOSTLES

ACROSS

1 Islam's founder, to close friends
5 Wagon of old
9 What the gate was in Acts 12:10
13 Object of worship
14 Architect Saarinen and namesakes
16 Angry
17 What Herod intended for church members (Acts 12:1; 3 wds.)
20 Arm straighteners
21 Stadiums
22 Fawn's mom
23 Cut a piece
24 Bugs's delight
28 Seated, prefix
29 Every prep. or transitive vb. should have one
32 Villain in Josh. 7
33 Disappointed
34 Anglo-Irish expletive
35 What the gate did in Acts 12:10 (4 wds.)
38 Forty of these make a furlong
39 Savings accts.
40 Peaceful name
41 Mouths (Lat.)
42 Like ____ ____ of bricks
43 Flats, for short
44 Evil (comb.)
45 Old hand
46 Ancient documents
49 Arouse passion
54 How Herod's admirers described his voice (Acts 12:22; 7 wds.)
57 Unperturbed
58 Painting holder
59 Alliance org.
60 Paris airport
61 Mary's gift (John 12:3)
62 Chemical endings

DOWN

1 Glove
2 Smell
3 New Mexican Indian
4 Actor Guinness
5 Herod was one
6 Pee Wee of the Brooklyn Dodgers
7 Trajectory
8 "Wrap your cloak around ____" (Acts 12:8, NIV)
9 "____ ____ ahead of the competition"
10 Mourning brother in Acts 12:2
11 Region
12 Sleep activities (abbr.)
15 Come to attention (2 wds.)
18 Decorated again
19 Cleveland's lake
23 Peasants
24 Where Sadat ruled
25 Hoffman or Olivier
26 Doorkeeper in Mary's house (Acts 12:13)
27 What Peter does at Mary's door? (Acts 12:13)
28 It's east of Chad
29 Gender-inclusive addendum, often (2 wds.)
30 Sportscaster Musberger
31 The king's victim in Acts 12:2
33 Villain in Acts 12
34 Gillette razor
36 Nitrogen compound
37 Scam
42 Flight, prefix
43 Schwarzeneggar or Benedict
44 Lilliputian
45 Ex-con, at the end of Acts 12
46 Little (Span.)
47 Distant
48 Lose strength
50 Penny, Memory, or Lois
51 "What can ____ ____ give in exchange for his soul?" (Matt. 16:26)
52 A win at chess, for short
53 Seth's son
55 First Lady in the 80s, for short
56 Augustinian's credentials: abbr.

(Solution on p. 216)

VARIOUS DENOMINATIONS

ACROSS

1 Church school Notre ____
5 Brightened star
9 Cadence count
12 "Sing them ____ again to me" (hymn)
13 Currier and ____
14 Tumor, suffix
15 Denomination #1 (2 wds.)
18 Put together to reach conclusion
19 Apocryphal book ____ and the Dragon
20 Ancient harplike instrument (Ps. 33:2)
21 Protestant synod
22 Follows *tight*
24 Ivy League college with seminary
27 Hansom for hire
28 Unaccounted combatant
31 Denomination #2 (3 wds.)
35 English legislators (abbr.)
36 "Morning by morning new mercies I ____" (hymn)
37 ____ mater (nourishing mother)
38 "____ Maria"
39 Bark
41 Freshwater fish
44 Supreme being (Gen. 1:1)
45 News source
48 Denomination #3 (2 wds.)

52 Church teacher's degree
53 Surprise search (1 Sam. 27:10)
54 Ready to pick (Gen. 15:15)
55 Guided
56 Forearm bone
57 Apple or faucet part

DOWN

1 Reformed Church school
2 Solemn promise to God (Gen. 31:13; 2 wds.)
3 Interoffice note
4 Time frame
5 Church council and creed city
6 President's office
7 Animal doctor
8 First Wednesday of Lent (Exod. 27:3)
9 God's pure character (Gen. 2:3)
10 Islamic chief
11 Movement rate
16 News source
17 Not recent
21 Several past popes
22 Active hostility (Gen. 14:2)
23 Goat's hair garment
24 ____ Kippur, Jewish holy day
25 Swiss mt.
26 Part of Mormon name: abbr.
27 Third letter
28 Thickness meas.
29 Doctrinal, suffix
30 Triumph cry

32 NCC USA's Bible
33 Fourth letter
34 Directions
38 Scripture distributor
39 Large Korean church
40 Public notices
41 Plymouth Brethren agency
42 Employ (Lev. 25:50)
43 Consumed
44 Broad smile
45 One (Exod. 26:6)
46 Head of 15-A
47 Same as before (Lat.)
49 Tulsa church school
50 Major carrier
51 Age markers: abbr.

(Solution on p. 217)

ACROSS

1 Mrs. Bush, among friends?
5 Sneeze
10 Scottish assent
13 Fever with chills
14 Hindu deity or Indian bull
16 Apollo's chariot
17 Main characters of these chapters (Acts 13:2; 3 wds.)
20 John Mark to Barnabas, acc. to Col. 4:10
21 ____ Cruces, NM
22 Often, the fat lady who sings
23 Site whence Saul was sent (Acts 13:1)
25 In Acts 15, it was whether Gentiles could be Christians
29 Eye problem
30 Some church members, acc. to Acts 13:1
33 ____ Sajak
35 Box
36 Stool pigeon
37 Apostles' actions (Acts 14:3; 2 wds.)
41 Priestly robe
42 Agrees to
43 Speedwagon
44 The missionaries' message (Acts 13:32; 2 wds.)
46 RR depot: abbr.
48 Famous violin, for short
49 A divided district (Acts 14:1, 4)
53 Trick
56 Huge amount
57 Dir. traveled in Acts 13:14
58 "We should not ____ ____ ____ for the Gentiles" (Acts 15:19, NIV)
63 Pub offering
64 "Saul has slain his thousands, and David his ____ ____ thousands" (1 Sam. 18:7, NIV)
65 A cheese
66 Yang's companion
67 Late-night host Jack and family
68 What some matches are made of

DOWN

1 Russian pastry
2 Once more
3 A kind of offering (Heb. 10:6)
4 Sun Yat-____, Chinese statesman
5 Monastic office
6 Collision
7 "What God promised our fathers he ____ fulfilled for us" (Acts 13:32-33, NIV)
8 The agriculture dept. in Columbus (abbr.)
9 Atlanta arena
10 Abijah's successor (2 Chron. 14:1)
11 "We too are only men, human like ____" (Acts 14:15, NIV)
12 Pipe elbow
15 Dear Abby columns
18 Much (2 wds.)
19 Belt
24 Spanish believer (comb.)
26 Grounds for a suit?
27 Heavenly (comb.)
28 Superlative endings
30 Belonging to actor Donahue?
31 Fragrant waters
32 Asbury Theol. Sem.
33 Captain
34 A lattice of vines and branches
35 Talon
37 Periodicals, for short
38 Passageway
39 A short guitar, for short
40 Hussein foe
45 Risk
46 What a jokester (like those in Acts 13:41) does
47 Brand of home permanent
49 "You intended to harm me, but God intended ____ ____ good" (Gen. 50:20, NIV)
50 Get used to
51 Dark
52 Divvies
54 Rung
55 Writer Ferber
58 "...that you ____ bring salvation to the ends of the earth" (Acts 13:47, NIV)
59 Boxing champ
60 Scope of knowledge
61 It comes before Jer.
62 Dan Rather's co.

(Solution on p. 216)

ACROSS

1 Napoleon's retreat
5 Base runners, usually
8 Alas companion
13 Telegraph wizard
15 The common mkt.
16 Showing ignorance
17 One of Apollos's teachers (Acts 18:26)
19 Actor Edward James ____
20 Paul's assurance (Acts 18:9; 4 wds.)
22 Abraham's wife, for short
23 NRC predecessor
24 A refugee from Italy (Acts 18:2)
29 Stray
30 Baby seal
33 Beyond, prefix
34 Alliance including U.S., Cuba, Haiti, and others
35 Dinner (Lat.)
36 Companions of Paul (Acts 18:5; 3 wds.)
40 Ireland
41 Far out, to eighties kids
42 Moses' dad
43 Vietnamese holiday
44 Withdrawn
45 Where Apollos excelled (Acts 18:28)
46 One ____ time (2 wds.)
47 ____ and feather
49 Paul's encouragement (Acts 18:9; 4 wds.)
56 Benefactor
57 What one couple did for Apollos (Acts 18:26)
59 Sign of life
60 Norma ____: Field vehicle
61 Avarice
62 More clever
63 Where there was no room for Joseph and Mary
64 Being (abbr.)

DOWN

1 Caesar or Charlemagne (abbr.)
2 The one who spoke to Paul in Acts 18:9-10
3 Verve
4 Org.
5 Peach dessert
6 A kind of fisherman
7 College sports org.
8 Fan
9 Flower famous in Lombard, Ill.
10 Hosea's child Lo-____, from the Heb. for "not my people" (Hos. 1:9)
11 Klutz
12 Florida's islands: abbr.
14 Environmental, prefix
18 "____ ____ Girl!"
21 Persian
24 Possession
25 One twentieth of a ream
26 Illuminated from behind or above
27 Where Reza Pahlavi once ruled
28 ____ Vegas
29 Wolf down
30 Christian "rock" group
31 Remove someone's fez
32 "____ ____ that thou owest" (Matt. 18:28, KJV)
34 Bizarre
35 Rooster feature
37 Enlightened Buddhist
38 No vote
39 In finance, Fanny or Ginny's last name
44 Pack rat
45 Bore through (arch.)
46 Win by ____ (2 wds.)
47 Perot or Bush
48 Ski resort
49 Dismal
50 "...he knew ____ the baptism of John" (Acts 18:25, NIV)
51 Half of a thiamine-deficiency disease
52 Fall behind
53 The Emerald Isle
54 Dirs. from Hebron to Jerusalem and from Ephesus to Thyatira
55 Golf needs
56 Dept. of Public Wks.
58 JFK's predecessor

(Solution on p. 217)

BAD GUYS

ACROSS

1 Explosive weapons
6 Derelicts (1 Sam. 1:15)
10 Slipped and ____
14 Be of use (Isa. 22:11)
15 Opposed stance
16 Fifty-seven, rom.
17 Amer. comedian ____ Bruce
18 Portent
19 After concession or million
20 Dry
21 Humor
22 Done to Christ on cross
   (Luke 23:38)
24 Programming language
25 Dog's best friend?
26 Destiny of the wicked (Rev.
   20:14)
27 Scorners (Prov. 21:24)
29 Mined mineral
30 Evil character
33 Tax collector
34 Goes with Gatos or Angeles
35 Cast ballot
36 Deprecate
39 Unhappy
40 God's Word (Ezra 7:10)
41 Moms and ____
42 Steal
43 Fluid-filled "bag"
44 Married, prefix
45 Comrade
46 Two crucified with Christ
   (Matt. 27:44, KJV)

50 Crossbar system
51 Lamprey, for one
52 Anger
53 Drunk: slang (Exod. 19:13)
56 Amer. Medical Assoc.
57 Duration
58 Prolonged unconsciousness
59 Wyatt ____
61 Heart and lung protector
   (Exod. 4:6)
62 Author Leon ____
63 Floating platform
64 Apple slicer
65 Wool eater
66 Talk back
67 Not neat

DOWN

1 Prophet who cursed Hebrews
   (Num. 22:5)
2 Carry to excess
3 A crazy person
4 Hard spot
5 Foxy
6 Washbowls
7 One of a number
8 Called gathering, in brief
9 "While we were yet ____,
   Christ died for us." (Rom. 5:8,
   KJV)
10 Beat with a stick (Isa. 28:27)
11 Wicked
12 Maltese monies
13 Misrepresented the truth
21 Armed aggressions

23 Beer, for example
25 Nothing more or less
26 Street gang member
28 Judas's betrayal act (Luke
   22:48)
30 Crosby or Dylan
31 Ocean: abbr.
32 River in Scotland
34 Drug experiment site
35 Organized crime
36 Tkt.
37 Tavern
38 Personnel or sales, e.g.
39 Convinced
40 Money posted for release
42 Surprise attackers (1 Sam. 13:17)
43 Singer George Beverly ____
45 Before sent or serve
46 Solicits to evil (James 1:13)
47 Snakes (Matt. 23:33)
48 Wipes slate clean
49 Guard
50 Grind teeth
53 Worthless person
54 Mower maker
55 Leave out
56 Dog's sounds
57 Wear it if it fits
60 Motorist's aid assoc.
61 Metric meas.

(Solution on p. 217)

ACROSS

1 "We receive a good income from ____ business" (Acts 19:25, NIV)
5 "They ____ out of that house naked and wounded" (Acts 19:16, KJV)
9 "So do what we ____ you" (Acts 21:23, NIV)
13 Jekyll's alter ego
14 St. ____, a Caribbean island near Barbados
16 A kind of code
17 What the Ephesians did about their evil deeds (Acts 19:18, NIV; 2 wds.)
20 More equipped
21 Frauds
22 Previous to
23 Mademoiselle
24 "Open your eyes and look at the ____! They are ripe for harvest" (John 4:35, NIV)
28 Wily or attractive
29 Dutch airline
32 Not greeted
33 Swelling
34 Altars (Lat.)
35 Paul's charge to the elders (Acts 20:31; NIV; 5 wds.)
38 Chemical endings
39 Wings
40 Draw out
41 German article

42 Wealthy athletes
43 Demetrius and friends (Acts 19)
44 "After I have ____ there, . . . I must visit Rome also" (Acts 19:21, NIV)
45 Visit Aspen
46 Brando's resort
49 Pascal's ruminations
54 Where Eutychus was, for a while (Acts 20:9, NIV; 4 wds.)
57 "Many of them also which used curious ____ brought their books together, and burned them" (Acts 19:19, KJV)
58 "May their table become a ____ and a trap" (Rom. 11:9, NIV)
59 Fire, prefix
60 Optimistic
61 Buck
62 Gnat or little brother

DOWN

1 Norse lightning technician
2 Puff
3 Philosophy
4 "Go; I will ____ you far away to the Gentiles" (Acts 22:21, NIV)
5 Lindros and company
6 Profit
7 Environmental, prefix
8 Hubbub
9 What Paul was given in Acts 20:24 and others like it
10 Gaelic

11 Amorous look
12 People like Eutychus
15 Glue, for one
18 Deceived (2 wds.)
19 Comfortable
23 The M in a criminal's m.o.
24 Welded together
25 Hole-____ - ____
26 Coal
27 Shelters
28 They rush in where angels fear to tread
29 What Hogan might rudely call Schultz
30 A tree
31 Darius and company
33 Hose material
34 Fancy car
36 Sea nymphs
37 Two-man spacecraft
42 Rose, for one
43 Run through
44 Companion of itsy
45 "Savage wolves . . . will not ____ the flock" (Acts 20:29, NIV)
46 Russian ruler in 1800s
47 Flight, prefix
48 Derbies and toques
50 Cut a corner
51 Rim
52 Ages
53 "M*A*S*H's" Loretta
55 Neighbor of Ill.
56 Natl. Assoc. of Evangelicals

CREATURES GREAT AND SMALL

1	2	3	4		5	6	7	8		9	10	11	12
13					14				15		16		
17					18						19		
20				21			22			23			
			24			25		26					
27	28	29							30			31	32	33
34						35	36	37			38		
39					40							41		
42			43		44						45		
46				47				48	49	50			
			51			52		53					
	54	55					56		57			58	59	60
61					62			63			64		
65					66						67		
68						69					70		

ACROSS

1 No longer available (Gen. 31:15)
5 Advertising and distribution dept.
9 Young horse
13 Bangkok's people
14 Famous fable fabricator
16 Great Lake
17 Points to shoot
18 Mix-up
19 Forty days before Easter
20 N.A. lynx
22 Crawler or creeper (Gen. 6:20)
24 Fail to include
26 Registered port of call
27 Fast, flightless bird (Lev. 11:16)
30 Captured on film
34 Falcon cover
35 Relaxation
38 Adam's job with all animals (Gen. 2:20)
39 S.A. country: abbr.
40 Ocean's ins and outs
41 English network
42 Not imagined
44 By mouth
45 Butter substitute
46 Delegate
48 Animal mistreaters
51 Sharp turns
53 Diced meat and potatoes
54 Jonathan Livingston _____ (Lev. 11:16)
57 Jewish Feast of Tabernacles

61 Mule or white-tailed
62 Overhangs
64 Greasy
65 Ancient embalming ointment (John 12:3)
66 Backbone
67 Break crisply
68 Prohibitionists
69 Deposited soil
70 Sharpen

DOWN

1 Puncture
2 Great Lake
3 Jesus is the _____ of God (John 1:29)
4 Contention (Prov. 6:19)
5 Glue
6 Bluegrass state, for short
7 Person of great authority
8 Odd-job employee
9 Fish-grabbing flyer (Lev. 11:18)
10 Pitcher _____ Hershiser
11 Ten's predecessor
12 Still
15 New dogs
21 _____ Pro computer program
23 Cat type
25 Possessive plural
27 Actress Maureen _____
28 Unhealed wounds
29 Roman cloaks
31 Roof type
32 Glowing log
33 Art forms

36 Amer. Diabetes Assoc.
37 Psalm ending (Ps. 4:4, KJV)
40 Languages (Gen. 10:20, KJV)
43 Geckos and iguanas (Prov. 30:28)
45 Wis. aviation center
47 Enforce secrecy
49 Hound type
50 Normally, in brief
52 Flathands
54 Brand with iron
55 Uncanny
56 Fifty-seven, rom.
58 German movie
59 Photographer _____ Mills
60 Printed characters
61 Popular adventure game: abbr.
63 Made bigger: abbr.

(Solution on p. 217)

ACTS 21–23

ACROSS

1 Walked
5 Dally
8 Craze
13 "We are ready to kill him before he gets _____ " (Acts 23:15, NIV)
14 Ecuador neighbor
15 Story
16 Fencing sword
17 Bad word, acc. to Matt. 5:22, NIV
18 Olfactory sense
19 "I am . . . a citizen of _____ _____ " (Acts 21:39, NIV)
22 Print measures
23 Precedes Josh.
24 Commandment word
27 "They built a _____ and welcomed us all because it was raining and cold" (Acts 28:2, NIV)
28 In the manner of (2 wds., Fr.)
31 Be a pedagogue
32 Swedish car
33 Parseghian and namesakes
34 "More than forty of them are _____ _____ _____ for him" (Acts 23:21, NIV)
37 _____ fair in love and war
38 Baseball's Mel and family
39 Gasoline or bowling
40 Draft org.
41 Yen
42 Pedigree
43 Colonnade

44 _____ generis (one of a kind)
45 How Paul described himself in Acts 21:39, NIV (4 wds.)
52 Desert plant
53 Jog
54 _____ _____ boy! (2 wds.)
55 Kareem or Magic
56 Actress Sommer
57 Brick oven
58 Ryan, of "Hillbillies" fame
59 Pumpernickel
60 Hiram's home

DOWN

1 "_____ everybody will know there is no truth in these reports about you" (Acts 21:24, NIV)
2 Take back a car that's not paid for, for short
3 A cookie
4 Follows rein or mule
5 Relies
6 Box (Lat.)
7 Parents or legal _____
8 Error
9 Give entrance
10 Boris's refusal
11 In a bad manner
12 "_____ the disciples and their wives and children accompanied us out of the city" (Acts 21:5, NIV)
14 What Gutenberg's machine did
20 Indian city

21 South American beverage
24 Navy counterterrorists
25 Greets
26 John follower
27 "He spoke about _____ in Christ Jesus" (Acts 24:24, NIV)
28 As _____ _____ (generally)
29 Emitted light
30 Pale
31 "_____ the night before Christmas"
32 Pvt. Gomer Pyle's boss (2 wds.)
33 "And at that very moment I was _____ to see him" (Acts 22:13, NIV)
35 "I am _____ _____ this world" (John 8:23, NIV)
36 The lead in West Side Story or Sound of Music
41 As _____ _____ (so to speak, 2 wds.)
42 Montana town
43 "Finding the disciples there, we stayed with them _____ days" (Acts 21:4, NIV)
44 Where there's _____, there's 27-across
45 Mold-growing environment
46 Dad of Joe, Ben, Rube, and nine other guys?
47 Paris airport
48 What occurred in Acts 21:30
49 Stop
50 Frmr. Russian nation
51 Fulfill
52 Boxing champ in 1974 and 1978

(Solution on p. 217)

WOMEN'S PAGE

ACROSS

1 Indebted for
5 Scholastic, for short
9 Critical cut
14 Function
15 Fly high
16 Driven in
17 Aquila's wife (Acts 18:2)
19 Meagerly surviving
20 Axlike tool
21 Negative decision (2 wds.)
22 Examine similarities: abbr.
24 Card
25 Mass. city
27 Stockpiled (Isa. 23:18)
29 Has-____: pl. (over the hill)
30 Gospel author (Col. 4:10)
31 Supervise (Nm 34:29)
33 Belly
37 Turned on
38 "They'll know we ____ Christians by our love" (chorus)
39 Home of Greek goddess
   Diana (Acts 19:26)
44 Came forth
48 Not fem.
49 Wanderer (Ps. 72:9)
50 Charmin, Cheer, and Crest
   maker
53 Not vegetables or minerals
   (Gen. 1:21)
56 Entertainment rm.
57 Uganda dictator Amin
58 Middle: abbr.
59 Keep upper stiff
60 Aquatic weasel
62 King Solomon's mother (2 Sam.
   12:24)
65 Christian vocalist ____ Susek
66 Eve's second son (Gen. 4:2)
67 Over again
68 Promotes (Exod. 22:1)
69 Refined woman
70 Swiss capital

DOWN

1 Ruth's sister-in-law (Ruth 1:4)
2 Too talkative
3 Mother of John the Baptist
   (Luke 1:13)
4 Precedes *Moines* or *Plaines*
5 Stupid and silly
6 N.T. Asian city
7 Aid Assoc. for Lutherans
8 Greek money (Ezra 2:69)
9 First American in space
10 Chinese cookery
11 Homer's work
12 Br. sum of money
13 Sidestepped (Ps. 149:6)
18 Seniors' sticks? (Zech.h 8:4)
23 Ruth's homeland (Ruth 1:4)
26 King Saul's uncle (1 Sam. 14:51)
28 Howard Hughes's studio
31 Triumph shout
32 Very important person
34 Jesus' friend, Mary ____
   (Matt. 27:56)
35 "When our strength has failed
____ the day is half done"
(hymn)
36 New English Dictionary
40 Einstein's theoretical letters
41 Ridiculous exposés?
42 Expended
43 Rel. to prof. copyist (Ezra 4:8)
44 Played out (2 Chron. 24:6)
45 Twelve times a year
46 Arab rulers
47 Ewe's mate (Gen. 22:13)
50 Nudges (Ezek. 19:9)
51 Fasten again
52 Base eight number
54 Claude Lorrain's ____ *Veritatis*
55 Give birth
61 Made bigger, in brief
63 Amer. Booksellers Assoc.
64 O.T. prophet: abbr. (Gal. 3:11)

(Solution on p. 217)

JAMES

ACROSS

1 Yankee who hit 61 in '61
6 Melt together
10 Get rid of
14 Part of an act
15 Khomeini's domain
16 Atop
17 The Father of lights is not like these (James 1:17, NIV; 2 wds.)
20 Direction from NYC to R.I.
21 Bishop's watch
22 Daze
23 College prog. for mil. brass
25 Non-erasable: abbr.
26 The decision of the judge
29 Shrub of the West Indies
32 Heir
33 Uttered a syllable for meditation?
35 *Nada*
36 The second Stooge, for short
37 Takes a guess
38 What a Bulova keeps
39 Capp and Capone
40 Actress Christine
41 Where Julius Erving went after college? (2 wds., with abbr.)
42 Hydrocarbon gas
44 James says the one who perseveres "will receive the ____ ____ life that God has promised" (James 1:12, NIV)
46 Steams
47 Bristle
48 In coll., fourth-yr. males (2 wds.)
49 Jimmy's successor
50 Knock
53 James says he's "unstable in all he does" (James 1:8, NIV; 2 wds.)
57 Seed covering
58 Do the contralto part
59 "If someone forces you to go ____ ____ with him, go with him two"
60 ____ *noire* (French pariah)
61 Droops
62 Get a second year of *Time*

DOWN

1 What an ed. edits
2 Hurt
3 Check
4 Second banana
5 Six wins for Sabatini
6 James prohibits special attention to men in this attire (James 2:2, NIV; 2 wds.)
7 Push
8 Scandinavian flight co.
9 Intensifies
10 James compares the tongue to this
11 Having to do with the Greek god of sunlight and poetry
12 "____ preach and so you believed" (1 Cor. 15:11, RSV)
13 Two make an em
18 Adherent (Span.)
19 Found a sum
24 Overnight nurse: abbr.
25 Sonnets put to music? (2 wds.)
26 Imam's *ism*
27 One of the things that fell from Saul's eyes (Acts 9:18)
28 James says God gave us birth so that we might be "a kind of ____ of all he created" (James 1:18, NIV; sing.)
30 Neither here nor there
31 "We all shrivel up like ____ ____, and like the wind our sins sweep us away" (Isa. 64:6, NIV)
34 Wrestling or welcome
37 One's right mind
38 In my direction (2 wds.)
40 Gill, prefix
41 Young'un
43 James says: "The brother in ____ circumstances ought to take pride in his high position" (James 1:9, NIV)
45 "____ your heart and not your garments" (Joel 2:13, NIV)
48 Angry
49 Tintinnabulate
51 Uganda's tyrant
52 Ashen
53 One of these will "do ya"
54 POW kin
55 What Jesus gave back to Malchus
56 "If anyone is in Christ, he is a ____ creation" (2 Cor 5:17, NIV)

(Solution on p. 217)

WORKING WORDS

ACROSS

1 Compass stabilizer
5 Actress Turner
9 Airplane part
13 Hawaiian banquet
14 Biggest weapon
16 Frost type
17 Leave out
18 Skin
19 Notice, in brief
20 Folk song (Judg. 5:11)
22 King (2 Chron. 1:1)
24 Mimic
25 Doing business as: abbr.
26 Administrator (Dan. 1:11)
30 Smoothed
34 Not his
35 Formerly before *while*
38 Hawaiian seaport
39 Musical adapter: abbr.
40 Entices (2 Pet. 2:18)
41 Commander, for short
42 Throat mucus (Exod. 8:2)
44 Forearm bone
45 Son of Noah (Gen. 5:32)
46 "Go, _____ _____ on the mountain" (hymn)
48 Harvesters (Ruth 2:2)
51 O.T. bk.
52 Constellation of Regulus
53 Jesus' occupation (Mark 4:38)
57 Wit
61 Process color
62 Decree (Exod. 20:1)
64 Business transaction
65 Church recess
66 Connect again
67 Earned run averages
68 Afrikaner
69 Henpecks (Judg. 16:16)
70 Dispatched

DOWN

1 Lump
2 Arizona city
3 Train track
4 Habitual criminals (Isa. 59:14)
5 Jacob's dream theme (Gen. 28:12, KJV)
6 Sixteenth U.S. president
7 Average
8 Shells: slang
9 Ancient Egyptian king (Gen. 12:15)
10 College military unit
11 Vow
12 As needed: phar.
15 Thieves (Judg. 11:3)
21 Amer. Psychol. Assoc.
23 Condensed, for short
26 Beam (Exod. 25:31)
27 _____ Haute, Ind.
28 Actor Flynn
29 Hand out
31 Suitable position
32 Church official (1 Pet. 5:1)
33 College houses
36 _____-Tin-Tin
37 Famous actress (Num. 24:17)
40 Part of baker and candle-stickmaker (Gen. 18:7)
43 Field scavenger (Ruth 2:8)
45 Mates
47 Interstate Commerce Comm.
49 Gives joy
50 Atomic Energy Comm.
53 Keying error
54 Freedom from work
55 Adam's workplace (Gen. 2:15)
56 Actress Hayworth
58 Moon plain
59 Vivacity
60 Graduated-size set (Prov. 27:8)
61 Two quarts: Heb. (2 Kings 6:25, KJV)
63 Weed: slang

(Solution on p. 217)

ARTIFACTS

ACROSS

1 Go first
5 Chimps
9 Arm or leg
13 "And by him we cry, '____, Father'" (Rom. 8:15, NIV)
14 A sample photo
16 Operatic air
17 Used to anoint Jesus' feet (John 12:3)
20 Criticized strongly
21 LA to NYC flight (hyph.)
22 1979 film: Norma ____
23 Rock of ____
24 Lord
28 Made angry
29 American Missionary Fellowship
32 Odor
33 "You ____ me together in my mother's womb" (Ps. 139:13, NIV)
34 Hodgepodge
35 King Jehoiakim cut and burned it (Jer. 36)
38 How to spell millenary, as opposed to millennium (2 wds.)
39 New York Information Exchange: abbr.
40 Had possession of
41 Did the marathon
42 Sting
43 Last letters
44 "____ first his kingdom" (Matt. 6:33, NIV)
45 Upon, prefix
46 New York island
49 Street sellers
54 Goliath's bane
57 One who fires people
58 Intelligentsia
59 Fifty shekels, in Bible times
60 How Judas betrayed Jesus
61 8,760 hours
62 "Those who hope in the Lord ... will ____ on wings like eagles" (Isa. 40:31, NIV)

DOWN

1 Passover beast
2 Biblical mount near Gerizim
3 Magic word
4 "There will be terrible times in the last ____" (2 Tim. 3:1, NIV)
5 "We must all ____ before the judgment seat of Christ" (2 Cor. 5:10, NIV)
6 It precedes a fall
7 A long time
8 Wino
9 Touches down
10 Dies ____ (day of wrath, Lat.)
11 "He brought me up ... out of the ____ clay" (Ps. 40:2, KJV)
12 Commanded
15 What an amnesiac does
18 "Let justice roll on like a river, righteousness like a never-failing ____" (Amos 5:24, NIV)
19 "____ my lambs" (John 21:15)
23 "____, shine, for your light has come" (Isa. 60:1, NIV)
24 Field of college study
25 Where Christians met lions
26 Philosopher Kierkegaard
27 Treasury agents
28 "____ ____ was life" (John 1:4, NIV)
29 "Merrily We Roll ____"
30 A ____ ____ minute
31 Bends, in fabric
33 Boat for one
34 "Whether we live ____ ____ die, we belong to the Lord" (Rom. 14:8, var.)
36 Odiferous offering
37 "Look, he is ____ with the clouds" (Rev. 1:7, NIV)
42 "The promises were spoken to Abraham and to his ____" (Gal. 3:16, NIV)
43 First line
44 Awakes
45 Webber musical
46 Pierre is its cap.
47 Cab
48 Rds.
50 Distinguished Service Medals (abbr.)
51 River dividing Indiana from Kentucky
52 Gossip monger Barrett
53 The sun, for one
55 Clever
56 Prevaricate

HIDDEN NAMES 2

ACROSS

1 Nuclear reduction negotiations, in the 1970s
5 A pay increase
10 Gem
14 Apple reddener
15 Charming, in a magical way
16 The Andrews Sisters, for one
17 Attend a bistro
18 "One Sabbath Jesus was ____ through the grainfields" (Mark 2:23, NIV)
19 Immaculate
20 How Eve's husband felt when she first told him
22 "But those . . . who say to ____, 'You are our gods,' will be turned back in utter shame" (Isa. 42:17, NIV)
24 A fur piece
25 TV reception problem
26 Muric or amino
27 What Jacob's brother liked best about his stew (2 wds.)
31 Delete
32 Al and Tipper
33 Negative, prefix
34 Leo or Urban
35 More recently created
36 Beginning to be in bloom
37 Intl. Monetary Exch.
38 Keep a library book for another few weeks
39 The first month (Span.)
40 The fisherman, when he got a job laying rugs
42 Flavored milk shake
43 Old maxims
44 Question put to Jesus (Matt. 26:22, KJV)
46 Bundle of energy
49 Adam to his remaining son: "God gave you brains, ____ ____!" (2 wds.)
51 A mil. absence
52 Ruddy (It.)
54 Vile
56 Trick
57 Cabbage dish
58 A word on Belshazzar's wall
59 Expressions of amusement
60 Places to keep valuables
61 Pi times the radius squared

DOWN

1 Down
2 Other things (Lat.)
3 One who plants bushes and sods lawns
4 A scholarly paper
5 Kingly
6 "Man does not live on bread ____" (Matt. 4:4, NIV)
7 ____ ____ ain't broke, don't fix it (2 wds.)
8 Missing God's mark
9 Manipulate
10 Canadian capital
11 Prim and uppity person
12 Part of an entourage
13 Actress Myrna and her family
21 Style
23 Not found on a rolling stone
25 A bird or nag
26 Bouquet
27 Babel building
28 "If some ____ invites you to a meal . . . , eat whatever is put before you" (1 Cor. 10:27, NIV)
29 Where Borg or Barkley plays
30 Inside (comb.)
31 The Iliad or Ivanhoe
32 Where DNA resides
35 CNN or Fox
36 Accursed (1 Cor. 16:22, KJV)
38 An amount of paper
39 Put out
41 Asaph wrote some
44 Progeny
45 Places in the mezzanine
46 100-yard race
47 Women's community org.
48 Father of Shem and Ham
49 Its acad. is in Colo. Spr.
50 "Vengeance is ____" (Rom. 12:19, KJV)
53 Mouths
55 Meadow

(Solution on p. 218)

OPPOSITES ATTRACT

ACROSS

1 Filled tortilla
5 0–7 number system
10 Solution hint
14 Bulky bovids (Gen. 12:16)
15 Analyze grammatically
16 Carefree adventure
17 Darius the ____ (Dan. 5:31)
18 Child's vehicle
19 Border
20 Opposites pair #1 (Deut. 30:1; 2 wds.)
23 Presbyterian Church in America
24 Ugly old woman
25 Wedding site (Gen. 8:20)
29 Test suite
32 Body gland
36 Suddenly attacked
38 Between million and trillion (abbr.)
40 Savings plan
41 Opposites pair #2: 2 wds. (Gen. 14:4; Eph. 1:21)
45 Mined mineral
46 Bee's follower
47 Push through
48 Recorded (Ezra 8:34)
51 Ems' predecessor
53 Heavy
54 Nuclear watchdog
56 Napoleon's Water____
58 Opposites pair #3 (Jer. 3:1; 2 wds.)
67 Look-alike: abbr.
68 Floating flavor
69 Oil of ____
70 Bowl, for one (Gen. 27:9)
71 More rational (Mark 5:15)
72 Large barrel
73 Murky black
74 Polishing medium
75 Prayer bender?

DOWN

1 Burial place (Acts 13:29)
2 Wheel holder
3 Grant, as a point
4 "Seeking the lost ____ he died to redeem" (hymn)
5 Lens
6 Not spiritual (Rom, 7:14, KJV)
7 Advanced geometry: abbr.
8 Requests
9 Sucker (Prov. 30:15)
10 Ministers (1 Sam. 22:17)
11 Boys
12 Entreat
13 Barely gets by
21 Outburst of activity
22 Commercial carrier: abbr.
25 Set fire
26 Cruise ship *Achille* ____
27 Chinese region
28 Noun modifier, in brief
30 Gamal ____ Nasser
31 Bible Literature Intl.
33 Bishop's hat (Exod. 28:4, KJV)
34 Confirmation
35 Sturdy
37 David C. Cook (pub. co.)
39 Cash register maker
42 Golf ball holder
43 Forbidden
44 Black denom.
49 Realistic (1 Cor. 15:47, KJV)
50 *"Domine Deus, Agnus ____, Filius Patris"* (Gloria)
52 Repulsive person: slang
55 Stop
57 Egg maker
58 Musical Instrument Digital Interface
59 Former Ugandan leader
60 Take chance
61 Eighth of an ounce
62 Finished
63 ____ and roll
64 Extended family
65 Relaxation
66 Dick or Jerry Van ____

(Solution on p. 218)

SPECIAL DAYS

ACROSS

1 Follows *door* or *place*
5 _____ hands, devil's workshop
9 Sarai's husband (Gen. 11:26)
14 Long for
15 Astronaut Armstrong
16 Dough: slang
17 Period of rain on Noah's ark (Gen. 7:4)
19 Re. sea power
20 Anger
21 "_____ Father in heaven" (Matt. 6:9)
22 Malt beverage
24 Before
25 "Easier for a camel to go through the eye of _____ _____" (Mark 10:25)
27 Relieves of hostility (Zech. 9:10)
29 Lowest, worst part
30 Nonakaline
31 Hawthorne's letter (Exod. 26:1)
33 Rabbi or Socrates
37 "Have you _____ room for Jesus?" (hymn)
38 Eggs
39 Standards (Ps. 74:4, KJV)
44 Sacrificed (Gen. 46:1)
48 Soft drink
49 Coffee accompaniment
50 Female flyer
53 Payola: slang (Hab. 1:3)
56 Parody
57 Undercover agency
58 Native or resident, suffix (Lev. 17:3)
59 Weeding tool
60 Slapping noise
62 Sabbaths (Mark 1:21)
65 Select body (1 Sam. 26:2)
66 Spanish custard dessert
67 French seaport resort (Ruth 3:3)
68 Impede
69 George Bush's alma mater
70 Mars

DOWN

1 Org. crime syndicate
2 Squash type
3 Time Christ in tomb (Matt. 27:63; 2 wds.)
4 Tennis match unit
5 Spoil (Lam. 1:9)
6 "I love that old cross where the _____ and best" (hymn; Ps. 35:25)
7 "Now I _____ me down to sleep" (child's prayer)
8 Egyptian pres. Anwar _____-
9 Memory lapse
10 Constrictor
11 Pirate ship
12 Danger signal
13 Fathers, e.g.
18 Swiss mountaineer's call
23 Dog parasites (Exod. 8:16)
26 To _____ is human
28 Aid to Dep. Chil.
31 Self-addressed envelope
32 News channel
34 Mane material
35 Night's predecessor
36 Extremist: abbr.
40 __ thyology, a fishy science
41 Pursue (1 Sam. 14:37; 2 wds.)
42 Natl. Labor Rel. Bd.
43 Make content
44 Reciprocal
45 Fame's ally?
46 Circular
47 Evangelical Literature Bd.
50 Carefully maneuvered
51 Macintosh maker
52 Ignited again
54 Follows 49-across
55 Votes for
61 Corroded
63 Huntsville's state
64 Chromosome constituent

(Solution on p. 218)

HEART CHECK

ACROSS

1 Nuclear energy source
5 Grieg's Peer _____ Suite
9 Crows' sounds
13 Actress Madlyn _____
14 Wife of Jacob (Gen. 29:16)
15 Exaggerated manliness
16 Data item
17 Gorbachev's old empire
18 Cooking coat
19 Quote (10 wds., Matt. 6:21, KJV; cont. 37-A)
22 "When our strength has failed _____ the day is half done" (hymn)
23 Seventh Greek letter
24 Cancel or postpone
28 Long narrow strip (John 11:44)
31 Decay
34 Head of Borland Intl.
35 Great Lake
36 Disgusting!
37 Quote (cont. 52-across)
42 Fifty-six
43 Fibbed
44 Appear
45 Mental perception
46 Bottomless pit (Rev. 9:1)
48 Telegraph inventor
49 106
50 News source
52 Quote (cont.)
60 Commercial carrier
61 Limbs
62 Charged particles
64 Strongly seasoned
65 Fit
66 Animal parasite
67 Many, many pounds
68 Strokes animal (Job 41:5)
69 Orient, e.g.

DOWN

1 Dog talk
2 Defrost
3 Hurt expression
4 Dole out (Ezek. 23:45)
5 Fastener
6 Enthusiastic positive response
7 Nose, prefix
8 In one end and out the other: infor.
9 It's a Wonderful Life director Frank _____
10 43,560 square feet
11 Horse command
12 Male children
15 One of 12 apostles (Luke 6:15)
20 Yiddish respect title
21 Make another bow
24 Lie in hiding
25 Slice
26 Swiss, German, and Dutch river
27 Single, prefix
29 Unwanted wild plants
30 Due time, in short
31 Measuring stick (Prov. 29:12)
32 Stares at
33 Mint
38 Bondage (Gen. 41:52)
39 Leg bone
40 Attention cry: slang
41 Film speed rating
47 Defer to another (Gal. 6:13)
48 Missing in action
49 Classy girls: slang
51 Pains in the neck: slang
52 Remove
53 Mail agency: abbr.
54 Parade spoiler
55 Grate
56 Agrees with reality
57 "Whoever has God's Son has _____" (1 John 5:12)
58 Reformers' cry, "_____ Scriptura!"
59 "O happy _____ and holy" (hymn)
63 College entrance exam

(Solution on p. 218)

LOST IN LUKE

1	2	3	4		5	6	7		8	9	10
11					12			13			
14			15				16				
		17				18					
19	20	21			22						
23				24				25	26	27	
28			29				30				
31			32				33				
		34				35					
36	37	38			39						
40				41				42	43	44	
45				46			47				
48				49			50				

ACROSS

1 To make someone or something ready, for short
5 Many miles away
8 School organization (abbr.)
11 Peruvian city
12 Poem
13 A kind of life insurance
14 Lost object #1 (Luke 15:6; 3 wds.)
17 Bit
18 Employable
19 Robot
22 Bird
23 "Bring the finest ____ in the house and put it on him" (Luke 15:22)
24 Piece of glass
25 Do camelback
28 Lost object #2 (Luke 15:8-10; 3 wds.)
31 Salary
32 Poverty
33 Grasp
34 Alpha Centauri, for one
35 In a pale appearance
36 Movie awards
39 Brain scan: abbr.
40 Lost object #3 (Luke 15:13; 3 wds.)
45 Charged particles
46 Toupee
47 Scottish isle
48 Small bed
49 Curve
50 Vladimir's veto

DOWN

1 Thickness
2 Brazilian city, for short
3 Flightless bird
4 ". . . wasted all his money on ____" (Luke 15:13)
5 "At home even the hired men have ____ enough" (Luke 15:17)
6 Notices
7 "So he ____ home to his father" (Luke 15:20)
8 Skin
9 Mulberry or linden
10 Boost the sound: abbr.
13 Emaciated
15 Young man
16 Direct
19 Let fall
20 Gossipmonger Barrett
21 Honor
22 Vacillate
24 What the younger son sought as he wasted money
25 Not long from now
26 "____ the calf we have in the fattening pen!" (Luke 15:23)
27 Site of a famous car race, for short
29 Prelude
30 What the older brother felt when the Prodigal returned
34 Utters
35 Tiny
36 Ear-oriented
37 Exclamation to an unwanted creature
38 Small monetary amount
39 Hen products
41 Greek letters
42 A bean or sauce
43 "If you had a hundred sheep and ____ of them strayed away" (Luke 15:3)
44 King Cole

(Solution on p. 218)

MY FAVORITE YEAR

1	2	3	4		5	6	7		8	9	10	11
12					13				14			
15			16				17					
		18			19							
20	21	22			23							
24				25				26	27	28	
29			30				31				
32			33				34				
		35				36					
	37	38			39						
40				41			42	43	44	
45				46			47			
48				49			50			

ACROSS

1 Song for three
5 Copy
8 Supervisor
12 Division
13 Zilch
14 Against
15 When the high priest would enter the Holy of Holies (Heb. 9:7; 4 wds.)
18 Hosts: abbr.
19 Fold
20 Used a broom
23 Outfitted one's feet
24 Roll to a runway
25 Navy or soy
26 As well
29 Burnt offering (Ezek. 46:13; 3 wds.)
32 Draft agency: abbr.
33 Clue
34 I wander (Lat.)
35 Sapient
36 Loose
37 Tilts
39 Owned
40 Every half century (Lev. 25:13; 3 wds.)
45 Comfort
46 Mideast alliance in the 1960s (abbr.)
47 Clean
48 Flats (abbr.)
49 Weight measure (abbr.)
50 Veep

DOWN

1 Number of Testaments
2 Sought office
3 Sick
4 Washington capital
5 Doll Raggedy and Antarctic Cape
6 Image, for short
7 Pachyderm
8 Howled at the moon
9 _____-_____-Day vitamins
10 Immediately
11 Term of address to a man
16 Tenth month (abbr.)
17 "It's ____ ____ Way to Tipperary"
20 RR depots
21 Methods
22 Former spouses
23 French river
25 Happy
26 Acidic
27 Ahab's father
28 Wind instrument
30 Horned pachyderm
31 Giving a loan
35 Salesman's stuff
36 College in Birmingham (abbr.)
37 What every fourth February does
38 Follower of Far, Middle, or due
39 Colors
40 Vote of approval
41 Short punch
42 Name for a lion
43 Attention
44 Summer (Fr.)

(Solution on p. 218)

O MY WORD!

ACROSS

1 Fill up
5 Government operative
8 Large jars
12 Originating in
13 Samuel's mentor
14 Spanish rio
15 Lumbering cry in Zech. 11:2 (3 wds.)
18 Erode
19 Dank
20 Sobbing
23 Entry
24 About (2 wds.)
25 Sword part
26 Resort
29 God's call to attention in Deut. 6:4 (3 wds.)
32 Understanding
33 A lord's consort
34 Lakelet
35 Tops
36 Egyptian Christians
37 Applies plaster
39 Fine
40 Open exclamation of Ps. 24:7 (3 wds.)
45 Con
46 Little one
47 Granny
48 Give nourishment to
49 James Bond, for one
50 Nervous

DOWN

1 Airline code for Frisco
2 Trajectory
3 Play with
4 Domitian or Charle-magne
5 These go into Reeboks
6 City trains
7 In a depressing way
8 Stanza
9 Aid
10 Three-point play
11 Call for emergency help
16 Charles of Diet Pepsi fame
17 _____-frutti
20 Grabbed
21 Lakeside Pennsylvania city
22 Organization: abbr.
23 Applies a golden veneer
25 Talking-and-listening devices worn by some operators
26 Octagonal sign
27 Held inside (with "up")
28 "No ifs, _____, or buts"
30 Explanation of whereabouts
31 Washington city
35 Clear
36 Machine part
37 Hamlet, for one
38 Previous to (comb.)
39 Lawyer: abbr.
40 Clod
41 M–Q connection
42 Bit
43 Official language of Australia: abbr.
44 Utter

(Solution on p. 218)

TWO BECOME ONE

[crossword grid]

ACROSS

1 Troubling aftereffect (Lev. 13:23)
5 Long cut
9 Single-cell cytoplasm
14 Explorer Marco
15 Follows Puerto
16 Victorian, e.g.
17 O.T. couple (Esther 8:1; 2 wds.)
20 Prayer chain
21 Christmas mo.
22 Level, for short
23 Louvre's Mona
25 "I'm So Lonesome I Could
     ____"
27 Sands, loams, or ____
30 After grand or petit
33 First Greek letter (Rev. 1:8)
37 Sawn or axed (Prov. 9:1)
38 Smithsonian is one
40 Extremist (infor.)
41 N.T. couple (Acts 5:1; 2 wds.)
44 Pine
45 Atlantic and Pacific
46 Pre-____ (displace)
47 Grant (Ps. 72:1)
49 Color (Exod. 25:5)
50 Delete
51 New American Bible: abbr.
53 Passé person
55 Play part (Deut. 17:10)
57 ____ de Triomphe
60 Most uncouth
64 N.T. couple (Acts 18:2; 2 wds.)
67 Yangon's country

68 Middle (comb.)
69 Shirt protector (Exod. 13:4;
     2 wds.)
70 Joshua's cohort (Num. 14:6)
71 Pure-white goose
72 Tennis match units

DOWN

1 Boxing match
2 Freshwater salmon
3 Juneau's state: abbr.
4 Mrs. Jimmy Carter
5 Middle tones
6 Breathing material
7 Iraqi missile
8 Stocking
9 Sales notices
10 Alcohol type
11 Reverberation (Hab. 2:11)
12 South African war
13 Mus. rescorer (Lev. 1:7)
18 American novelist Leon ____
19 O.T. book: abbr.
24 Entertained
26 Incline
27 Warm by rubbing
28 Soviet premier after WWI
29 Tribute (2 Tim. 4:8)
31 Analyze content
32 Inclined
34 ____ donna
35 Harmonicas, for short
36 Booking (2 wds.)
38 Apple computer
39 Package carrier

42 Des Moines's state
43 Salome's mother (Matt. 14:3)
48 Punctual (2 wds.)
50 Schooling, in brief
52 Sheep's bleat
54 Filmmaker Welles
55 Water-related
56 Form ringlets
58 Rotations meas.
59 Work group
61 Czechoslovakian river
62 Cut
63 Space stoppers
64 Network's initials
65 Short retriever
66 O.T. major prophet: abbr.

(Solution on p. 218)

CATCHING SOME Z'S

ACROSS

1 Boyfriend
5 Eleventh king of Judah (2 Kings 16)
9 Jerusalem mount (Ps. 48)
13 Oven
14 Rodent
15 Keys
17 Continent
18 Classic work
19 Prepare dough
20 Prophet who follows Habakkuk
22 Takes merchandise from a damaged store
23 Greek letters
24 Former basketball league
26 Photo finish
29 Did a '60s dance
33 Brief ruler of Israel (1 Kings 16:9-20)
34 Site of a King Jehoram battle (2 Kings 8:21)
35 As to (2 wds.)
37 Jacob's sibling
38 Cellophane wrap
39 Throw a pitch at a batter's head
40 Nod off
41 School at Chapel Hill, N.C. (abbr., with U.)
42 Some houseplants
43 Employment

45 David's high priest (2 Sam. 15:24-36)
46 Follower of Galatians: abbr.
47 Emerge victorious
48 Amplified light beam
52 Painkiller
58 Put on clothing
59 Marshall Wyatt
60 City near Sodom and Gomorrah (Gen. 14)
61 Paris river
62 Annapolis institution: abbr.
63 Frost
64 Greek god of war
65 Belt
66 Wings (Lat.)

DOWN

1 Ruth's husband
2 Convenience
3 A short drink (2 wds.)
4 Salt Lake site
5 Street
6 Some New Mexicans
7 Inter ____ (among other things, Lat.)
8 Penultimate Old Testament prophet
9 David's headquarters, for a time (1 Sam. 27:6-12)
10 "There ____ ____ other name for men to call upon to save them" (Acts 4:12)
11 Margarine
12 Tidy

16 Students for a Democratic Society: abbr.
21 Prefix for matter, ballistic, or disestablishmentarianism
25 Set fire to
26 Soy and grain food pastes
27 Baffle
28 More thoroughly factual
29 Broad comedy
30 Teased
31 A winter month in Juarez
32 Had a Coke
33 The letter Z
34 Tax collector who encountered Jesus (Luke 19)
36 Half ems
38 Cut a corner
42 Weapon for vampire or wolf
44 Stanzas
45 A concubine of Jacob (Gen. 30:9-12)
47 Admonishes
48 Mormon: abbr.
49 Vicinity
50 Edomite mountain (Deut. 2)
51 Serf
53 Organization for Armstrong, Aldrin, and Collins: abbr.
54 Nehemiah preceder
55 Dirt
56 Paul's claim: "But ____ ____ ____ citizen by birth!" (Acts 22:28)
57 Saskatchewan Indian

(Solution on p. 218)

ISAIAH 53

ACROSS

1 A pinch of a recipe ingredient
5 Atlantic City casino
8 Humane org.: abbr.
12 Armbone
13 Bill of fare
14 Musical exercise
15 Armor
16 Auto pioneer
17 More unusual
18 What the "man of sorrows" was acquainted with (Isa. 53:3)
21 Tyrannosaurus or Oedipus
22 One of the plotters of (2 wds.)
23 Sandwich salads
26 A long way off
27 "A _____ of sorrows" (Isa. 53:3)
30 Veins
31 French rulers
32 "Yet it was our grief he _____" (Isa. 53:4)
33 "He was lashed— _____ _____ _____ _____" (Isa. 53:5)
36 Appropriate, formerly
37 The backs of boats
38 Slimfast and Weight Watchers
39 Exclamation of a cold person
40 Jazz singer Fitzgerald
41 Sign of life
42 Transaction
43 Pouch
44 "But in our eyes there was no _____ at all" (Isa. 53:2)
51 Spook
52 Musical sound
53 Hebrew letter
54 Vocally
55 Operator of a RR train: abbr.
56 A word on Belshazzar's wall
57 What man was made from
58 Expires
59 Being (Lat.)

DOWN

1 "As a sheep before her shearers is _____, so he stood silent" (Isa. 53:7)
2 Jai-_____
3 Dither
4 Desist
5 Electronic communique
6 Companion of ifs and buts
7 Makes right (Isa. 53:11)
8 Spot
9 Clean
10 B–G filling
11 _____ Lingus (Irish airline)
13 Customs
14 Gaffe
19 Wipe out
20 Grind teeth
23 Photocopier supply
24 Where milk comes from
25 Eft
26 Major artery
27 Spies on the inside
28 Sharp ridge
29 Beatty and Rorem
30 "He was brought as a _____ to the slaughter" (Isa. 53:7)
31 Sent back light
32 Bond
34 _____ Walla, Washington
35 Draw out
40 Like some vases
41 Cement workers
42 March ostentatiously
43 Burn slightly
44 Human rights watchdog: abbr.
45 New Mexico town
46 Home permanent
47 Handle
48 "In God's _____ he was like a tender green shoot" (Isa. 53:2)
49 "But he was wounded and bruised for our _____" (Isa. 53:5)
50 Dirk
51 Depressed

(Solution on p. 218)

GOOD FRIDAY

ACROSS

1 Happen again
6 Partly open
10 Affectedly dainty in Britain
14 Pay for sin (Dan. 9:24)
15 Bud's joint
16 Prickly pink plant (Song 2:1)
17 Christian message (pt. 1, 1 Cor. 15:3; 2 wds.)
19 Evangelist Roberts
20 Musician Medema
21 Ripped
22 Departure, as from Egypt (Heb. 11:22)
24 Foxy
25 Bears a debt (Philem. 1:18)
26 Trade show (infor.)
27 Sphere
28 Bel-_____ (Guy de Maupassant novel)
29 Fellowship of Christian Athletes: abbr.
32 Matthew or Mark, e.g.
35 Legal right
36 Self-images
37 Despair cry (Joel 1:15)
38 Mountain train
39 Dads and _____
40 Story
41 Purchase
42 Good _____ (when Jesus was crucified)
44 Abbr. letter holder
45 Energy
46 White South African
47 "So be it" (Num. 5:22)
49 Xs (1 Sam. 18:7)
50 German cathedral
53 Grown up (James 1:4)
55 Missionary Praying John _____
56 She sheep
57 Pivot point
58 Christian message (pt. 2, 1 Cor. 15:3; 3 wds.)
61 Blood block
62 Same, for short
63 Flowerpots
64 Egg layers
65 How Palmer got the ball off
66 Way in

DOWN

1 Antlers (Isa. 21:3)
2 Singer Waters
3 Hokey
4 Before cycle or form
5 Give back (Neh. 4:2)
6 Del Sarto, Mantegna, or Sansovino
7 Marries (Hos. 7:5)
8 Add to lemon and drink
9 Buys back (Lev. 27:15)
10 Band (2 Sam. 18:29)
11 Holy Scriptures (John 10:35; 3 wds.)
12 Birthright bargainer (Gen. 25:34)
13 Lampreys, for example
18 Cloth dryer
23 Legal age in Rome
27 Church recess
28 Eighth mo.
30 Unconsciousness
31 Set of parts, in short
32 Race starting point
33 Photographer Mills
34 Deliverance (Eph. 6:17)
35 Delight (Ps. 100:1)
36 Head of Qatar
38 "Fill My _____, Lord" (chorus)
41 Advantage
42 Hot cheese dip
43 Emergency fund
45 For each
46 Surpassing (Mic. 2:10)
48 Necessities (Gen. 2:17)
49 Days Jesus was in tomb (Matt. 27:63)
50 Theist by reason alone
51 Admitter (Matt. 13:52)
52 Untidy
53 Speed relative to sound
54 Wheel holder (1 Kings 7:30)
59 Pindaric or sapphic
60 Before Bernardino

(Solution on p. 213)

UP, UP, AND AWAY

ACROSS

1 Ray
5 Medics
9 Namesakes of David's prophet, for short
14 ____ Mater
15 In a poor manner
16 Clean a board
17 Went diving into second
18 Arabian port
19 Heron
20 How Paul wanted men to pray (2 Tim. 2:8; 3 wds.)
23 Bee follower
24 In good health
25 Less
28 Head (Fr.)
29 Color
32 British comic Michael
33 ____-Rooter
34 Minus
35 Jesus' prediction (John 3:14; 5 wds.)
38 Surrender
39 With (Fr.)
40 Aired again
41 Summer cooler
42 Landed
43 Agrarian
44 Irish
45 Recline
46 Where God has taken our sins (Ps. 103:12; 4 wds.)
52 Belonging to which person
54 Sin
55 Master
56 Tends
57 Philosopher Descartes
58 Altars (Lat.)
59 Melt ore
60 Droops
61 Short howl

DOWN

1 Slug
2 Scat singer Fitzgerald
3 Ugandan dictator
4 Anti-intoxication group (abbr.)
5 Phone feature
6 Song from the '50s
7 Music notation
8 Man-made
9 Tease
10 Cavil
11 Covering
12 Direction from the apostle Paul's place of death to his hometown
13 TV ____
21 Aroma
22 Garden command: "When you ____ ____ it you will surely die" (Gen. 2:17, NIV)
25 Renowned
26 Escape
27 Learned
28 Sign on an apartment (2 wds.)
29 Geometrical figures (comb.)
30 Ordinary
31 Cable channel of Chris Berman
32 Type size
33 Siskel and Ebert, for instance
34 A lecher's look
36 Light wood
37 More loyal
42 Nab
43 Winchesters
44 Painter's stand
45 Deceiving
46 Golf cry
47 What's one block away from Blvd. B? (2 wds.)
48 First two words of a well-known anthem (var.)
49 Goo
50 Asian mountain range
51 Ooze
52 British bathrooms: abbr.
53 A son of Noah

(Solution on p. 213)

THE WELL

ACROSS

1 First father
5 Skin (comb.)
9 Pre-owned
13 "All too ____!" (John 4:17)
14 Bacchan cry
15 Winter month in Madrid
16 Toodles!
17 Ponce de ____
18 Map collection
19 "If you only knew what ____ ____ ____ God has for you" (John 4:10)
22 Beam
23 Road payment
24 Group of eight
27 Only
28 Rather's network
31 Sweeping device
32 Altar area in an Eastern church
33 Upset
34 Water drawer in John 4
37 Do or *sol*
38 Press
39 Lift
40 Printer's measures
41 Interested in
42 What the disciples went into Sychar for
43 *D–I* connectors
44 "If you only knew . . . who ____ ____" (John 4:10)
45 Jesus' declaration about his Father (John 4:24; 4 wds.)
52 Duplication, for short
53 Dance, photography, poetry, etc.
54 "Well, at least I know that the Messiah will ____" (John 4:25)
55 Warhorse
56 Prestigious university
57 *Beowulf* or the *Aeneid*
58 Care for
59 Directions from SF to LA and Chi to Atl
60 Son of 1-across

DOWN

1 ____ boy!
2 What the woman intended to do (John 4:7)
3 Kind of biography or mobile
4 Average
5 Remove a polluting substance from gasoline
6 Each
7 Housetop
8 Colonial soldier
9 Up to that time
10 Ego
11 Part of q.e.d.
12 *Seis* divided by *tres*
15 Bird of prey
20 Piece of theater
21 Navigation system
24 Welles or Bean
25 Overwear
26 Volume
27 Tagalong statement (2 wds.)
28 Funny
29 Bold
30 "My nourishment comes from doing the will of God who ____ me" (John 4:34)
31 Tragic factor
32 Yearly celebrations
33 In a short time
35 The Beatles' drummer
36 Wallop
41 "____ ____ is on our side, who can ever be against us?" (Rom. 8:31)
42 Young women
43 Goofed
44 Basket fiber
45 Celebration
46 Shop sign
47 Savings funds: abbr.
48 Frosts
49 "But you don't have a ____ or a bucket" (John 4:11)
50 A copy: abbr.
51 Engineering school, for short
52 What's between *Q* and *U*

(Solution on p. 215)

WATER, WATER EVERYWHERE

1	2	3	4		5	6	7	8		9	10	11	12	13
14					15					16				
17					18					19				
	20			21					22					
			23					24						
	25	26	27					28				29	30	31
32					33	34				35				
36				37					38					
39				40					41					
42			43					44						
		45					46							
47	48	49				50				51	52	53		
54					55					56				57
58					59					60				
61					62					63				

ACROSS

1 A basic beam in a building frame or wall
5 Nonunion strikebreaker
9 Throat ailment
14 South African bishop
15 Scat singer Fitzgerald
16 Snapshot
17 Dirk
18 Play a musical intro repeatedly
19 Tidbits
20 When the ark floated (Gen. 7:18; 4 wds.)
23 Alternatives
24 Victor's words (2 wds.)
25 Serf
28 Acne problem
29 Onto
32 One at _____ _____ (2 wds.)
33 Ireland
35 A greater amount
36 What Jesus promised the Samaritan woman (John 4:10; 3 wds.)
39 Deadlocked
40 Made melody
41 Spy
42 Cub/Dodger third baseman Ron
43 Alley's companion
44 Spry
45 The scoop
46 Fear
47 What Moses got by hitting a stone (Num. 20:8; 4 wds.)
54 Post-opera cry
55 State
56 Wind indicator
58 Duplicator, for short
59 Care for
60 Seth's son
61 Awake and aware
62 Associates of odds
63 Soaks

DOWN

1 Augustine, Francis, and Ignatius, among many others: abbr.
2 Canned fish
3 Southwestern Native Americans
4 Song for two
5 Harsh
6 Talons
7 _____ Mater
8 John's water activity
9 The one who was "hovering over the waters" (Gen. 1:2, NIV)
10 Piercer of Paul and Jesus
11 _____-Rooter
12 Greek letters
13 What models do
21 Shack
22 J. R. or Patrick
25 What you often find atop a 50-down
26 Tar
27 You said it!
29 Sheraton or Four Seasons
30 Peaceful name
31 Cute and sassy
32 "Just _____ _____!" (Wait a moment)
33 What water does in heat
34 First name of a TV shepherd
35 Visitors of the Christ child
37 Has been canceled (2 wds.)
38 Bet
43 Homonym for en route (2 wds.)
44 Emmy and Oscar
45 "Why was _____ _____ born?" (Jer. 20:18)
46 Change
47 West Bend Military Academy (abbr.)
48 Seed covering
49 Domesticated
50 Kiln
51 Turn the page
52 Crutch, of sorts
53 Boy Scout subject
57 Curve

(Solution on p. 219)

OPTICAL ILLUSIONS

ACROSS

1 Plant with spikes of flowers (abbr.)
5 Wedding ring (Ps. 22:16)
9 Double laugh (Luke 4:34)
13 Heavily burden (Song 8:14)
14 Addict
15 Counterfeit
16 Goes with ends
17 Father of Edomites (Obad. 1:6)
18 Top of the line
19 Maxim (pt. 1; 4 wds.)
22 Three-way pipe joint
23 Indian's shoe (abbr.)
24 Enticed
28 Abnormal prefix
29 Christian Booksellers Assn.
30 Before California's Alto
31 Preside over meeting
34 Intoxicated
36 Cat's "hand"
37 Bedding
38 Performers' suffix
39 Select group (Ezek. 23:7)
41 "____ Can It Be" (hymn)
42 Alphabet's first quintet
44 Swiss call
45 View (Acts 12:9)
47 Earthy prefix
48 Letter addenda, in brief
49 Conduct error
51 "The Raven" author
52 "____, though I walk through the valley of the shadow of death" (Ps. 23:4, KJV)
55 Maxim (pt. 2; 2 wds.)
58 Old Testament prophet (Rom. 9:25)
61 Promissory notes
62 Murderous frenzy
63 Nonactive
64 Aware of true motive
65 Formally surrender
66 Faculty head
67 Lighted sign
68 Was certain

DOWN

1 Crow over
2 Molten metal transport
3 Mentally confused
4 Actor Arnaz
5 Part of Argentina's capital
6 Short group
7 Organized
8 Shooting heroin, e.g. (2 wds.)
9 Bank robbery
10 Salesperson, for short (Neh. 11:24)
11 Lew Wallace's Ben ____
12 This king of Judah wanted to be friends with Syria (1 Kings 15:8)
15 Michael Jordan is one
20 One of Asia's seven churches (Rev. 1:11)
21 Nation's photographer, ____ Mills
25 Quick (Ezra 5:8)
26 Cause joy (1 Sam. 11:9)
27 Round rod
28 Mold (Jon. 1:14)
29 Belief statement
31 Gold miner's stake
32 Official language in New Delhi
33 South American mountains
34 Trickery (2 Cor. 4:2)
35 Door handle and lock
40 Before Gatos near San Jose
43 Billy Graham Evang. Assn.
46 Behind the boat
48 How Socrates died (James 3:8)
50 "O ____ will be glory for me" (hymn)
51 Ninth planet from sun
52 Sanaa's country
53 Wear away
54 Crooked
56 Ruined (Lam. 1:3)
57 Pinup item
58 Secreted
59 Single
60 Great quantity (Gen. 1:21)

(Solution on p. 219)

PEOPLE R US

ACROSS

1 Explosive
4 Distant
8 Syria
12 Predisposition
14 Chimney
15 Descartes
16 Record
18 Boaz's love
19 Russian ruler
20 Israel's oldest
22 Kick
24 Resident (comb.)
25 Fusses
27 Cereal fiber
29 Wear out
32 Get dirty
33 Paul's friend in Rome (Rom. 15:13)
34 Actress Perlman
36 Speech impediment
40 Hen product
41 "Just as you ____ ____ ____ and I am in you, so they will be in us" (John 17:21)
44 Small amount of money (Fr.)
45 U.S. job safety watchdog (abbr.)
47 Internal (comb.)
48 Radiology pictures
50 Arrived
52 Isaac's love
54 A Midianite king (Num. 31:8)
55 Dirk

56 "Happy ____ ____ clam"
58 Society
61 A daughter of Laban
65 Author of three New Testament letters
67 Formerly Persia
69 She answered Peter's knock (Acts 12:13)
70 Wings (Lat.)
71 Hydration for Julio
72 Bad sign
73 Bathwear
74 Actress Lamar
75 Conclusion

DOWN

1 Ski lift
2 Place for Cleopatra's barge
3 Something you mustn't do
4 Europe's neighbor: abbr.
5 Gaffe
6 Product of 13-down
7 Solomon's successor
8 Curve
9 Threat to Ahaz (Isa. 7:1)
10 Medical school subject: abbr.
11 Only
13 Car company
17 A Gorgon
21 What Bingo cards have, besides letters: abbr.
23 Thrice (comb.)
26 Peaceful
28 Everyone
29 Sandwich cookie

30 Cavities in rocks
31 D–I connection
32 Sirs, in Sonora
35 Concealed
37 Out of Africa author Dinesen
38 Protein bean
39 What often comes to shove
42 Father of King Pekah (2 Kings 15:25)
43 What Walter Payton was, after retiring (hyph.)
46 Star pilot
49 Sound again, and again
51 "As easy as ____"
53 Number of students in a school (abbr.)
54 Spy-saver in Jericho
56 Partly open
57 Unaccompanied
59 Encourage
60 Computer transmission rate
62 Where the heart is
63 Biblical garden
64 Alight
66 Originally named
68 A vote no

(Solution on p. 219)

CAUTION QUESTION

ACROSS

1 Not likely to happen
4 Social stratum
9 Rascal
14 O.T. bk.
15 Pentecostal teacher Kenneth ____
16 Currency
17 Central European river
18 Mexican friend
19 Up to that time (Lev. 8:33)
20 Obvious question (pt. 1; Prov. 6:27; 5 wds.)
23 Indian warrior's trophy
24 Buck
25 Beat
28 Harder of hearing
33 Idle chatter
36 Death notices
39 "____! and Did My Savior Bleed?" (hymn)
40 Obvious question (pt. 2; 3 wds.)
44 "Friends, Romans . . . ____ me your ears" (Luke 6:34)
45 Ominous
46 Fifth bk. of Moses
47 Drug user
50 Author Ferber
52 Rich friable soil
55 Grab
59 Obvious question (pt. 3; 4 wds.)

65 City in Kentucky, Ohio, and So. Carolina (Acts 20:4)
66 Mr. Sadat
67 Energy unit
68 New development (Jer. 4:3)
69 Asinine
70 Annabel Lee author
71 Long dismal cries
72 Pried into (Prov. 30:33)
73 Comp. pgm. instantly available

DOWN

1 Compact and laser
2 Rebekah's husband (Gen. 24:67)
3 Bread from heaven (Num. 11:6)
4 Goliath was one (1 Sam. 17:4)
5 Dalai ____ (Tibetan monk)
6 Opposed in the South
7 Audible breaths (Mark 7:34)
8 Condescending person (infor.)
9 Dirty mark
10 Secret, for short (Judg. 16:15)
11 Opposed
12 Former Israeli leader Golda ____
13 Gomer ____ (TV series)
21 "____ the Way My Savior Leads Me" (hymn)
22 Young chap
26 Major network
27 Go fly a ____
29 Satisfied saying
30 Escaped
31 Carefree
32 Four before vee

33 Festive occasion
34 Mellow (Gen. 43:27)
35 Wedding ring
37 "For God so loved ____ world" (John 3:16, NIV)
38 The Universe Next Door author James ____
41 Ugandan dictator Amin
42 The Whipping Boy author Fleischman
43 Officially reprimanded
48 Outer wraps (Acts 22:23)
49 Small child
51 ____ Lingus (Irish carrier)
53 Encore! (John 20:21)
54 Church reformer ____ Simons
56 Bungling
57 Ciphers
58 Lawn trimmer
59 Dear ____ (advice column)
60 Rome's fiddler emperor
61 Pulled up (Mark 14:47)
62 Astronaut Armstrong
63 "____ the night before Christmas"
64 Destroyer

(Solution on p. 219)

HOW MANY?

ACROSS

1 Skip
5 Info
9 Turf covers
14 Window
15 Send
16 Racetracks, often
17 "____ Homo" ("Behold the man," Lat.)
18 Lincoln portrait
19 Aired again
20 What false prophets will do (Matt. 24:11; 3 wds.)
23 Billboards
24 Former newscaster Huntley
25 Witch who hounded Odysseus
28 Snow runners
29 Make a cat sound
32 Columbus's hometown
33 ____-do-well
34 Defiled
35 These will be last (Matt. 19:30; 4 wds.)
38 A condition of an object being sold (2 wds.)
39 Some are carpenters
40 Runs an engine without driving anywhere
41 Born (fem.)
42 Takes a small drink
43 Dog pests
44 Mister, in Munchen
45 Metal deposit

46 Jesus gave his life to be this (Mark 10:45; 4 wds.)
53 Persona non ____
54 Tirades
55 Margarine
56 Bolt
57 "____ ____ him on a Monday and my heart stood still"
58 Headliner
59 Omit
60 Hamilton portraits
61 Sped

DOWN

1 European car
2 Criminal stopper
3 South American tribe
4 Started a golf game (with off)
5 120 months
6 Approvals
7 Wee
8 Those who commit violence
9 Pastries
10 Steer clear of
11 ____ avis
12 Button on a tape recorder
13 A government-issued number: abbr.
21 Parrot
22 British county
25 Desist
26 A kind of navel
27 Rogers and Clark
28 Places in a theater

29 The first name of Trump's second wife
30 Curves
31 Moistens
32 Fed
33 What many charitable groups are
34 Wait
36 Things split by legalists
37 A secretary, many times
42 One hundred Washington leaders
43 Poet Robert
44 Despised
45 Many times
46 Seed covering
47 Sitarist Shankar
48 Ape
49 The majority
50 She sings the low part
51 Approach
52 Past
53 Test for higher education: abbr.

(Solution on p. 219)

TEACHING

ACROSS

1 Disaster area
5 Thrust
9 Release
14 Resound
15 Where Lima's been
16 Twelves
17 Trolley
18 Petrol cartel
19 Air sacs
20 What Paul warned about (Col. 2:22; 2 wds.)
23 Liver (comb.)
24 High signs
25 Hot
28 ____ of the Thousand Days
29 A male cat
32 What Flynn might buckle
33 Got an A
34 Siamese
35 What God's people must be (2 Tim. 2:24; 2 wds.)
38 Quantities
39 Trip (Lat.)
40 Some lagomorphs
41 Do undercover work
42 Playwright Bagnold
43 Cylindral, but pointed
44 What follows Zech. and Mal.
45 Hawaiian dish
46 Disciples' request (Luke 11:1; 4 wds.)
53 Shell
54 Morse code components
55 Darius, for one
56 One of Jesus' closest disciples, in Spanish
57 Other
58 Gold medal gymnast in 1972
59 Standoffish
60 Utters
61 Winter vehicle

DOWN

1 An adherent of John Wesley's teachings (abbr.)
2 Neutral color
3 Hoax
4 Body (Gk.)
5 Not consistent
6 Plains Indian dwelling
7 Province
8 Tampa Bay gridder
9 Different
10 Subjects or objects, usually
11 Part of a grabbing utensil
12 Gerund endings
13 Curve
21 Place to be
22 Carmaker
25 Fen
26 Lump of beef
27 Egyptian goddess
28 Played Polonius
29 "Where two or three gather together . . . I will be right ____ among them" (Matt. 18:20)
30 Like a rowboat
31 Mademoiselle
32 Places to relax
33 Outlooks
34 Compared to
36 Last inning
37 Vocal ensemble
42 "Yes, ____ us will give an account of himself to God" (Rom. 14:12; 2 wds.)
43 Groves
44 Big or total (comb.)
45 Fall guy
46 Sign in a Chicago transport station (2 wds.)
47 Internal (comb.)
48 ____ Scriptura
49 A shepherd-forester from Tekoa
50 Holler
51 Move slowly
52 Skim or scan
53 A number-cruncher (abbr.)

(Solution on p. 219)

NO WAY

ACROSS

1 Employer
5 Each of these has 10 milligrams: abbr.
9 Nothings, to Nina
14 Skin opening
15 "I smell _____ _____"
16 Feel
17 *Thirtysomething's* Ken
18 Emperor who launched Roman persecution of Christians
19 Walked in the water
20 What believers have (Rom. 8:1; 2 wds.)
23 Charged particle
24 Black
25 Having more mental health
28 A kind of song or dive
29 Hesitations in speech
32 Prank
33 "_____ _____ I say, not as I do"
34 Skiing need
35 Psalmist's plight (Ps. 142:4; 5 wds.)
38 Transgression (hyph.)
39 Sin
40 Elizabeth or Wilhelmina
41 Orang
42 Cleaner
43 Cavelike
44 Guns an engine
45 CCC divided by C
46 Situation of those who reject God (Isa. 57:21; 4 wds.)
53 Object
54 Jewel
55 Wagon
56 Multitude
57 How many are righteous (Rom. 3:10, KJV)
58 Editor's note: abbr.
59 Attire
60 Editor's note to undo 58-across
61 Sweet potatoes

DOWN

1 Informed about (2 wds.)
2 Individual effort
3 Norse hero
4 Attorney General
5 Openness
6 Environmental
7 Jam substitute: abbr.
8 Confederate general Jackson
9 Physicist Isaac
10 Mightily or speedily
11 Extinct creature
12 Perfect score for Nadia (2 wds.)
13 But (Lat.)
21 Sister's daughter
22 Embarrass
25 Pry
26 Pay for
27 Spanish boy
28 What a frozen liquid becomes
29 Remove a fastener
30 Domestic
31 Swedish man's name
32 Admirer of baby Jesus (Luke 2:36)
33 What sports leagues often have
34 Belt
36 Use a shuttle
37 Arm
42 Unites
43 Purplish flower
44 Tears
45 Wacky
46 Norse god
47 Employ
48 Espy
49 Whirlpool
50 Region
51 Irenic
52 Windows to the soul
53 A degree in biblical studies

(Solution on p. 219)

Old Testament Occupations

```
T E A C H   B A N K E R S
R   B   E   O   O   X   Y
O P H E L   W E A V E R S
P   O   M   M   H   C   T
H E R D S M E N   J U D E
Y   M   N   J   T   M
  S P I E S   B A K E R
M   R   N   A   N     A
A M O S   A D V I S O R S
D   P   K   D   T   R   T
E N H A N C E   O W N E R
U   E   E   R   R   A   A
P O T T E R S   S U N N Y
```

Building a House

```
  C H E S T S   S I T E
N   E   U   T   A   E   U
A G A T E   A W N I N G S
I   R   V   D   A   U
L A T T I C E S   A N E R
S   D   S   H   T   Y
  T O O L   L E G S
C   E   L   S   L     A
R A R E   S K Y L I G H T
Y   R   S   I     A   T
P L A S T E R   S I N A I
T   C   E   T   I   G   C
P E E P   S T R E S S
```

Too Many Titles

```
M O S E S   B E G G A R S
I   M   E   U   A   C   E
C R I E R   G E N E R A L
H   T   G   L   G   E   L
A T H L E T E S   M A T E
L   A   R   P   G   R
  A G E N T   G R E E D
E A T   S   I     E
M A T S   A P O S T L E S
B   E   B   I   O   Y   C
A R M O R E D   N E C H O
L   E   A   E   E   I   R
M A N A G E R   R O A S T
```

Neighbors

```
  W I N N O W   J A M E S
A   B   O   I   O   I   K
G A Z E D   Z E B E D E E
U   A     A   S   W   T
R A N C H E R S   D I S C
S   U   D   H   F   H
  S I N S   H I K E   I
F   T   R   R       I
L U R K   J E W E L E R S
O   V   A   I     D   E
C H A S T E N   A B I H U
K   N   A   E   P   C   E
S A T E D   D E P U T Y
```

Grab Bag

```
A S K S   A B B R   E R A
B L A U   A B E E   T A N
D A M N   A L M I G H T Y
A B I D E   A G R I
  A P E D   N A O M I
D E C E I V E D   S P I N
E A R   C I L I A   I N G
U S E D   L A N G U A G E
S T A R S   Y A R N
  T A K E   O I N K S
O R I G I N A L   Q U I P
C O O   D A D O   U L N A
T E N   S M O G   E L K S
```

Stuck in Sin

```
T E M P T   T O B I J A H
H   A   R   Y   U   E   E
R O G U E   R E M O R S E
E   I   A   A   S   I   D
A C C U S I N G   A C H E
T   U   T   I   H   D
  S W O R E   I D I O T
B   I   E   A   O
A R T S   A D U L T E R Y
L   C   O   A   A   X   E
A S H A M E D   T I T A N
A   E   R   A   R   R   A
M E S S I A H   Y E A R S
```

Bible Animals

```
R E D U G   S E A G U L L
I   E   A   H   N   N   A
T O P A Z   E N T I C E D
U   O   E   S   L   D
A N T E L O P E   L E V I
L   L   S   S   A   E
  A S H E S   S W I N E
S   T   S   Q   A     O
A T A D   B U L L O C K S
L   B   U   A   L   E   P
M A L A C H I   O L D E R
O   E   A   L   W   A   E
N E S T L E   S T R A Y
```

In the Courtroom

```
R E C O R D   M E D D L E
L   P   E   V   E   O   A
B E L I E F   R E N O W N
  C   N   R   I   O   Y
E T U I   A T T O R N E Y
  O   U   U     R
B A N N E D   M O L E S T
C       O   E
A C C I D E N T   G A S P
U   M   V   I   A   T
E S T A T E   V A L U E S
E   G   N A E   L   R
A S S E R T   S P Y I N G
```

Tricky Ones

```
C A S A B A   P E N I E L
A N T H E M   E Q U A T E
U N R U L Y   R U B T H E
D U O M O   F A I R E R
A L L A N D   E L A I N E
D I L I G E N C E   C E D
      S E T
C R T   E P H E S I A N S
A H A S A I   D A C R O N
L Y I N G S   M E N T A
E M P A L E   D A C O I T
S E A R E R   B R A N C H
A R N E S S   L A P S E S
```

Sheep and Shepherds

```
C L O S E R   S T A F F S
  A   H   E   W   N   E
M Y S E L F   A L T A R S
  E   P   R   M     T
A R C H   E P I D E M I C
  E   S     X   L
W E A R E H I S S H E E P
X   D     C   A
P A S S O V E R   U T A H
M     I   A   S   P
S P R I N G   W A T E R S
L   N   O   N   E   I
L E A D E R   Y O D E L S
```

Hidden Message

```
P A R A D E   S T O R M S
  B   L   X   T   W   E
P U B L I C   A V E N G E
S   I   L   M     I
S E L A   A P P L A U D S
  N   I     E   E
I A M C O M I N G S O O N
S   E     E   E
S U N S H I N E   M E A L
N     S   D   B   N
I D E A L S   I S L A N D
E   I   U   N   E   I
P R I N C E   G A D F L Y
```

Bible Foreigners

```
S Y R I A   C R E T A N S
U   E   M   Y   X   R   A
N E C H O   R E P H A I M
D   T   R   E   O   M   S
A R A B I A N S   H A L O
Y     T   E   B   I   N
  M E D E S   E R E C H
M   D   S   G   A     E
O D O R   A R A M E A N S
S   M   T   E   B   R   T
A B I L E N E   L Y N C H
I   T   M   K   E   O   E
C A E S A R S   S E N I R
```

Bible Wars

```
A R M I E S   C L A S P S
U   N   O O H S   S   I
G R O V E L   I M P A L E
A   A   D   E       G
F L E D   I N F A N T R Y
  E   E       X   I
T E R R O R   L E G U M E
  N   H   O   O
I G N O M I N Y   L O T S
  I   S   A     I   R
A N N A L S   L E A G U E
  E   S   U L T   T   C
E S C A P E   Y A H W E H
```

Sing to the Lord

```
  A N T H E M   A M E N
D   A   I   A I   L   B
R O B E S   R E J O I C E
U   A   V   A   P   A
M E L O D I E S   W H E T
S     U L   C A S
    L Y R E   B O A Z
B   E   A D   M       P
L E A D   T I M B R E L S
O   P   S   R       Z A
W H I S T L E   J U B A L
N   N   A   C   O   O M
  A G U R   T R Y I N G
```

Personality Characteristics

```
R E J E C T S   D R E A M
E   O U E   O   R   R
N A K E D   L O G G E R S
T   D     F   C
  J E H O V A H   A H A Z
S A B   S   W       E
C O M P A S S I O N A T E
U   L   U   R   N   B
M I N D   P R E D I C T
  E     A   I     O
C R I M S O N   Y I E L D
O   G O C   E   N E
R A H A B   E X A L T E D
```

God's Work

```
B E H A L F   A R A B A H
A   D   R O B   H   R
S T A D I A   I S A I A H
E   I   M   H       M
K N I T   E D U C A T E D
  I   U       B   A
A C C O M P L I S H I N G
  A   N       N   O
A P O S T L E S   R A G E
  A   E   T   E
A B L A Z E   A G E N C Y
  L   M   K I N   N   K
B E G I N S   T A T T O O
```

Beached

```
Z E P H   B A R   R A F T
E Z R A   U R E   E B E R
A R O D   R O C   M E T A
L I F E T I M E   E L A M
      H E A D E D
R E P A I R   E M I G R E
A G I N G   B E A U S
G O E T H E   I O D I N E
      I S L A N D
A M E N   B U S Y B O D Y
H E R O   O R E   A B I A
A M A M   W A C   L A C K
B O N Y   S S T   I D E A
```

Old Testament Hodgepodge

```
A A R P   F E E   H A L I
S C A R   O W L   O B E R
I N K Y   R E Y   S E B A
S E E I N G   M A H L O N
      N E E   A P E
P L I G H T   S T A V E S
G I L             I R I
M E L O N S   J A S P E R
      C A I   E L I
C A L E B S   W I N N O W
A R E A   E Y E   F A M E
S C A N   R E L   U N I V
H O D S   A S S   L A T E
```

Truth or Consequence

```
J E T H R O   B A N I S H
A   O   U S E   U   W
A G H A S T   A U T H O R
L   R   C R   L
B E E F   R A D I C A L S
  R   O   O   E
A C C O M P A N I M E N T
  A   S   E   M
A B S T A I N S   O I L S
I   B   T   T   O
S N A T C H   I D I O T S
E   I   A I N   O   H
S T U P O R   G E N D E R
```

The Cornerstone

```
C H R I S T   E L D E R S
H O O R A H   A O R T I C
U P S O M E   C R E E P Y
R H I N O   H E A R S T
C R E E S H   A D N A H
H A R D   A M A L   E W E
        T O M
S A A   T H A I   G A D E
P L U M E   D R I V E N
I G N O R E   A F A C E
R E T I N A   K I T T I M
I R I S E S   U N E A S Y
T S E T S E   H Y D R O S
```

The I's Have It

```
A L T A R S   C H A R M S
I   R   U R I   L   A
K N O C K S   V I L E L Y
E   H   T I   A
A N T I   A L L I A N C E
  P   I       B   H
C O M P A N I O N S H I P
  B   U   V   T
C A P S T O N E   A D D S
  D   A   R I   A
B I R T H S   F I N I N G
  A   E   E V E   E   C
C H E A T S   D O D G E D
```

Proverbial Potpourri

```
  C A F E   A T O M
H I R E D   G E R A R
D E R I D E   R E E L E D
R A C A   N O I   N A Z I
I L L   A S A P H   W I N
P S E U D   O P E N I N G
  S A M   A A A
V I N E G A R   R E A C H
O N E   E D I C T   D O E
E D A M   N B A   C U L T
T I R A D E   B A A L A H
  A B Y S S   A B E T S
  Y A M S   L E N S
```

Jacob and Esau

```
  I S A A C S   G U S H
S   L   S A   O   M
T E E T H   N E W B O R N
E   E   I   N   T   E
A P P E T I T E   C H E W
K   O   Y   H   E   S
  D I E S   H E A R
E   E S   S L
B A L D   A C C I D E N T
B   I   T U   N   A
S U L P H U R   C H O I R
A   I   V C   C   K
  C H I N   Y O U T H S
```

Women of the Word

```
L A U G H E D   D O Z E N
I   N   I   I R A   U   O
F R I N G E S   U Z Z I A
E   F   H   C G   I   H
  T Y P E   S C H E M E S
R   S   S   T   N
B U R N T O F F E R I N G
  E   R     R   U
P R I V A C Y   I L A I
A   R   N   E N   L   O
C R A C K   A L L O T E D
K   Q   E R S   A   A D
S H I E D   T H W A R T S
```

204

Politics

```
D I S B A N D   N O R T H
I   H   D   E O   E   O
P R O P O R T I O N A T E
S   V     E   K   C
  B E A R E R S   C H E F
P   L   A   M   C     I
A S S A S S I N A T I O N
U   H   N   L   M     D
L E A D   G A L L O P S
  N   E   T     L   A
D E N U N C I A T I O N S
A   U   D   O   O   R K
M A L E S   N E P H E W S
```

Leaders

```
A R D   O P E N   J O A B
R O E   C A R E   E N C L
B A L   K N O B   W E T S
A D I N   E S A U S
    G O B L E T S   V A S
A B H O R     E R A S E
N O T S O     F E L I X
S L E E K     U N I F Y
A D D   E L T O L A D
    S N O R T   L A B S
W O V E   T A T A   T A M
E M I R   A C E D   E C U
B A S E   N E R O   D A G
```

The Ministry of Jesus

```
C H R I S T   P R E A C H
O   C   H   A   A   O
I N V O K E   N A T U R E
O   N   U   I   E   I
A R N I   D O C T R I N E
    U   A           T
P A T M O S   W O R T H Y
B           A       E
M I R A C L E S   V O W S
L   R   I   H   I   I
R I M M O N   I N V E S T
T   O   U   N   E   E
C Y P R U S   G A D A R A
```

Cross My Heart

```
K N O C K S   L I M P I D
O   E   I D O   A   S
O B T A I N   O F F E R S
L   S   C   S   A
M E T E   E X E M P T E D
    L   R   R   L
C O M E B E F O R E H I M
V   S       B   S
P E R S U A D E   E S A U
R   L   Y   R   N
A D M I R E   I N V O K E
U   F   R U N   E   L
S E C R E T   G U S H E D
```

Hard Times

```
C H E R U B   B A L A A M
A   E   E A R   A   B
C L O S E T   O R P H A N
V   E   H   O   N
B E A R   C O M M A N D S
E   V   A   I   O
E N C O U R A G E M E N T
E   I   E   L   R
B A R R A C K S   E A S Y
R   A   T   S   C
B E A T E N   U N S E E N
S   O   A I R   L   N
S T R O L L   E G Y P T S
```

Sunday Morning

```
C H A P E L   S C O F F S
U   R   A M I   F   R
E R R A N D   N A T H A N
R   Y   D   C   N
T Y R E   E L E V E N T H
R   R   L       I
S E L F A S S U R A N C E
D   U   N       B
B I L L O W E D   O N C E
F   O   E   R   R
D I S A R M   R E A D E R
E   D   B E G   T   T
O D I O U S   O B E Y E D
```

Attitude Check

```
S E N S E S   R E J E C T
L   H   C O O   O   O
B E W A R E   L A Y I N G
C   R   N   L   T
S T E P   T R I C K E R Y
E   E   N   N   O
O B E Y H I M G L A D L Y
E   E   N       P
H A R D S H I P   S O W S
R   E   E   A   I
V I C T O R   A C C E S S
N   E   I C K   E
A G H A S T   E N S U R E
```

Almost There

```
M A S C A R A   W A G E D
O   C   R   P E L   U
O V E R E M P H A S I Z E
D   N   R   K   D
  S T A T I O N   B E L T
B   E   O X   S     I
U N D I S C I P L I N E D
D   S   M   U   E   E
S O B S   H A R R O W S
  O   T   T     B   U
I N S U R R E C T I O N S
N   O   O   L   E R   E
N A M E D   Y E A R N E D
```

What to Do

```
A I R   S H R I   I C E S
F L A   H E A D   B A R I
A I N   E M P O W E R E D
R A S           L O X
  A B R E A S T   W E D
R E C O U N T     H A Y
A S K A N D R E C E I V E
M A E   E S C A P E D
A U D   R E E Q U I P
    A E C         I R U
B A T H S H E B A   N A G
U R E A   E L A H   G I L
Z E E B   D Y A N   S L Y
```

Obscure Old Testament Men

```
S H E D   T A P   G E T S
C A V E   A W L   A C H E
A R I P   S E E   N C A A
R E L E N T   A R D E N T
    N I E     S A H
E X O D U S   E D I B L E
G I L           E A R
G I D D E L   P L E D G E
  A P E     E R R
A H I M A N   A C R O S S
R I C A   G U R   A B E L
A D O G   T A L   N E B O
B E N E   H R S   D R A B
```

Desert Discovery

```
P L U M P   R A F T E R S
I   N   E   O A   Q   E
L A T E R   B E D O U I N
A   I   S   U   E A
T R E S P A S S   A L S O
E   I   T   F E   R
  S O R R Y   M A I D S
R   M   E   O M   B
A R I D   A F F I N I T Y
V   T   A   S S   W
I N T E N S E   H O S E A
N   E   E N   E   U   Y
E N D O W E D   D E E P S
```

Old Testament Stories

```
  A S A H E L   J E H U
S   C   A   E   A   I U
H O O K S   P A R A D E S
I   U   E   S   E   U
P I T C H E R S   T O U R
S   I   S   C   U   P
    M U L E   C A R T
O   A   T   H M   C
F O R D   W E A P O N R Y
F   C   W   L   A   R
E P H R A I M   R A P H U
R   E   R   E   E   S
U S E S   T H I R S T
```

Search for Truth

```
B E L I E F ■ C H O R D S
■ V ■ G ■ O A R ■ U ■ O ■
B A N N E R ■ U N R U L Y
■ D ■ O ■ E ■ M ■ ■ P ■ ■
D E A R ■ S A B B A T H S ■
■ A ■ A ■ ■ G ■ I ■ ■
A C K N O W L E D G I N G
■ A ■ C ■ ■ N ■ R ■ ■
A P P E A L E D ■ E A C H
■ T ■ ■ A ■ L S ■ H ■
D I G E S T ■ E A S I E R
■ V ■ L ■ ■ I T S ■ O A
D E S I G N ■ S E R A P H
```

Areas of Caution

```
C H I S L E U ■ L A T C H
U ■ C I ■ N E ■ I ■ I
B R O K E N H E A R T E D
S ■ N ■ E ■ F ■ H ■
■ B I G T H A N ■ D E A F
E ■ U A ■ L ■ Y ■ I
D E M O N S T R A T I N G
O ■ K ■ H ■ R ■ M ■ S
M I C E ■ K I D N A P S
■ H ■ A ■ N ■ O ■ E
B L A S P H E M O U S L Y
I ■ I ■ E ■ S D ■ E ■ E
D A R E S ■ S P E E D E D
```

Murderers

```
R E M ■ L O A F ■ A F A R
A X E ■ O N C E ■ D O P E
C O N T R I T E ■ O R E B
A D D E D ■ ■ D A B S ■
■ ■ A S C I ■ D E A L S
B A R K ■ A M M I ■ K I T
A S A ■ H I L E N ■ E R E
R I B ■ E N A N ■ E N A M
N A B A L ■ H O A R ■ ■
■ I B I D ■ ■ M A S S A
C A N A ■ R E G I S T E R
A M I N ■ A M O S ■ A B C
A U C A ■ B U G S ■ B A H
```

School Daze

```
T O T E M ■ D A N G L E D
I ■ Y ■ E R A ■ A ■ A ■ O
P L I E D ■ N O M A D I C
P ■ N ■ I C E D ■ ■ I ■
E N G R A V E R ■ H E R O
D ■ ■ T ■ D ■ C R R ■
T U T O R ■ P O S S E ■
C ■ N ■ R Q N ■ ■ A ■
R A C E ■ Q U A V E R E D
A ■ O G O ■ ■ E E M ■
F L U T I S T ■ R A B B I
T ■ T L ■ A P T ■ E R ■
S C H O O L S ■ S O L V E
```

Gifts of God

```
■ ■ W A X ■ A M I S S ■
Y ■ P ■ U ■ ■ O A ■ D
A R R A N G E ■ U L C E R
N ■ O T ■ D N ■ K A ■
K E P T ■ R U S T ■ S A P
■ E ■ C C A ■ ■ ■ E ■
P E R S O N A L I T I E S
L ■ ■ U T ■ ■ N N ■ ■
A X E ■ N A I N ■ C L A P
Z ■ L S ■ O U A ■ I ■
A L I V E ■ N A G G I N G
S ■ H L ■ ■ L D S ■ ■
N U R S E ■ E Y E ■ ■
```

King David

```
S T Y E ■ H A R P ■ P E A
C O E N ■ A M A L ■ C A I
A G A G ■ T A L E N T E D
G A R E B ■ D E A L ■ ■
■ ■ D A D ■ ■ D R E S S
N A Z I R I T E ■ B L E W
A C E ■ B L E N D ■ A L A
M A S K ■ L A V I S H L Y
E N T R Y ■ ■ Y E H ■ ■
■ A A A L ■ D A V I D
B R A N C H E S ■ D I R E
O A R ■ H A K E ■ O N A N
W P M ■ T B S P ■ W E N T
```

Life and Death

```
B A N D ■ V A T ■ B A T E
A L O E ■ E A R ■ A H E R
W E E P ■ S H E ■ R I N G
D E L A Y S ■ A A R O N S
■ ■ R O E ■ T H E ■ ■
L I N T E L ■ Y A N K E D
Y A O ■ ■ ■ I R A ■
E M B A L M ■ W A N D E R
■ ■ P E A ■ I S A ■ ■
W E A P O N ■ S A B T A H
A B E L ■ G A D ■ O I L Y
G O R E ■ E X O ■ T R A P
E N O S ■ R E M ■ H E R E
```

Unhealthy Relationships

```
H E M ■ P A N E ■ D A L E
A X E ■ I R A D ■ E N A M
D E L I L A H ■ T S A D E
■ ■ B E D ■ L O I N ■ ■
N A K E D ■ B E G G I N G
A M E X ■ R O A N ■ A I
S A G ■ C R A N E ■ D B A
A S ■ P R A Y ■ B E A N
L A W L E S S ■ D E A L T
■ ■ E A S E ■ B O A ■ ■
E N A C T ■ W I L D E S T
C O V E ■ B A D E ■ H A M
U S E D ■ E B E D ■ I C H
```

Being Wise

```
■ A D V I C E ■ R I F T ■
I ■ O ■ N ■ L U I ■ S
D R U N K ■ I N S I G H T
E ■ B ■ ■ A ■ E ■ U A
A T T I T U D E ■ I R O N
S ■ ■ A ■ A ■ L ■ E ■ D
■ B L A M E ■ S E N S E
Y ■ E ■ E H ■ V ■ A
O R A L ■ B E L I E V E S
U ■ R ■ W ■ L ■ A ■ K
C O N F I R M ■ F A L S E
H ■ E ■ S E ■ O ■ I D
■ I D L E ■ T R E A D S ■
```

For Example

```
B E T R A Y ■ W A F E R S
L A Z U L I ■ I D U M E A
A R A B L E ■ N A M I N G
U N R E A L ■ T H E M E S
■ ■ ■ D I E ■ ■ ■
M O D E L S ■ R A T T L E
A B A S E ■ ■ S H E A F
D E B T O R ■ T H U M B S
■ ■ ■ E G O ■ ■ ■
G O S S I P ■ B A A S H A
O B L A T E ■ I B L E A M
R A I S I N ■ A B L A Z E
E L D E S T ■ H A S T E N
```

People Aplenty

```
S W O O P ■ I C H A B O D
A ■ P ■ H I S ■ E ■ U ■ E
L A H M I ■ A N A N I A S
O ■ I ■ L ■ I L ■ L E ■
M O R D E C A I ■ E D E R
E ■ M H ■ I ■ U T ■ ■
■ J A C O B ■ A S A P H
S ■ L N ■ M C ■ ■ E ■
T Y P E ■ B A R A B B A S
R ■ H M H ■ R L H ■ ■
E Z E K I E L ■ I S A A C
A ■ U ■ C ■ A G O ■ C ■ O
M E S H A C H ■ T E K E L
```

In the Family

```
H A S T E ■ N U R T U R E
A ■ W ■ X ■ A ■ A ■ N ■ A
R E A C T ■ R A I D E R S
A ■ M ■ E R ■ N ■ Q ■ I
S U P E R I O R ■ C U R E
S ■ ■ N ■ W ■ A ■ A ■ R
■ L O Y A L ■ A N K L E
E ■ B ■ L ■ G ■ C ■ M
M I L E ■ A L L E G O R Y
B ■ I A ■ A ■ S ■ R R
A N G E R E D ■ T I G H T
L ■ E T ■ L ■ O A ■ L
M O D E S T Y ■ R A N G E
```

Details, Details

```
R I P P I N G   T E S T S
U   R   N   R   R   M   E
T H O R N   A D A M A N T
H   V       N   Y   R
  B E D S I D E   S T A R
B   R   U   D   I       I
E M B A R R A S S M E N T
A   F   U   L   N   E
R A C E   A G R E E T H
A   A   H       E   D
U N K E M P T   C A R V E
S   E   I   E   A   E   N
E A S E D   R A P I D L Y
```

To God Be the Glory

```
C R I T I C   B E R E F T
  E   A   A H I   U   L
D A M S E L   B E G G A R
  C   T   K   L   T
S H O E   I D E N T I T Y
I   L   N       E   E
S T R E N G T H E N I N G
  H   S       A   D   A
B U R S T I N G   E A S Y
  N       T   G R I   L
A D H E R E   A M E N D S
  E   R   M A R   S   E
B R E E D   D E T E S T
```

God Is in Control

```
K I D N A P   A C C E P T
  T   I   I T S   A   E
C A N C E L   K I N D L E
  L   O   G   E   L
D Y E D   R A D I A N C E
  E   I       N   A
C O M M E M O R A T I N G
  V   U       E   I
R E A S S I G N   Q U I T
  R       B   E U   S
I D B A S H   W H I L S T
  U   G   A S A T   U
D E T O U R   L A Y M E N
```

Time to Move

```
G L A S S   F O L I A G E
R   N   C   A   E   R   X
I N N E R   M O N A R C H
E   U   E   I   D   I   O
V A L U A B L E   O V E R
E   M   Y   U   A   T
  B O X E S   K N E L T
B   B   D   P   B       F
L A S H   A L I E N A T E
O   C   D   A   L   H   L
C   U   I   Y   I   E   L
K   R   R   E   E   A   E
S C E P T E R   F A D E D
```

The Power of God

```
  A W E   A F O O T
C B A   A   A   C C
A M A S S E S   I N C U R
N   K   H   Y   R   U   U
A R I D   O M E N   R A M
  N   E   B   E       B
R I G H T E O U S N E S S
A   E   L       S   A
R I M   R E I N   E G G S
E   I   N   Z   A   L   A
S I N A I   E A S T E R N
T   C   T       I   S   D
  B E R Y L   B A Y
```

Strong Beliefs

```
S A T   C L A N   C R O W
A B O   L I R E   H A V E
I B M   E B E R   A D A R
L A B O R   A V E R
    A G E   E A G L E S
M A R T Y R S   S E E L E
I C U   A I D   N I B
M E T A L   M A H A T M A
E S H C O L   D U P
    C O A L   R E A L M
S A V E   B A I L   N A Y
A S A P   A C R E   A N N
D A R T   N E E D   K E A
```

Wisdom and Folly

```
L I B Y A N S   M A D L Y
I   A   I   U   A   R   E
C O N T R I B U T I O N S
K   Q   S   E   O
  N U G G E T S   S P E D
B   E   A   I   A       A
A U T O M A T I C A L L Y
S       E   U   H   O   S
K E P T   S T R E E T S
  I   S   I   T       U
M A L I C I O U S N E S S
A   O   A   N   I   R   E
P E T E R   S T R A Y E D
```

Name Game

```
P E T S   I D D O   O P P
A C R O   S E E D   N E R
C O U P   A B E D N E G O
E L E A Z A R   S O S
    T A C I T   W I S P
L A S E R   S I S   M E A
A B I R A M   S A M U E L
M A L   H E N   T A S K S
A D V T   N E B A T
    A U G   P O N T I U S
S Y N T Y C H E   H O R A
I O U   P E E R   E W E S
B U S   S A W S   W A Y S
```

Time to Go

```
E J E C T E D   C L A S P
D   A   A   E   A   N   U
E R R O R   T A L E N T S
N   N       E   F   E
  C E L L A R S   O X E N
W   R   O   M   K       O
I N S I G N I F I C A N T
F       S   N   N   M   E
E N V Y   B A R G A I N
  E   L   T       T   B
I S R A E L I   E N T E R
L   G   A   O   L   A   A
L E E C H   N A I L I N G
```

Taking a Risk

```
B L O W U P   A D V I C E
A   H   A C T   I   O
S T R O N G   O P E N L Y
  E   L   E   N       O
F R E E   A B E D N E G O
  N       A   N
O P P O R T U N I T I E S
  E   M   A       H
S O M E W H A T   A I R S
  P   E   I N     U
P L A Y E R   O R A C L E
  E   O   B E N   E   E
I S S U E S   S A L A R Y
```

Bad Habits

```
G E M   E A C H   A G A G
A M A   B I L E   B A D E
Z I P P O R A H   I D D O
A R S O N   D E A D
    A Y E   H A B I T
D I S C   Z I O N   A L E
A D A H   E N D   C L A N
R E G   T R A D   L E I S
A S A P H   S B A
    L E A F   L I A R S
Z I Z A   N E H E M I A H
A T I C   T A O S   A C A
G A P E   S L I T   H A D
```

Qualities

```
B R A V E S T   A S I A
A   D   N   I D   S   C
C U D D L E D   M O R A L
K   E   I   A   A   O
  D R A G   L E N D E R S
A   H       I   L   E
R E L A T I O N S H I P S
R   A   E       T   T
I N T E N D S   E C H O
V   T   M   C R A   K
A L I K E   A M I A B L E
L   C   N   N   N I   E
  B E S T   T I G H T E N
```

Signs and Wonders

```
  A R K   A P P L E  
G A   A   S   O   B
A R R A N G E   A T O N E
R   I   G   M   L   S   L
B A S E   S P O T   E X O
  E   F   O   E       N
W O N D E R W O R K I N G
R   A   E   Y   D
E B B   R A R E   A I R S
T   A   S   E   A   O   I
C A R G O   D E M O T E D
H   N   M     E   S   E
  A S H E N   I N K  
```

Major Problems

```
S U P   R E B A   L E B O
E R R   O R E B   A G E D
L I E   E S T R A N G E D
A S S     A N D  
  E C O N O M Y   H O E
I G N O R E D   A S K  
V A T S   B O O   F R E E
A L L   U N A I D E D  
H E Y   P A R E N T S  
  S E A     H A D  
A R B I T R A T E   I I I
H E A R   O R A L   P A N
A D D S   N E R I   S H E
```

Call the Doctor

```
S U P E R B   B L E A C H
  N   X   A I R   A   A
L I S T E N   A C T I N G
  F   R   D   N   T  
T Y P E   I N D E B T E D
    M   T     E   E  
U N D E R S T A N D I N G
  I   L     S   R  
E N V Y I N G S   I D E A
E   E     I   D   R  
A V E N G E   G I D E O N
E   E   D E N   E   D  
S H A W L S   S E N S E S
```

Family Relations

```
C A S T I N G   B A B E S
A   U   L   R A A   I
L A B E L   A B A N D O N
F   C   N   L   G  
  A L M O N D S   B E A K
S   A   W   C   H   I
T E N D E R H E A R T E D
E   S   I   I   H   S
M A I L   A L A R M E D  
  D   S   D     A   G
B O L S T E R   S A T A N
A   E   A   E   E   R   A
R I S K Y   N E A R E S T
```

The End Is Near

```
Z E A L O T   U N H O L Y
I   R   O   N   E   O  
O N C E   D I C T A T O R
N   H   A   L   P   S  
  M A R T Y R E D   B E G
S   N   H   E   R   L
T I G R I S   E M P I R E
A   E   R   O   M   E
B E L   D A R K N E S S  
  N   A   D   N   T  
O V E R C O M E   R O M E
  O   B   P E   N   L
T Y R A N T   L A M E N T
```

Taking Shape

```
D E P A R T   I S A I A H
  X   R   R A N   B   B
C I R C L E   C R I S I S
  L   H   A   U     S  
L E V I   S T R A I G H T
O   P   O     N   A  
C O M P A N I O N S H I P
A   U   B   I   E  
C R E S C E N T   S I G N
S     N   A   T   O  
A M A Z E D   I D E A L S
E   I   O W N   N   A  
U N F A I R   S A T A N S
```

Lead Us Not into Temptation ...

```
E G G S   W A D E   B R O
R I O T   O A R S   A A B
A S E R   R A I S I N G S
S T R U C K   E A T E S T
    T A M   D Y E  
O C T   B E D   S M A L L
G A A L   N B A   S C A B
S T E E D   A R D   A B S
  V A L   R E A  
S E R E N E   A L T E R S
A D U L T E R Y   O B E Y
D A G   E C C E   N A I N
A M A   S H A D   E L S E
```

Bad News

```
I N L A I D   B A R U C H
  I   C   U S E   E   O
B E A C O N   S A D D L E
  C   O   G   O     O
M E N U   E A R L I E S T
U   N   O   N   S  
D I S T I N G U I S H E D
  M   E     N   C   U
E P I D E M I C   R O B E
A     A   Q   I   I
S L E E P Y   U N B I N D
E   R   B E T   E G  
A D H E R E   H E D G E D
```

The Word

```
    C R Y   A R R A Y  
L   A   O   E   M   E
A F F E C T S   L A B A N
M   F   K   A   I   E   A
B O I L   S T A G   R I B
R   P   I   I     L
C O M P A S S I O N A T E
A   R   F   N   L  
N U N   D R I P   S K I P
N   E   O   E   O   A   O
O R G A N   S A D D L E D
N   E     E     O   I   S
  A B I D E   F R O  
```

Add It Up

```
T R A I N   C O L U M N S
I   M   I L L   I   E   I
T H O R N   O N E H A L F
H   N   E   V   S   S T  
E I G H T E E N   J U N E
S     E   N   F   R   D
  W I V E S   D O Z E N  
T   N   N   M   R     T
E A S Y   F I F T I E T H
M   T   M   N   I   I  
P L A T E A U   E A G E R
L   N   R   T A T   H   T
E X T R E M E   H O T L Y
```

Affirmations

```
D E N I E D   L A B O R S
  Q   L   I   O   U   E
P U B L I C   G U I L T Y
A   E   T   I   L  
F L O G   A C C I D E N T
  A   T       U  
T W E L V E   P R O V E D
I     A   F  
S T R A T E G Y   F I R M
N   V   D   M   I  
D E B A T E   E X C U S E
S   I     N   N   E   T
P S A L M S   T H R U S T
```

The Big Party

```
S U P E R B   S H A G G Y
L   V   A L L   I   L
S C R E E N   A R M F U L
E   E   R   Q N  
B R A G   U L T I M A T E
E   R   E     E   O  
E N T E R T A I N M E N T
E   E   L     L   O   A
M A I N S A I L   R E A R
R   A   I   A     A  
R E P A I R   C U B I T S
S   R   O N I   L   I  
A T T A I N   T R E N C H
```

Bible Fill-Ins

```
A B J E C T S . C A L E B
R . A . U . H . L . E . E
C O V E T . A B A D D O N
H . E . . R . Y . G . . .
. A L E R T E D . B E A M
C . I . A . C . C . . . I
H A N D K E R C H I E F S
E . . E . O . I . U . . T
F A C E . O P E N I N G .
A . B . P . . . U . B . .
E M B R A C E . C Y C L E
N . I . B . R . O . H . V
D A N C E . S A T I S F Y
```

A Comforting Truth

```
J E W . N A B . B P S
A P E . C E O . R E T
W H A T A F R I E N D
. D O A . E L A N . .
S N O W . B A L T I C
O U R . C A L . H E B
P R E C U T . B O S S
. S T I R . C E F . .
W E H A V E I N G O D
E R E . E A T . O R E
B Y E . D R Y . D U O
```

Bible Greenery

```
L A M E C H . G R A P E
A C A C I A S . H I R A M
C O M F O R T . I B M P C
E R M A . A A A . L Y E .
D N A . S Y C A M O R E .
. . . R A S . C R O C U S
. B L A B . . A R K S . .
P L A C I D . A B E . . .
R O S E B U D S . C P M .
A S A . B A T . S A R A .
I S L E T . N E T T L E S
S O L I D . G R E A V E S
E M E N D . . S E R E N E
```

Solving Problems

```
B L E S S . L E C T U R E
L . X . C O O . O . N . N
U R I A H . V E I L I N G
R . S . O . E . N . F . A
T A T T L E R S . S O N G
. S . A S . P . R . E . .
. F I E R Y . S H A M E .
T . N . S . E . I . . A .
O A K S . E X P L O R E D
N . L . O . C . I . E . H
G L I M P S E . P A S T E
U . N . E . S I P . T . R
E N G I N E S . I S S U E
```

Wear It

```
. L A M E . E T H A N .
P U M I C E . S W E D E .
C O R O L L A . S E L M A
N E C K L A C E . E M I T
N T H . S I H O R . E R E
. . C T R . F E S T E R .
. C O L O . . C U S S . .
N O V E N A . H U B . . .
I S A . E L M E R . E A T
E T T A . E A R R I N G S
C U I N G . A M E N D E R
E M O T E . M E N T O R .
S E N S E . . S T O W . .
```

Tones

```
H A R M . B U S . B O L T
I D E A . A L P . U S E R
C O N T R I T E . S H E A
. . . U A L . C S H A R P
A D O R N . C I T E . . .
H A L E . H U M I L I T Y
A N A . B O R E R . D E O
B E F A L L E N . M E E K
. . . B A I T . D O N N E
A U T U M N . C O R . . .
P R O S . E D U C A T E D
O G R E . S E T . L A K E
D E E D . S U E . S T E W
```

Church-Related

```
C A M P . A B C D
A R I A . S O A R
S A N S . S U R E
A B S T A I N E D
. . T O A S T . .
N A R R A T I O N
A R E A . E F M A
M A L T . R U S S
E L S E . S L I T
```

Women at Work

```
I M E L D A . S A M O A
M A D O N N A . O M E R S
P R E P A I D . W I D T H
L I M E . M O B . D I E T
Y E A . A B B A . U G O
. . S A L E S W O M A N .
. . M I C . . L A S . . .
P R O P H E T E S S . . .
L I T . Y A R N . B A M .
A C H E . R A D . F E T E
S H E R D . C A R A V A N
M E R G E . T R A D E R S
A R S O N . A M E L I A
```

Animal Boat

```
S T A G . A R F . S W E D
H O M O . C I I . H A R E
L E O P A R D S . R I L E
. . . H U E . H E I F E R
I N D E X . S H A M . . .
R E A R . S C O R P I O N
A C T . C H A O S . C U E
N O A H S A R K . W E S T
. . . A W L S . P E S T S
P R O P Y L . B A A . . .
L O O P . O F A S S I S I
A D Z E . T E L . E D E N
T E E N . S E E . L A W N
```

His

```
P A P A . C H A S M S
A L U M . P I S T O N
P A R E . U N T R U E
A M E N . . E A S E .
L O R D S S U P P E R
. . . T E A . . . . .
L O R D S P R A Y E R
A V E R . . M A R E .
M E T A L S . A C R E
P R I M A L . S H E D
S T E A D Y . S T D S
```

Biblical Parts

```
L A B A N . B A A . R F D
O B E S E . O B L . E L I
C H R I S . B E T . B A T
. O L D T E S T A M E N T
. R E E L S . R A C K O .
. . . E S T H . A C E S .
. S U E . E X A . M A D .
D O N A . S T I R . . . .
A M A S S . . F A C I A .
N E W T E S T A M E N T .
I D A . A L A . A D L A I
E A R . L I D . D E E R S
L Y E . S P A . A S T I R
```

On the Farm

```
P A W S . K I D . B A L M
O B I T . A C E . A R I D
P U R R . I H S . R E F S
S T E E R S . E S T A T E
. . . A Y E . R T E . . .
F A R M E R . T U R T L E
U S O . . . . . . I C E .
R A T T L E . F I E L D S
. . . H O N . A S S . . .
S P R O U T . L O C U S T
H A I R . R E L . O K L A
I C O N . A G O . R E A P
P E T S . P O W . T S P S
```

Judgments

```
HAIRDO · STOCK
ALTOONA · ERROR
STEPHEN · VALUE
TAME MGM · MARS
YRS · CALIF · NAG
· DONOTJUDGE
DOES · OBOE
DONOTWORRY
ROE · ACNED · MED
ERMA · COL · CAPE
AMISH · FINANCE
MALTA · FEARGOD
SNEAD · SHEETS
```

Sad and Glad

```
TUNE ITS EDOM
ANAB NET PARE
LIVE SEA IRAD
ETERNITY DALE
· ADHERE
APIECE DAMAGE
SERAH · RIDER
PRISON BECOME
· TRADES
VIEW GRATEFUL
ADNA GOT BACA
TEAR AWE ETAM
SAND INN ZELA
```

Daniel and His Friends

```
HIP FOGS SOBS
AIR ALTO ABLE
LIONSDEN NODE
PATS ORDERS
HGHTS PFUI
OREL SEGS COT
BIC SHOOK HAH
SPY HAND JAKE
BEDS PULSE
APPEAR DEAD
LILA ABEDNEGO
APOC COCA ANN
NETH HAIL NUT
```

The E's Have It

```
EAVE SAG CEDE
AXED ELA RARE
SING AIR OREL
ESTEEMED SPGS
AENEAS
IMPUGN NIBBLE
SPELL MARES
AGATES HEROES
ESTHER
ENTR EGGSHELL
VIII WHO OBEY
ANNO ETA MAIM
LEER DST ELSE
```

The Reverend

```
HARP BOW CORE
OVER OWE AMEN
REVEREND LINT
AOR DOCTOR
SPACE BID
HASH HANDBALL
ANTE ARG AQUI
HEARINGS PULL
CDE ITALY
AGENCY SCI
LACE MINISTER
MIRE ADA MARE
STUD NAG SLED
```

Some Old, Some New

```
VINE SHE OMAR
EVEN COR VALE
NARD ASA ENAN
THISTLES REST
AENEAS
NADABS DREADS
AROSE MEDIA
PANNAG GIRDED
ALLURE
SLIP ONESIMUS
POMP VIE NICE
ABLE ETC CLAN
NEAR SEE HELD
```

O Holy Night

```
MBI LORD ASAP
RAM ANTE DINO
EMMANUEL LMNO
ARCS ISAIAH
ANNIE LVII
BAUD COED ROB
EVE MADRE OBA
DEL ALES SCOW
AGES BIKED
VIRGIN ALMA
IDEA DECEMBER
SOFT ALAS YAY
ELSE RIDS ERE
```

Being Neighborly

```
INFO ELF CBMC
LEAP GOO OREO
LOVEYOURNEIGH
SNORES GODMAN
RAN MIDI
DAIS COVETOUS
AFT COLES BAG
PRESENTS PERT
ADVS PED
ANNLEE ADRIAN
BORASYOURSELF
RETD ECC INTL
ALAS DIA ATAD
```

Mixed Bag

```
WEST MOB SAFE
IDLE ONE TROD
SEAM WOE ACRE
ENGEDI RICHER
NON ACT
GAPING HEEDED
ODE IVE
DORCAS VIRGIN
ESH III
SHEPHO EMBERS
PUSH BOW ABEL
ULLA AWE LEBO
ELIS LED DRAW
```

Heaven and Earth

```
SIZE BAN EBAL
ORAL ODE NAME
WARM DOR GNAT
SMASHING RIMS
ELIADA
BETRAY LEVELS
AHEAD PELAH
DIADEM STRIDE
IDALAH
BELA KINSFOLK
AVEN EVI ADIN
DISC SET COME
ELSE TRY TREE
```

Church Talk

```
BLOT ADD AJAR
MARY BEE TAME
AMEN BAA ANON
BODYOFCHRIST
ART OBIT
FALLS MNO OVA
BRAE FOS PRAY
ICU BUD PESTS
SEEN BAN
EVANGELICALS
BIND RIB NAME
BANE ALL CRUX
SLED LYE EDGE
```

People and Places

```
MILE SAG WANT
OBED ELA ODOR
RING AIR RISE
ESTEEMED KNEE
AENEAS
DESIGN NAHARI
URIEL ROMAN
GRAZES COPING
ESHBAN
BEAR ELISHAMA
ABDI BAN ANAN
BEAT ARA CODE
EDRE HEN KNEW
```

What to Do

```
NEED  ADD  FEAR
AIDE  MOO  AMSO
TRUSTINCHRIST
RECITE  TACTIC
   ARY  TRUE
HATE  TOILSOME
EVE  SHUNS  VAN
MEDITATE  SECT
   GENS  APR
AMALEK  ERICAS
BECONSIDERATE
INTO  TOG  AMEN
BUSS  ONE  LEST
```

On Death and Doom

```
LAMB  OBED  WEB
AMAL  DEAR  AWE
IOTA  DECEASED
DRESS   SHAM
    TAR  MICAH
CRESCENT  DUCE
RIB  KNEEL  FLA
ESAU  DREADFUL
WELLS   DIE
   AMOS  RABBI
RADIANCE  CORN
AGE  STAR  OLAF
DON  HONE  NONO
```

It's Clear

```
ILL  CLAD  DARA
SEE  HERO  APES
UNABATED  RODS
ITHAI   OLDS
   CRIB  EATEN
REBA  TOPS  AVA
ASA  JESUS  SEM
MAD  AMON  LYRE
PULSE   MYRA
   AILS  ACBOR
HIND  PERCEIVE
AIDE  AREA  TEA
MISS  TEIL  END
```

Rod and Staff

```
TBSP  NOTE  ABE
HALL  AAHS  RUN
AGOODSHEPHERD
IST  PAUL  OARS
   AIL  INC
OBEY  FOE  ABC
LAYSDOWNHISLI
DYE  CMD  LAID
   NEA  BBL
OPEC  SALK  HMS
FEFORTHESHEEP
FEM  CEES  ULNA
SPA  ARMS  SPUN
```

Going Fishin'

```
RAM  FAST  ACES
AGE  ACCO  HOWL
CUD  THEN  OBEY
ARID  AVITH
  TERRACE  FED
ADAMI  AGILE
SATAN  MASSA
PRESS  ETHER
SAD  ELEADAH
  ADULT  MOST
TASK  SITE  ONI
IDEA  THIS  KIN
EDEN  SUCH  SPY
```

Authorities

```
LASH  RAW  CHUB
UNTO  EVE  RAZE
KEEP  SEA  ORAL
EMPERORS  SAIL
    ALTERS
AFRAID  LABORS
DOERS   MANEH
DRIVEN  PARODY
    ARARAT
WOOD  TELHARSA
AMMI  HAT  DAUB
FRET  AIR  ACRE
TIRE  NAY  HEEL
```

Name the Preacher

```
SHAW  SBC  ACRE
MARY  CIS  BRED
USER  OBL  AIDE
PATROBERTSON
  ZEP  WHEW
ETHEL  MIC  EPA
ASON  JOS  PLAN
REF  EBB  DELTA
  FLEA  EUR
JAMESKENNEDY
OMAR  KOA  TEAR
LMNO  ENC  TALC
TONY  RST  IDEA
```

Old Testament

```
EAT  CALM  BASE
TWO  AGEE  EBER
CLEANED  AGATE
   PAD  SIGN
BABEL  RELEASE
ALAS  EBED  AH
LUD  ACCAD  IRU
AS  SHOA  ARAD
CHILEAB  ANAHS
   BEAT  FRO
EASED  RAINBOW
TRAP  MESS  ONE
HEMS  RITE  GOD
```

People and Places

```
ARTS  HAD  SHOP
MOAN  ARE  HARA
APHARSACHITES
MEARAH  LAMENT
   NET  JAIR
THIS  WARRIORS
HIT  RAGES  VIE
EPENETUS  VENT
   AHER  WAR
PASHUR  CASSIA
ACCOMPLISHERS
SCAR  OAT  TEAS
SOBS  TYE  ISNT
```

Strictly Personal

```
EDGE  ERR  HELL
LOAD  RUE  ASIA
SORE  ELA  NAAM
EMBRACED  DURA
    ITSELF
BOWELS  REUMAH
URINE   BLADE
LENGTH  CASTOR
    AHIMAN
STAG  DEBATERS
LEVI  ELI  OVAL
AMEN  TEN  MIRE
GANG  HES  BLEW
```

Stocks and Bonds

```
LAW  SEBA  TRAY
AGO  AVEN  RACE
SUR  LEAN  ANTS
TEKOA  RAID
   WHO  NEARS
SAVE  MARK  CAP
TROD  RUE  AHIO
ABI  PILE  RENT
BADGE  DAM
   AGAG  ASAPH
WADI  BOAR  BAY
IRON  INTO  DIM
TENS  BEEN  INN
```

Old Testament Prophets

```
FAIR  RAPS  MOM
URGE  EDIT  IKE
SAND  CAKY  SLC
ELISHA  ELIJAH
   EOL  ICU
MIRACLES  EDDY
ERA  EGO  GOD
NAIN  DARKNESS
   NAB  CEE
DEFEAT  EGGERS
EVA  BEAR  AGUE
AIL  ERLE  TADA
DEL  LAIR  EDEN
```

Places

```
A D S . A L M S . A R C H
T A N . C O A T . W A C O
A M A . T U N A . H Y M N
P E P S I . Y F C I . . .
. . P O P . F O R B A D .
A T L A N T A . G L O B E
I R A . A B S . . C A N .
R A C E R . C A L V A R Y
E Y E L E T . M A E . . .
. A B U T . N E A R S . .
A B E T . B A N D . L A W
A B L E . A M O R . P C A
A C I D . S P R Y . S K Y
```

Men of Olde

```
A D A M . C O G . D E A R
S I N O . A N I . W A G E
A C T S . R E D . A R E A
P H I L I P . E A R N E D
. . E M U . O A F . . . .
T H O M A S . N A S H O N
H E B . . . . . . E L I .
E L I A D A . A S A H E L
. . A B S . N A B . . . .
C E P H A S . D E D A N S
U L A I . H U R . I B I D
R U I N . U S E . E L L A
B L D G . R A W . L E E K
```

Desirables

```
G O D . C H A D . C A I N
A L I . R A C E . L I R E
D E S S E R T S . E D A R
. . C O T E . O F F E N D
P R I M E . S L A T . . .
H O P E . G O A T S K I N
U A L . E L A T E . I T A
T R E A S U R E . S N A G
. . T A T S . M A D L Y .
S P R O U T . B O R N . .
A E O N . O B E D I E N T
G A L E . N A V E . S A W
E K E D . S A Y S . S B A
```

Alive and Well

```
Z E A L . P U N . S C A B
I D D O . A P E . H A I R
O R E N . L I P . R U D E
N E R G A L . H A U L E D
. . E R I . E B B . . . .
B A N D E D . G I S H P A
E X O . . . . . . O A R .
T E B E T H . B E H I N D
. . S E A . L A Y . . . .
S P R A N G . O R E G O N
E L O I . A D O . N A P E
R A M A . B A D . A G E R
E Y E S . A N Y . S E N D
```

Cross Talk

```
A B B A . P A W . C L A D
L O A F . O M A . Y A L E
T O U R . N A T . R O M E
I N D I C T . C A E S A R
. . C H I . H I N . . . .
L A Z A R U S . D E A T H
A L A . S I T . . D E O .
M I G H T . T H I E V E S
. . E A T . I S M . . . .
G A M B L E . R O B B E R
O V E R . A D S . A E R O
D O M E . C I T . L A G S
S N O W . H A Y . M U S E
```

At the Right Time

```
T O O . A B B A . Y E A
I N N . P A I L S . O A R
R A T . P R E M A T U R E
E N O C H . R U L E . . .
. . A I D . G E S H A N .
K A R N A I M . S T A T E
I R A . D A M . Z A R .
S A G E S . P E R I O D S
S H E L A H . N A Y . . .
. . I L A I . N E B A I .
C O M M A N D E D . E B B
O N I . H E L L O . K I R
W E D . S E A M . A B I
```

Heady Things

```
K I S S . A P T . S A P H
O N A M . R U E . A B I A
A N T I . A R M . T I N Y
. . L A M . A N Y . . . .
A B N E R . . . U R G E S
L I E . D A G O N . R A T
O N E . C O W . . A R A .
F E D . U T T E R . P L Y
T A S T E . . . O B E Y S
. . A L L . T W O . . . .
A R A B . U S E . A H A B
R A I L . S E E . R O S E
T Y R E . H A M . D E A L
```

Bible Men

```
C R Y . O M E R . P R E Y
H O E . P I L E . R A R E
E P A P H R A S . O M E N
F A R S I . S T E W . . .
. . A R K . S L I N G . .
U Z A L . N E S T . D I A
F A R M . I K E . T O L L
O C T . S T E P . U L L A
S H Y E R . . . T A L . .
. . A I J A . W I E L D .
H U N G . O S N A P P A R
E L S E . K I S S . H W Y
B E A R . E A C H . A N S
```

Big Events

```
L A W . C O P Y . M O T H
E L A . A R E A . I O W A
H A S . B E T R O T H A L
I S H . . . D U E . . . .
. . B A P T I S T . A G O
A C A C I A S . M I X .
H O S T . C A D . P A L E
A M I . A I J A L O N . .
B E N . D E C E A S E . .
. . R I B . . . . K I T .
R E M E M B E R S . I R I
O V E N . E L O I . T O E
T E N T . D I E T . E N D
```

Around the House

```
. . F I G . C A N . . . .
. . F A C E . L I E N . .
G A R E B . A M R A M . .
B A D . A R M . . B Y E .
O D E . L A P . . A R T .
R I D E R . M E H O L A H
. . A I N . D A N . . . .
B O A R D E D . D E A L S
E N D . S E M . K O A . .
L A D . T W O . K I D . .
M A H L I . L A B A N . .
N A I N . I R A D . . . .
. . P E G . D A Y . . . .
```

Holy Moses

```
. B A P T . P L O P . . .
M A L T A . R A I L S . .
E L I A B . I N L A W . .
B R A G . L E M . G A B .
I R A N . E R E . F U M E
G Y M . M T G . S L E P T
. . C P S . J O Y . . . .
L A M B S . B A Y . C I V
A M I N . C O W . M A D E
W A R . H A B . O N Y X .
. S I N A I . O C T A L .
. S A W E D . N A T A L .
. M A C E . E C O N . . .
```

Archaeology

```
P A S S . M A M A . B A R
U L A I . A D A H . O R E
R A Y S . O B T A I N E D
E S S E N C E . B I D . .
. . R A H E L . I M L A .
B A R A K . L A D . A U L
A B A S E D . H A T I T A
A B I . D I G . T I D E D
L A N D . M E R E D . . .
. . F A N . D E S I G N S
A N A M I T E S . N O A H
C O L . C A R E . G A M E
T E L . E R A N . S L E W
```

Judges and Samuel

```
AGAG  GAAL  ROME
BENO  ANNAS AMOS
EBAL  LEAVY MITE
DANIEL KERIOTH
  AHIO  RIOT
BASTION  ATHLAI
ANAH  ADINA  YON
RAM AI AS  IRK
ANO ABRAM  ANTE
KISHIS SHAMGAR
  EDAM OOGA
CHISLON  DOZENS
DOEG OLIVE  ISIT
ETCH MENES  ARBA
BSKT SETH  HOST
```

Believers' Names

```
FETA  BUSHY  STYE
ACED  ENTER  TROW
CHRISTIANS  RAKE
TONNE SIS  CAVES
  ARMOR  CAPE
CTY VAN ART  LSA
LOOSEN APOSTLES
ARKS DATES  HERS
STEWARDS SWERVE
PSF NEO BEE SOT
  EVIL LOSER
SALIM RYA  PINTA
OSLO POSSESSORS
BIOL AMITY  EVAP
SAWS TENSE  SAYS
```

Vacation Destination

```
POW PERU  FLOW
ADA RAIL  ROAR
COD IRON  OPRY
TREAD  ARG
  FEB  ASSET
FRET ARID  IRA
LOS IUD  LIB
ALA FLEE  BLEU
GLUED  ALE
  MAD  ATTIC
RESP RACK  UNO
EMIT ISLE  BKT
LUCY PARS  EYE
```

Plants in God's Plan

```
AGE  RIPE  VILE
BALT AARON  IDOL
BLAH DIANA  NETS
ALMONDS DISEASE
  RESIN MAG
ENG NOW  BAKER
SWAYED BEL  RISE
PIG BIG TOW  LAN
USED GAP  WALNUT
DERRY GUM  TES
  OAT RAVEN
MATURED NARTHEX
ABUG CRAGS  ISLE
NIGH TABLE  LIAR
EAST AGEE  ANO
```

Beauty and the Beast

```
SAFE DOLE  ALL
OVAL AREA  SEE
FOND YEARLING
ANGELS KNEADS
  RAM SEA
ACT DAM  DREAD
POEM NIB  NAME
TRAYS DRY  TIN
  RCC OAF
EMINOR WHACKY
CATALOGS  DONA
CGA DUNE  EZEK
LIL SPUD  DYES
```

Christian Qualities

```
STAR YARD  ALL
HOKE OHIO  CAB
UNIV KINDNESS
NINEVEH  OIL
  REDUG ADAM
EDREI DAB  AGO
NEEDLE CALMED
DEW SAL  LOADS
SPAN REKEY
  RAZ PARABLE
REDEEMER LEAD
AXE PARA  TAME
GOD HOST  YUAN
```

Good Friday

```
RECUR AJAR  TWEE
ATONE NODE  ROSE
CHRISTDIED  ORAL
KEN TORN  EXODUS
SLY OWES  EXPO
  AREA AMI  FCA
GOSPEL JUS  EGOS
ALAS COG  MOMS
TALE BUY  FRIDAY
ENV PEP BOER
  AMEN TENS  DOM
MATURE HYDE  EWE
AXIS FOURSINS
CLOT IDEN  VASES
HENS TEED  ENTRY
```

Crime and Punishment

```
CUT BUMP  AURA
ANY USER  MSEC
TIP INTO  EACH
STEAL SPAN
  ITS IDEAL
AGED ALMA  DUE
GAZE FIE  CANE
FIR DEBS  ARTS
ATARI HAM
  APED BEACH
LAMP REDO  BAY
EVIE ABBR  DIM
TEND STAT  INN
```

Men and Women

```
LEHI RAMA  OAR
OVEN AHAZ  VIE
NERS MARINER
GROUP AZOR
  LIFE APHIK
BIGTHANA HAVE
ALL ARABS  NAP
GAAL MIDNIGHT
SIDON MAAM
  DOES PACES
FEMALES GOAH
TEN RARE  ELSE
HES SPEW  STEM
```

Up, Up, and Away

```
BEAM DOCS  NATES
ALMA ILLY  ERASE
SLID ADEN  EGRET
HANDSLIFTEDUP
  CEE HALE
FEWER TETE  HUE
PALIN ROTO  LESS
IMUSTBELIFTEDUP
CEDE AVEC  RERAN
ADE ALIT  RURAL
  ERSE LIE
  FARAWAYFROMUS
WHOSE EVIL  SIRE
CARES RENE  ARAE
SMELT SAGS  YELP
```

Ye Men of Olde

```
  ROE PAL
SAUL  HIEL
ZIMRI  ARIEH
YEH HUR  HOI
MEO UNA  EBB
ABNER SOLOMON
VIA HUL
AGRIPPA  ZADOK
UNE ONE  AHI
GAZ LIL  VER
TIDAL  DEVIL
NERO  EHUD
BKS  RIG
```

Animals in the Bible

```
FLA CYAN  PREY
LEG HOLE  RARE
EWELAMBS  OMEN
ADDER STEW
  ADE SLING
BODS GOAT  DON
UTAH GAS  IOTA
LTD TSKS  SLAT
LOOSE NRA
  HEAD EAGLE
CAGE COCKCROW
WISE HOPE  ACE
TRAP EMMY  DOS
```

Denomination Information

```
E A G L E   H U G       S E L F
S T O O P   E R A   S A M O A
S O U T H E R N B A P T I S T
A N T S   L B S   C O A R S E
Y E S   E D S   A T T N
      A X E   A R E S   B D S
E L A B O R A T E D   R E A P
P A L E D   R O N   H I N D U
I M P L   A R M A G E D D O N
C B S   A M O S   A L E
    F L O W   A R M   V I A
M O S A I C   T L B   T E N S
E P I S C O P A L C H U R C H
D A N T E   E P A   E N S U E
E L K S   N E H   M E A R S
```

Firmly Planted

```
B R I E R   A G E S   G R E W
R E T R O   M O T E   R O S E
A V E R T   A L O E   A L T A
N E R S   O L D   P O P L A R
C R U   O N E   B A N E
H E M L O C K   E G O   S A P
    A P E   N A E   P A D S
H E R B S   B U N   R E E D S
A M O S   B A T   T O A
B U D   N U L   C Y P R E S S
    A B L E   E R E   D A T
P I L L A R   O D E   B I L E
I D O L   U Z Z A   A R B O R
N E B O   S E E R   M E L O N
E A S T   H E M S   E D E N S
```

Civil Rights

```
S H A G   W H A P
C O C O   R A C E
A R E A   O I L S
M A R T I N L U T
      S I G
H E R K I N G J R
A L I I   E R I E
T E N N   S A G S
E C G S   S Y S T
```

Namesake Evangelist

```
M O N O       A D M   C A M P
O M E R   M A R I A   O L E O
A S I A   A M I S H   B E L L
B I L L Y G R A H A M   P E A
    R A N   L U T H E R
C R O O K E D   A I D E
L I M B   T A M P A   S T E W
A C N E   R C A   T A R E
M E I R   H E A R T   I R I S
    T H E S   T R U M P E T
C O N S U L   U S O
A B A   B I L L Y S U N D A Y
L E S T   C O U R T   I O T A
E S A U   A M I S S   E N T R
B E L T   L B S   S E N D
```

Acts of the Apostles

```
P E W   S L A B   F A D E
A D I N   S T E L E   E B E R
L I F E   L O V E S   R E A R
S T E P H E N   S E R V E R S
    H E W E D   T E E
N E R   S O P   U N I T E
P L O W O X   G A P   T R A P
H A B   D I E   W A S   A T E
A I L S   V O W   U N I Q U E
T R E A D   S E A   A M I
    B A M   S C A R P
H U M B L E D   T H E U D A S
A R E A   L Y D I A   R A C E
L A S T   B E N O B   E R A N
E L A H   A R A N   E N D
```

Animal, Vegetable, Or . . .

```
S O N S   B B B   S L A M
O P E N   E A R   H U L A
D E C A   A D A   A L A R
A C O R N S   I M M U N E
    E A T   N A E
C H A S M S   S E S A M E
N O R       C A P
N E C T A R   S C O T C H
    O R U   A D C
A P L O M B   T S E T S E
F A I L   B A Y   A R E A
A G E E   E R R   N E A R
R E N D   R E S   S E L L
```

Commands to Obey

```
A C H A N   A C C   B A C H
B L A M E   B O A   C A C H E
H O N O R Y O U R F A T H E R
O N E S   E M P   A D H E R E
R E S   L A B   S I R E
    O A S   P I L E   M P H
A N D M O T H E R   T I R O
C A R E S   E K E   S H E O L
A M E N   D O N O T E N V Y
D E G   C A G E   U A E
    T Y R E   A G T   D P I
A F F I R M   U G H   S O L D
Y O U M U S T N O T S T E A L
E A S E S   S I N   B O R N E
S L E D   P T Y   A P S E S
```

Whose Responsibility?

```
W A L E S   T B A   S H O O
A B O V E   E U R   S T A K E
G I V E T H A N K S T O H I M
O D E S   A C K   H O R S E S
N E R   A S H   N A R Y
    A C T   W O R M   G D S
I A M T H E G A T E   P L E A
S P A T E   U S C   S L E E P
M E I N   W I T H S T A N D S
S S N   H O L E   W O N
    G I F I   T A P   M A S
P H A L L U   S U R   A A R P
H E W I L L D I R E C T Y O U
Y A R D S   I N N   A T O L E
S T Y E   G A S   R A R E D
```

Women Namesakes

```
A L M S   M A R Y   R O B
L E A H   E V I E   U S E
M A R Y A N D M A R T H A
A N Y   C U P   C H A R
    J C S   W A C
A N N A   C A B   B A D
M A R Y M A G D A L E N E
A H A   A V A   T E A M
    A D E   E A R
A D A M   E N D   M A C
M A R Y A N D J O S E P H
I L K   N A N O   I D E A
D E S   S P A Y   T E X T
```

All God's Creatures

```
S E A L   A B E A T   F I S H
K I N E   B L A M E   I N T O
I D D O   A A R O N   T S A R
S E R P E N T   U N I C O R N
    A B A T   R E S H
A G O R A   E I S   L E E C H
B R I D L E R S   N E S T L E
B A L   U S A G E   H A B
A D O R A M   A N T E L O P E
S E N A L   C C A   D I S T R
    G E B A   T R E K
B A D G E R S   L I N A G E S
A B E E   A S S I N   B A S T
L I E D   S I L K S   L A T E
M A R Y   S A Y E E   E L E M
```

Jesus Our Lord

```
S A D   S A F E   S W A N
T R O D   G I V E N   T A C O
O B O E   O M E N S   R I L E
P A R A B L E   D U T I F U L
    T U D O R   E O P
P H T   N A P   P E T E R
G U E S T S   M I D   S E L A
O L D   E O N   G A S   A S P
A N E R   N E T   S P I C E S
L A S E A   R A W   A S H
    A H A   D E V I L
S H I P H M A   D O N A T E D
E A S E   A R O D I   N I N E
A L U R   S A V E D   D R A B
L O P S   A B A D   E N T
```

Creator's Character

```
S A G   T A C O   C A G Y
M N O   A D A M   O D O R
U N O   R O M E   N O B S
G O D I S L I G H T
    A U F   A E R A T E
A T O M S   M O R A L
M A L T   L I R A
O M A H A   O L D E N
R E N E G E   I C E
    G O D I S T R U T H
A B B A   I D L E   F O O
B E A T   F E A T   O I L
B E D E   Y A M S   S L Y
```

Gospel Quotes

```
C A L L   S A G A     D R U M
O B O E   U S E S T   E A S E
S L A G   M E L A H   A V E N
T E D I U M   S C O F F E R
    O S E E   K N E E
S I N N E R S   G E N T L E
A M O S   T O M E S   H E Y
T A T   B E D A D   O P E
A G E   H E R D S   A S E R
N E S T E D   S E L L E R S
    E A R S   A L O E
U N S T O P S   D O R C A S
T R O T   L O O S E   T A L E
A G E E   L I M B S   E R A S
W E L D   L E N T   D E S T
```

Catholic Church

```
E L V I S   C I T E D   R E B
C A I N E   A C H O O   O D E
F R A N C I S C A N S   M I A
A D D   E L E C T   A B A C K
    O D D L Y   A G E N T S
V A L U E S   E M B E D
I R O N S   B L O B S   V A C
S I R E   P R I C Y   H A L O
A A A   A O R T A   V I T A L
    S C O R E   D E F I N E
C H U R C H   B O R I C
E E R I E   H A I T I   A I A
N A B   P R O T E S T A N T S
T V A   T A M A R   A L I A S
S Y N   S H E D S   S P I L T
```

Missions

```
S C O T   C O D     C O P
P A G E   A M O     O L A Y
I S L E   L S D     N E R D
T H E N A V I G A T O R S
    C I I     E Y E
O R P H A N   M E X I C O
N C A A     T R U E
T A Y L O R   A M U S E R
    L I E   N R A
P R E E V A N G E L I S M
B O R N   P O E   I D E A
S W I G   E S L   Z E E S
  S E E   R E S   E N D S
```

Books of the Bible

```
M A G I   A R A B   F A C T S
O B I T   L I L A   A C H A N
L E V I T I C U S   T E R R I
E D E M A   A S T   S T O T T
    O X Y   H E R O I N E S
U N C T I O N   A S C I
P O O H   W E L S H   C Y L
O N L Y   I O U   A L O E
N E O   B L U R B   N E G S
    S Y S T   G E N E S I S
I I S A M U E L   L A C
C A I N E   P E E   I D A H O
O S A K A   C A M F L O R I A
M I N E R   O K I E   T E N T
E S S E S   T Y R E   E A T S
```

Special Days

```
G R A B   M A S S   C R A M
L O C O   F L O O D   D A Z E
O A H U   R I F L E   S P U R
W R E N S   B A S E D   I S R
    C H R I S T M A S D A Y
D U R Y E A   I S L E
A G E   A S S O C   E A G L E
S L A W   H E W E D   L I V Y
H Y P E D   B E S E T   V I E
    P I T A   A E N E I D
E A S T E R S U N D A Y
M G T   T I T L E   K L U G E
P O E T   P I T C H   O R A L
T R E E   P A R K A   N I L E
Y A L E   N A S H   S C A M
```

War and Peace

```
S P E D   W O E   A R M Y
E A S E   A D D   V A S E
E C C L   L E G   E G G S
    A W L   E A R
L I B Y A   S T A T E
I D O   D E B T S   N O V
M I R   R A W   G N I
B O N   E N D O R   E E L
S M E L T   Y A R D S
    A C T   B E G
C L U B   W A R   L U K E
R I L E   I S A   O K E D
Y E L L   N A G   W E N D
```

What They Did Then

```
O P A L   W I N E   W H O R E
C O N Y   I D O L   R U M O R
T E N N   D Y E S   I R A T E
T A X C O L L E C T O R S
    O W L   H E N
N I C A D S   A F A R   R F D
O D O R   A G I N   M E R E
T E A C H E R O F T H E L A W
R A T S   L A N E   N I N E
E S S   B E B E   K L U T Z Y
    K E G   C I A
M O N E Y C H A N G E R S
F I L E T   H A R D   P O P E
I D E A L   E C O L   I B E X
D I O D E   W K L Y   C E D E
```

Book of Books

```
A D A M   S P A S   S W A B
B A A E D   E A S T   P O G O
B I B L E V E R S E   A R E A
S C I F I   C Y L I N D E R
    T A K E   R A D I O
M E N A C I N G   R E E F S
A M I   E N D O R   A L L A H
R O N   G O N E R   I R E
S T E W S   W A G E D   F A A
E T H O S   D I V I D E N D
    Y E M E N   S A G E
S O F T E N E D   M I D A S
O B I T   S C R I P T U R E S
L O V E   E R O S   S C A L D
D E E R   S O P H   T B L S
```

Warning Signs

```
B A W L   S O D   R A R E
E C H O   P A Y   E B A L
A N E W   I C E   A B I B
D E N I E D   I M P A L E
    N Y E   N E E
D A N G E R   G A R D E N
E P H       I O U
E R A S E D   U R G E N T
    A W E   N E R
L I L I E S   K N E A D S
E D E N   I I I   E C R U
N E S T   R A N   K H A N
T A T S   E N D   S E W S
```

At the Cross

```
O P T S   C H A D   C L O D
M O O T   R A C E S   R I P E
A S A P   I B M P C   U S A F
R E D E E M   E T H I C A L
    T E E D   H E L I
V I N E G A R   M A F F I A
A V E R   E L B E   Y A M S
D O C   R A B I D   T A P
I R K S   E D I T   C A G E
S Y S T E M   S W O L L E N
    R O O F   Y I P E
T H I E V E S   S P A C E D
C H I P   A W A R E   N A V E
B A D E   L E V E L   E R I E
S W E D   R E L Y   R E E D
```

The Well

```
A D A M   D E R M   U S E D
T R U E   E V O I   E N E R O
T A T A   L E O N   A T L A S
A W O N D E R F U L G I F T
    R A Y   T O L L
O C T A D   M E R E   C B S
B R O O M   B E M A   S O R E
A S A M A R I T A N W O M A N
N O T E   I R O N   H O I S T
E N S   I N T O   L U N C H
    E F G H   I A M
F O R G O D I S S P I R I T
R E P R O   A R T S   C O M E
S T E E D   Y A L E   E P I C
T E N D   S S E S   S E T H
```

Nourishment and Raiment

```
E L M   C H A R   T I D E
H O E   L I T E   I D E A
U N I   A C A D   T E N T
D E R B Y   P O O H
    A S A   W E A V E
W H O S   N A M E   D A M
W O R K   E L I   D E L I
I R E   E W E S   U S E R
I N G O D   C O L
    L A S S   A L G U M
R E N D   A P E S   A C E
E L B E   M A T E   T A G
F L A N   E N D S   E L A
```

215

Best-Seller

```
TAME  PRAY   SWAM
EXEC  SURE   STOIC
KINGJAMES    TERRA
OAS  ALBS  BALDY
ALABAMA    CELLO
   IRS  WYCLIFFE
SIGNS  BACKS  GAB
ONUS  RAILS  MOCA
OCT  SUITE  FIDEL
THEBIBLE   ANN
  NOELS  STATUTE
ABASE  SCAM  RAS
BLEST  PHONETICS
AORTA  GOOD  RAKE
LEGS   APPT  WHYS
```

Match Mates

```
HATCH  UPPED   PSI
AGORA  PAOLO   EIN
DINAH  BROIDERED
ELIZABETH   OLIVE
SECY  CAN   FLEX
    PETERED
CARTA  RADIANCE
OVERLAP  PSALTER
TABLETOP   LAMER
    DEPENDS
IRIS   NEA   WEAR
SEMIS  BATHSHEBA
APPLICANT  CARAT
ALE  PEACE  ALICE
CYL  SOLED  REEKS
```

Minor Prophets

```
NOTPROPHESY
RAH  ERA  VIE
CREATE   TENS
   SIS  JARS
PEEL  MARL  E
AMP  COB  APT
R  EDOM  ASIA
 KOOP  BLT
RIPS  DEFILE
AWL  PIT  NEA
FIERCEANGER
```

Second Person

```
OSHA  CAPT   ACHT
CLUE  HUES   OBOES
COMFORTER   CLUCK
UPI  VIOL  STUNK
REDRESS   FLOSS
  ART  PROPHETS
SECTS  HAITI  LAP
LAOS  MICAH  BORA
USN  LINER  CARES
REVEALER   PLN
  IDYLS  CRUSADE
MCGEE  LEAN  BOX
CATER  HOLYGHOST
BIERS  BALE  AVER
ADDS   ODOR  MESA
```

Double Son

```
BEATS  GARTH  CPA
ATRIP  LEARY  HEW
THESONOFGOD  EAR
HEN  TAB  SORCERY
ERA  LIED  POCK
  BEL  ABE  IBID
COTES  AMID  OCR
HGHTS  CPR  CANOE
IRE  TEED  AMEND
CECE  EDS  APA
HORA  TINS  ALL
PERFECT  JOT  DEO
OCI  THESONOFMAN
UHS  REACH  NAIVE
TOT  ORRIN  ENTER
```

1 & 2 Timothy

```
SASS   FEDS   PTB
ALEC   UNIT   RUE
PIERCED    ROOTS
   OIL    INPUT
SHALT   GONER
EARLY  LAG  IMP
RIGS  PER  SEAL
FLU  PAN  INTRO
MAILS   TOYED
SWELL   SCR
TONAL  EPHESUS
ART  APSE  RUSE
RMS  REED  SEAT
```

Christian Service

```
WEVE  CLAN   MATRI
HAIL  LOVE   ABHOR
ERGO  OWES   ROUSE
ANQINT  STY  USES
TSR  AHA  SOWN
  AREAS  KADESH
DAVID  ROLES  DOE
EVER  ROBED  HELL
EVA  RENEW  TUNED
DALLAS   RIVER
  ANTS  SFX  PSA
LAMB  SOD  STRONG
UNION  NAPS  AWOL
STERN  GLUE  PERE
TENSE  SELL  TREE
```

Bible People

```
ADO   DUEL   ISIS
TURN  TABLE  STOP
AREA  STILT  HALO
DEBORAH  SHAMGAR
  MORAL  ELA
FAIT  NOW  PETER
SAMSON  TAT  LAMA
ABO  RAN  RAM  MBS
CLUB  PAI  RIZPAH
SERAH  ELI  LIAR
  PAT  KNELL
PONTIUS  STEPHEN
ALAI  BASIC  AIDE
LEGS  ALUSH  HEGE
LOST  LENT  LED
```

Jude

```
COME   NUB   GOAD
ALOT   OKE   ONCE
RESERVED    ETNA
  TRIO   RUSHED
KAHNS   COMTE
ASOAK  OOP  GOB
PILL  SAM  ARLO
HAY  TLC  SNEER
  FLOAT  ADAGE
CRAYON   TILT
HAIR  DISLODGE
ANTE  EVA  VARA
RAHS  RYR  EYER
```

Acts 13–15

```
BABS  ACHOO   AYE
AGUE  BRAHMA  SOL
BARNABASANDSAUL
KIN  LAS  DIVA
ANTIOCH   ISSUE
  STY  TEACHERS
PAT  CRATE  RAT
MIRACULOUSSIGNS
ALB  OKAYS  REO
GOODNEWS   STA
STRAD  ICONIUM
  RUSE  TON  NNE
MAKEITDIFFICULT
ALE  TENSOF  BRIE
YIN  PAARS  SETS
```

Acts of the Apostles

```
MOHA  DRAY   AJAR
IDOL  EEROS  SORE
TOPERSECUTETHEM
TRICEPS   ARENAS
  DOE   SNIP
CARROT  SEDE  OBJ
ACHAN  HURT  ARRA
ITOPENEDFORTHEM
RODS  IRAS  IRENE
ORA  ATON  APARTS
  PERD  PRO
PAPYRI  ENFLAME
OFAGODNOTOFAMAN
CALM  EASEL  NATO
ORLY  NARD  ENES
```

Philemon

```
AREA  APES   REF
DAYS  MAME   ESE
ONESIMUS   AFAR
  IDOL   RERUN
ERASE   ALICE
AORTA  PUN  SWF
SACS  ERG  OHIO
EDH  POI  SWELL
  IRONS  ENDED
APPLE   OATH
POPS  INCHAINS
SOU  OWER  NOAH
ELS  FORE  DUPE
```

Acts 18

```
E L B A   M E N   A L A C K
M O R S E   E E C   D I M L Y
P R I S C I L L A   O L M O S
  D O N O T B E A F R A I D
    S A R   A E C
A Q U I L A   E R R   P U P
S U P R A   O A S   C E N A
S I L A S A N D T I M O T H Y
E R I N   R A D   A M R A M
T E T   S H Y   D E B A T E
    A T A   T A R
  D O N O T B E S I L E N T
D O N O R   E X P L A I N E D
P U L S E   R A E   G R E E D
W R Y E R   I N N   E S S E
```

Acts 21–23

```
T R O D   L A G   M A N I A
H E R E   P E R U   I D Y L L
E P E E   R A C A   S M E L L
N O O R D I N A R Y C I T Y
    E N S   D E U T
S H A L T   F I R E   A L A
T E A C H   S A A B   A R A S
W A I T I N G I N A M B U S H
A L L S   O T T S   A L L E Y
S S S   I T C H   B R E E D
    S T O A   S U I
A J E W F R O M T A R S U S
A G A V E   T R O T   I T S A
L A K E R   E L K E   O A S T
I R E N E   R Y E   T Y R E
```

Evangelistic Trio

```
W O E   B A D   B O D S
C A P   B E B E   O M I T
C H A R L E S F I N N E Y
C U P I D S   I G N I T E
  H C R   B A L E
P A R E   R E N O   I C C
C H A R L E S C O L S O N
B A S   A G E E   I R O N
  S P I T   P E A
E S T E E M   S I R E N S
C H A R L E S W E S L E Y
C O N G   N E A R   I B S
E D G E   T A G   S O T
```

Bad Guys

```
B O M B S   B U M S   F E L L
A V A I L   A N T I   L V I I
L E N N Y   S I G N   A I R E
A R I D   W I T   N A I L E D
A D A   M A N   H E L L
M O C K E R S   O R E   B A D
  I R S   L O S   V O T E
A B A S E   S A D   B I B L E
D A D S   R O B   S A C
M R S   P A L   T H I E V E S
  G R I D   E E L   I R E
S T O N E D   A M A   S P A N
C O M A   E A R P   C H E S T
U R I S   R A F T   C O R E R
M O T H   S A S S   M E S S Y
```

Women's Page

```
O W E D   A C A D   S W I P E
R O L E   S O A R   H O L E D
P R I S C I L L A   E K I N G
A D Z   A N O   C M P   A C E
H Y A N N I S   H O A R D E D
  B E E N S   M A R K
O V E R S E E   A B D O M E N
L I T           A R E
E P H E S U S   E M E R G E D
    M A S C   N O M A D
P R O C T E R   A N I M A L S
R E C   I D I   C T R   L I P
O T T E R   B A T H S H E B A
D I A N E   A B E L   A N E W
S E L L S   L A D Y   B E R N
```

Philippians

```
S A N G   P A L O   B B B
A L A R   A M E N   L E A
C L E A N U P S   I A M B
  S E L L   A L M A Y
G R A P E   Y O D L E
O I L E D   S U E   L C A
B O L D   S U R   C E L L
I T T   S O P   A L S O P
  H E T U P   T E S T S
S H I N Y   L O O M
P E N D   F I G M E N T S
R A G   B R E L   N O O K
Y D S   A I D E   T R O Y
```

Acts 19–20

```
T H I S   F L E D   T E L L
H Y D E   L U C I A   A R E A
O P E N L Y C O N F E S S E D
R E A D I E R   F A K E R S
    E R E   M I S S
F I E L D S   F O X Y   K L M
U N M E T   N O D E   A R A E
S O B E O N Y O U R G U A R D
E N E S   E L L S   E D U C E
D E R   P R O S   S M I T H S
  B E E N   S K I
T A H I T I   P E N S E E S
S E A T E D I N A W I N D O W
A R T S   S N A R E   I G N I
R O S Y   D E E R   P E S T
```

James

```
M A R I S   F U S E   R A S E
S C E N E   I R A N   U P O N
S H I F T I N G S H A D O W S
E N E   S E E   A D D L E
  R O T C   I N D E L
I S F I N A L   A C E R O L A
S C I O N   O M M E D   N I L
L A R R   S T A B S   T I M E
A L S   L A H T I   T O A B A
M E T H A N E   C R O W N O F
  F U M E S   S E T A
S R M E N   R O N   R A P
D O U B L E M I N D E D M A N
A R I L   S I N G   A M I L E
B E T E   S A G S   R E N E W
```

Going Places

```
M O A B   A N A   M A S C
A M B I   R A N   I T A L
K E E L   A M C   Z O L A
E N T O M B   Y A P P E D
  X I I   R C A
A F R I C A   A C H A I A
L I E         M T V
A R A R A T   A S S I S I
  A M A   T E T
C A N C E R   H E A V E N
A L I I   S U E   T I L E
I S B N   U S N   E A S E
N O S E   S O S   S L E D
```

Creatures Great and Small

```
S O L D   M K T G   P O N Y
T H A I   A E S O P   E R I E
A I M S   S N A F U   L E N T
B O B C A T   R E P T I L E
  O M I T   R P O C
O S T R I C H   I M A G E D
H O O D   E A S E   N A M E
A R G   T I D E S   B B C
R E A L   O R A L   O L E O
A S S I G N   A B U S E R S
  Z A G S   H A S H
S E A G U L L   S U K K O T
D E E R   E A V E S   O I L Y
N A R D   S P I N E   S N A P
D R Y S   S I L T   H O N E
```

Working Words

```
G Y R O   L A N A   P R O P
L U A U   A B O M B   H O A R
O M I T   D E R M A   A T T N
B A L L A D   M O N A R C H
  A P E   D B A
S T E W A R D   I R O N E D
H E R S   E R S T   H I L O
A R R   B A I T S   C D R
F R O G   U L N A   S H E M
T E L L I T   R E A P E R S
  E C C   L E O
T E A C H E R   A C U M E N
C Y A N   E D I C T   S A L E
A P S E   R E T I E   E R A S
B O E R   N A G S   S E N T
```

Various Denominations

```
D A M E   N O V A   H E P
O V E R   I V E S   O M A
R O M A N C A T H O L I C
T W O   B E L   L Y R E
  L C A   W A D
Y A L E   C A B   M I A
O L D O R D E R A M I S H
M P S   S E E   A L M A
  A V E   Y A P
C H U B   G O D   U P I
M I S S O U R I S Y N O D
M R E   R A I D   R I P E
L E D   U L N A   S T E M
```

Artifacts

```
L E A D . A P E S . L I M B
A B B A . P R O O F . A R I A
M A R Y S P I N T O F N A R D
B L A S T E D . R E D E Y E .
. . R A E . A G E S . . . .
M A S T E R . I R E D . A M F
A R O M A . K N I T . O L I O
J E R E M I A H S S C R O L L
O N E N . N Y I E . O W N E D
R A N . S C A M . O M E G A S
. . S E E K . E P I . . . .
S T A T E N . V E N D O R S .
D A V I D S S L I N G S H O T
A X E R . E L I T E . M I N A
K I S S . . Y E A R . S O A R
```

Catching Some Z's

```
B E A U . A H A Z . Z I O N .
O A S T . V O L E . I S L E S
A S I A . E P I C . K N E A D
Z E P H A N I A H . L O O T S
. . . N U S . A B A . . . .
M A T T E . F R U G G E D .
Z I M R I . Z A I R . I N R E
E S A U . S A R A N . B E A N
D O Z E . N C C H . F E R N S
. S E R V I C E . Z A D O K .
. . E P H . W I N . . . .
L A S E R . A N A L G E S I C
D R E S S . E A R P . Z O A R
S E I N E . U S N A . R I M E
. A R E S . S A S H . A L A E
```

Lost in Luke

```
P R E P . F A R . . P T A .
L I M A . O D E . T E R M .
Y O U R L O S T S H E E P .
. . T A D . U T I L E . .
D R O I D . W R E N . . .
R O B E . P A N E . S K I .
O N E S I L V E R C O I N .
P A Y . N E E D . H O L D .
. . S T A R . W A N L Y .
O S C A R S . E E G . . .
T H E Y O U N G E R S O N .
I O N S . R U G . I O N A .
C O T . E S S . N Y E T .
```

Hidden Names 2

```
S A L T . R A I S E . O P A L
A L A R . E L F I N . T R I O
D I N E . G O I N G . T I D Y
. A D A M A N T . I M A G E S
. . S T O L E . S N O W . .
. A C I D . T H E S A U C E .
E R A S E . G O R E S . N O N
P O P E . N E W E R . A B U D
I M E . R E N E W . E N E R O
C A R P E T E R . M A L T .
. . S A W S . I S I T I . .
D Y N A M O . U S E T H E M .
A W O L . R O S S A . E V I L
S C A M . K R A U T . M E N E
H A H S . S A F E S . A R E A
```

Special Days

```
M A T S . I D L E . A B R A M
A C H E . N E A L . M O O L A
F O R T Y D A Y S . N A V A L
I R E . O U R . A L E . E R E
A N E E D L E . D I S A R M S
. D R E G S . A C I D . .
S C A R L E T . T E A C H E R
A N Y . . . O V A .
E N S I G N S . O F F E R E D
. C O L A . R O L L S . .
E A R H A R T . B R I B E R Y
A P E . F B I . I T E . H O E
S P L A T . S A T U R D A Y S
E L I T E . F L A N . N I C E
D E T E R . Y A L E . A R E S
```

My Favorite Year

```
T R I O . A P E . B O S S
W A L L . N I L . A N T I
O N L Y O N C E A Y E A R .
. . M C S . P L E A T .
S W E P T . S H O D . .
T A X I . B E A N . T O O
A Y E A R L I N G L A M B .
S S S . H I N T . E R R O
. . W I S E . U N T I E
. L E A N S . H A D . .
Y E A R O F J U B I L E E
E A S E . U A E . N E A T
A P T S . L B S . G O R E
```

Opposites Attract

```
T A C O . O C T A L . C L U E
O X E N . P A R S E . L A R K
M E D E . T R I K E . E D G E
B L E S S I N G S C U R S E S
. . P C A . H A G . .
A L T A R . L A B . L Y M P H
R A I D E D . B L N . I R A
S U B J E C T D I C T A T O R
O R E . C E E . R A M R O D
N O T E D . E L S . B E E F Y
. . A E C . L O O . .
M A R R I E D D I V O R C E D
I M I T . A R O M A . O L A Y
D I S H . S A N E R . C A S K
I N K Y . E M E R Y . K N E E
```

Heart Check

```
A T O M . G Y N T . C A W S
R H U E . L E A H . M A C H O
F A C T . U S S R . A P R O N
W H E R E Y O U R T R E A S
. . E R E . E T A . .
S C R U B . S W A T H . R O T
K A H N . E R I E . U G H
U R E I S T H E R E W I L L Y
L V I . L I E D . S E E M
K E N . A B Y S S . M O R S E
. . G V I . U P I . .
O U R H E A R T B E A L S O
U S A I R . A R M S . I O N S
S P I C Y . S U I T . F L E A
T O N S . P E T S . E A S T
```

O My Word!

```
S A T E . F E D . V A T S
F R O M . E L I . E B R O
O C Y P R E S S T R E E S
. . E A T . M U S T Y .
T E A R Y . G A T E . .
O R S O . H I L T . S P A
O I S R A E L L I S T E N
K E N . L A D Y . P O N D
. . L I D S . C O P T S
. D A U B S . A O K . .
O A N C I E N T G A T E S
A N T I . T O T . N A N A
F E E D . S P Y . E D G Y
```

Two Become One

```
S C A R . G A S H . A M E B A
P O L O . R I C O . D E C O R
A H A S U E R U S E S T H E R
R O S A R Y . D E C . H O R .
. . L I S A . C R Y . .
C L A Y S . M A L . A L P H A
H E W N . M U S E U M . R A D
A N A N I A S S A P P H I R A
F I R . O C E A N S . E M P T
E N D O W . D Y E . E R A S E
. . N A B . D O D O . .
A C T . A R C . R U D E S T
A Q U I L A P R I S C I L L A
B U R M A . M E S O . A B I B
C A L E B . S W A N . S E T S
```

Isaiah 53

```
D A S H . T A J . S P C A
U L N A . M E N U . E T U D E
M A I L . O L D S . R A R E R
B I T T E R E S T G R I E F .
. . R E X . I N O N . .
T U N A S . A F A R . M A N
L O D E S . R O I S . B O R E
A N D W E W E R E H E A L E D
M E E T . A F T S . D I E T S
B R R . E L L A . P U L S E
. S A L E . S A C . .
A T T R A C T I V E N E S S
S C A R E . T O N E . A Y I N
A L O U D . E N G R . M E N E
D U S T . D I E S . E S S E
```

Travel Things

```
A S H . M I C A . A D A R
H O E . A R I D . B A R E
A R A . D I S D A I N E D
B E D . . A S A . .
. B E R E A N S . C A B
A N A N I A S . A G O
B E N D . R A P . O R E N
L A D . . P A I N T E D
E R S . J A H D I E L .
. . B A D . O A K
J E H O H A N A N . A H I
A L A S . M A D E . D O N
R I M S . S P O T . S H E
```